INDIVIDUAL CASE
FORMULATION

INDIVIDUAL CASE FORMULATION

RICHARD S. HALLAM

Visiting Professor of Clinical Psychology,
University of Greenwich, London, UK

Amsterdam • Boston • Heidelberg • London • New York • Oxford
Paris • San Diego • San Francisco • Singapore • Sydney • Tokyo
Academic Press is an Imprint of Elsevier

Academic Press is an imprint of Elsevier
225 Wyman Street, Waltham, MA 02451, USA
The Boulevard, Langford Lane, Kidlington, Oxford, OX5 1GB, UK

Notices
Knowledge and best practice in this field are constantly changing. As new research and
experience broaden our understanding, changes in research methods, professional practices,
or medical treatment may become necessary.

Practitioners and researchers must always rely on their own experience and knowledge in
evaluating and using any information, methods, compounds, or experiments described
herein. In using such information or methods they should be mindful of their own safety
and the safety of others, including parties for whom they have a professional responsibility.

To the fullest extent of the law, neither the Publisher nor the authors, contributors,
or editors, assume any liability for any injury and/or damage to persons or property as a
matter of products liability, negligence or otherwise, or from any use or operation of any
methods, products, instructions, or ideas contained in the material herein.

Library of Congress Cataloging-in-Publication Data
A catalog record for this book is available from the Library of Congress.

British Library Cataloguing-in-Publication Data
A catalogue record for this book is available from the British Library.

ISBN: 978-0-12-398269-8

Printed and bound by CPI Group (UK) Ltd, Croydon, CR0 4YY
Transferred to digital print 2012

Working together to grow
libraries in developing countries

www.elsevier.com | www.bookaid.org | www.sabre.org

ELSEVIER   BOOK AID
International   Sabre Foundation

CONTENTS

It is not unusual to volunteer a summary opinion about the personality and life circumstances of someone you have known well for years. The opinion might take the form of "she never forgave her mother" or "he was unable to take advantage of his opportunities" or "she was always too impulsive to follow through with anything." These summary statements are given with a surprising degree of confidence considering the difficulty of producing a succinct account of all the influences that may have contributed to a person's life. Yet this is more or less what is expected of a psychotherapy assessment that takes place over a few hours with a complete stranger.

In both situations there is clearly the risk of a glib analysis—a partial picture based on selective attention to the evidence. Despite brief acquaintance, the psychotherapist has at least the advantage of offering a confidential service—the person "you know well" may reveal information to a therapist that has never been divulged to anyone else before. This book addresses the need for a set of guidelines that ensure conceptual clarity and greater objectivity when conducting an interview assessment and producing an individual case formulation. The problem is similar to the one faced by historians. They have to attempt to disentangle the personal idiosyncrasies of historical figures from customs prevailing at the time, taking account of a variety of changing external circumstances. Consequently, historians have paid considerable attention to their methods. Similarly in case formulation it is necessary to consider nature and nurture and their interaction. A person with a distinct genetic make-up has been exposed to a unique set of conditions, and is also the product of his or her culture, its norms and beliefs, and the opportunities afforded by his or her social environment.

This book first reviews different perspectives on formulation and then takes a position on a way forward. The final section of the book consists of a set of practical guidelines for undertaking an interview with a new client, illustrated with examples. The primary audience for this book is therefore professionals who routinely perform this kind of assessment task, in other words, therapists, counselors, psychiatrists, social workers, and others doing related work. The book focuses on one-to-one therapy with adults but many of the issues discussed within it are found in other assessment contexts.

In writing this book it became evident to me that not much has been written about case formulation from a "disinterested" perspective. By disinterested, I mean endorsing the notion that the task of formulation should be undertaken with tolerance for uncertainty and a willingness to suspend allegiance to any belief, theory, or ulterior motive. There are a number of fairly obvious reasons for the existence of partiality in this area. First and foremost is the pressure to label persons and assign problems to categories. A label has the advantage of simplifying thought and decision making. "The client is a Type-A personality and pathological gambler." This is the sort of opinion that is often asked for but it stifles any inclination to inquire further.

I do not take the position that all classificatory reasoning is valueless but I do err on the side of avoiding it when possible. For instance, there are rather few references in this book to psychiatric disorders or personality systems. Nevertheless, it seems highly likely that there are bio-psycho-social predisposing factors to a range of problems that result in characteristic patterns of behavior that are now frequently labeled as "disorders." However, these labels rarely carry with them an accompanying causal explanation and they do not help greatly when devising a therapeutic strategy. To rectify this situation researchers have developed theoretical models to explain the main features of each "disorder." These "disorder-specific models" have guided research and greatly facilitated the development of therapeutic guidelines. Some models are now "trans-diagnostic" in the sense of providing a general theoretical understanding of a collection of "disorders."

While recognizing the benefits of this strategy, I criticize it in this book and argue for an approach to formulation that is led by general principles. Labeling problems as disorders leads inevitably to an emphasis on diagnostic and theoretical templates, and ultimately to manualized therapy. The standardization of formulation and therapy is clearly advantageous to health-care management systems because they can then assign a client's problem to a fixed category and a "proven" intervention. This book offers an alternative to an overly rational and technical approach to the provision of therapy and points to the advantages of treating each client's problem as unique.

A second reason for the absence of a disinterested perspective in the field of formulation is the fact that case formulations are produced in a competitive professional and commercial environment. The assessment methods that have been suggested, and their potential end products, have become aspects of branding and marketing. This is not to claim that no one has attempted to produce a more impartial language for problem description and analysis. This book draws heavily on previous efforts, and they are acknowledged in the text. It is quite understandable that there are a variety of approaches to formulation and there is no reason to object to competition as such. Theories are usually held for good reasons and, for the most part, the intention is to help a client deal with a problem successfully. However, competition between therapeutic methods is meaningless in the absence of a measure of agreement about the nature of problems, how to describe them, and criteria for claiming that they have been resolved. In other words, to draw a comparison with brands of detergents, competition rests on generally agreed criteria for "dirty" and "clean." There are attempts to warp these criteria (e.g. "deep stains," "the existence of hidden germs," "the association of clean with sweet smelling," etc.) but they are kept in check by a general social consensus. Ideally, this consensus should be reached by a rational debate between parties in dialog. There are many examples of analogous debates in medicine, such as the criteria for deciding the level at which blood cholesterol becomes unhealthy, but rather fewer in the field of psychological problems.

The situation here is more like a free-for-all. Consequently, the definition of a problem and how it should be resolved is bound to be influenced by idiosyncratic and cultural factors. In a free market with willing payers and a ready supply of therapists, anything can be stated as a legitimate complaint. However, this freedom becomes problematic when therapy is funded by insurance or national welfare schemes. As noted above, the primary response has been to view psychological problems as analogous to medical disorders and to rely on psychiatric classification. This amounts to "naturalizing" problems, making them into pathologies largely caused by biological dysfunctions. This ploy is wearing thin for most of the problems that psychotherapists have to deal with. There are undoubtedly some universal biological determinants of problems but it is argued in this book that these are often of little relevance to the problem presented. In any case, they are not sufficiently well delineated or understood to form the basis of a typology for psychological problems. Given the obvious role of adverse environmental events, trauma, and sheer misfortune in problem causation, it is unlikely that anything that is strictly comparable to a medical classification scheme will ever suffice for psychological problems.

At present, there is no clear alternative. There is genuine and understandable conceptual disagreement about the causes of problems or even whether a causal framework for formulation is appropriate at all. My response to this issue, explained at length in this book, is to develop a method for laying out the reasoning a therapist employs during the formulation process in order to render it more transparent, thereby opening it up for public debate. I argue that all formulations contain a narrative element and that problems can only be defined in relation to a set of social circumstances. However, I try to reconcile social and language-based approaches to formulation with deterministic causal models.

The guidelines I have arrived at for individual case formulation have grown out of several decades of teaching formulation skills and supervision of trainees. My orientation has been predominantly cognitive-behavioral and the rules I have developed for constructing a case formulation diagram, and explaining the interrelationship between its elements, have their origin in some very familiar functional concepts. However, I suggest that the method I employ when going about describing the nature of a problem is compatible with a variety of conceptual interpretations. In other words, the proposed framework is *theoretically eclectic* provided some basic rules are followed when making observations and deciding on "the facts of the case." This is not a form of *technical eclecticism*, an approach that is essentially pragmatic and grounded in generalizations about which techniques are effective for a certain category of problem.

Thus, the approach described in this book is not wedded to cognitive-behavioral theories or techniques because a general functional description of a problem is compatible with different causal interpretations. The main consideration from a functional perspective is whether there are theoretical grounds (or other relevant forms of knowledge) for predicting that the action taken will have a beneficial effect. In this way, formulation is led by careful reasoning based on general principles. I devote two chapters to a description of formulation from this individual standpoint.

To some extent the chapters of this book stand alone and can be read independently. However, the sections of the Guidelines should be read in sequence and preferably in conjunction with Chapter 8, which explains functional and systemic concepts in greater detail. Compared to other books on the subject, this one takes a definite position on the *process* of formulation while being theoretically eclectic. At the level of observed phenomena, the proposed system is a flexible way of organizing information and helps to reveal gaps in understanding. Unlike many other organizing frameworks (cognitive, existential, psychodynamic, etc.) it makes fewer foundational assumptions.

As already noted, case formulation is a fiercely contested area, and so shifts from currently held positions are likely to be slow. Despite a manifest lack of consensus, the ability to formulate a person's problems is held up by the professions as a key therapeutic skill, if not the pre-eminent one. Members of the public (apart from those who have not unreasonably become thoroughly skeptical) are excited by the prospect of meeting someone who might "read their mind." Perhaps the chief lesson of this book is that there is nothing esoteric about case formulation; it is a hard-won skill that depends on methodical investigation, careful reasoning, and receptivity to the unexpected.

ACKNOWLEDGMENTS

I owe a debt of gratitude to all those colleagues and clients who have contributed to the set of ideas I have put forward in this book. There are also many people, far too many to mention, who have generously exchanged views on what it means to provide and receive psychotherapy. I would like to single out a few colleagues who have helped me especially in the various stages of giving shape to this book: Mary Boyle, Michael Bruch, Gordon Cree, Chris Lee, Kieron O'Connor, Clare Penney, and Glenn Shean.

CHAPTER 1

Formulation—the Main Issues

The topic of case formulation immediately brings to the surface a number of simmering and unresolved issues in the field of psychotherapy. This chapter introduces the issues and outlines how this book will deal with them. A major paradox is the disparity between the high esteem in which case formulation is held and the lack of any serious attempt to investigate how it is conducted in practice. Of course, all of the many forms of psychotherapy make recommendations as to how a therapist should assess and formulate a client's problem. However, formulation is so closely linked to a particular model of practice that the common features of the moment-to-moment process of formulation are rarely studied. One contentious issue concerns the role of diagnosis in formulation. Many psychotherapists, especially advocates of evidence-based practice, consider that formulation should include assigning a client's difficulties to a type of psychological disorder, usually one specified by a psychiatric classification scheme. The rationale is that a diagnosis connects a client's difficulties to a large evidence base of scientific knowledge about "psychopathology."

The position I adopt in this book is that psychopathology does not constitute a science in its own right. I assert this on the grounds that the problems a client presents are rarely produced by dysfunctions of natural processes that differentiate "normal" from "disordered" people. Consequently, I will avoid terminology with a medical resonance such as "symptom," "disorder," "patient," and "clinician" and substitute the terms "problem," "difficulty," "client," and "practitioner." However, this resort to non-medical language is not an anti-scientific stance. In fact, I will put forward formulation as a process that draws heavily on scientific knowledge, and maintain that the process of formulation can be compared to a form of scientific inquiry.

The terminology I adopt implies that psychotherapy is a form of problem solving rather than treatment of a psychological disorder. This is a fundamental difference of view and not one that is easily bridged. It is not a difference stemming from a belief that general psychological theory is not needed for case formulation. Rather, a problem is understood to exist at a higher level of analysis; it is a kind of obstacle or lack of something that prevents a client from satisfying their aims or, more simply, from living

Individual Case Formulation
http://dx.doi.org/10.1016/B978-0-12-398269-8.00001-6

without distress. A problem occurs in a personal, social, and moral context, and so its causes need to be formulated at a level in which the meaning of someone's life can be grasped. The term "problem" leaves open what framework of meaning is employed, although this book proposes a functional view (see Chapter 8). Narrative and textual approaches to case formulation are discussed in Chapter 6.

One implication of a problem-solving perspective is that reasoning in case formulation takes a hybrid form. Principles that derive from an understanding of natural processes and their technological application are relevant, but so, also, is the kind of reasoning that enters into anyone's reflections on a moral dilemma or a choice in life. Not all psychotherapists would want to endorse a problem-solving terminology, but I suspect that most therapeutic tasks could be understood in this way. Even exploration and reflection come to an end when a client feels that he or she has explored enough or concludes that he or she is no longer learning anything useful. This process could be reframed as "clarifying a problem" or "making a decision about whether there really is a problem to be solved." Thus, case formulation is not a morally neutral activity, nor need it be assumed that there is only one set of "real causes" of a problem. Presumably, construing a problem in different ways has different causal effects, some of which are intended to be beneficial. It is possible that one beneficial effect of solving a problem in a certain way is to disguise its "true causes" as seen from another perspective.

This book advances the claim that producing a good individual case formulation (ICF) is one of the key elements of therapeutic success. To put this differently, however much a general model of therapeutic change has been supported by evidence, it is its detailed translation for the individual that is of paramount importance. This places considerable responsibility on the therapist and her or his independent judgment. However, in the light of very little evidence concerning the merits of individually tailored therapy over standardized protocols, a case has to be made to justify it. The individual approach does not mean that every client will receive a different intervention. There is a body of knowledge that informs the analysis of problems that certainly does have implications for the selection of a method designed to solve them. Practice that is led by ICF is guided by an evidence base as well as by other forms of knowledge.

The significance I attach to independent judgment places the psychotherapist in the position of an expert. Naturally, a therapist does not "take control," decide on a client's goals, or direct a client what to do. Ultimately, it is the client who has to take matters into his or her own hands by thinking or acting differently. Formulation has to be a collaborative activity. Some forms of therapy do not pretend to offer an expert analysis derived from a therapist's stock of knowledge and I discuss these "non-expert" styles in Chapter 6. I will now give a general outline of case formulation and the tasks in which it is embedded.

CASE FORMULATION IN CONTEXT

On first acquaintance with a new client, a therapist is bound to wonder "Why has this person come?" "Why has she come right now?" "What is the real nature of the problem?" and "Am I able to offer what this client is looking for?" These questions begin to be answered when a therapist has constructed a case formulation. There is no widely accepted definition of a case formulation but most authors would include the following elements: a descriptive summary of the main problems broken down into their constituent components and situational triggers; how the components relate to one another, informed by a therapist's conceptual framework; an understanding of how a problem developed and is currently maintained; and some indication of a plan for how a problem can be resolved, based on a considered rationale.

Formulation skills are held in high regard in all forms of psychotherapy. This esteem acknowledges the complexity of problems and the contribution that a good formulation can make to the success of therapy. Therapists believe it to be unethical to intervene without a rationale for what they are trying to achieve—it gives a therapist confidence that she or he can respond appropriately. Although an initial formulation is usually revised later on, there is a brief initial stage in which a therapist is under pressure to decide whether he or she feels competent to deal with a problem or whether a client should be referred on for a different kind of service.

What happens in these first few sessions when problems are formulated is likely to be critical for later success. Although in recent years there has been a marked increase in the number of books published on case formulation, there is still a wide gap between the esteem in which it is held and the availability of a hands-on description of what it entails. When therapy does not go smoothly, a therapist is advised to make a careful and comprehensive appraisal of all the factors that could account for the difficulty. But there are rather few accounts of the process to which a therapist can turn. This may explain why novices are advised (and usually required) to seek out regular supervision from someone "more experienced." However, experience does not always count—it is easy enough to fail to appreciate the significance of an aspect of a client's situation or simply to get things wrong. It is for this reason that highly experienced therapists still seek out peer supervision. What ought to be of help here is a "method"—a systematic way of carefully reflecting on the circumstances surrounding a problem.

It is possible, but rather unlikely, that therapeutic success depends on accidental factors, such as a happy match between the personalities of therapist and client, or events occurring, as if by chance, in a client's life. These may be important contributors to outcome but evidence of consistent differences in the success rates of different therapists (see below) points to therapeutic skill. I will assume that at least one component of being a therapist who achieves good results is a skill in case formulation. This skill may not be sufficient by itself but its importance can hardly be denied. My aim is to present a method for structuring the process of formulation within a functional framework that is intended to be compatible with a wide range of conceptual models. It is clearly unsatisfactory to leave the ability to formulate in the position of an occult craft, and what follows is a step toward making it transparent.

The chief justification for good case formulation is pragmatic—that the analysis of a problem assists both therapist and client to work effectively toward its solution. Formulation, as noted, is a collaborative activity. There has to be a sharing of perspectives on what the problem is and how to approach it, otherwise therapy would never get started. The process involves a gradual, mutual shaping of an understanding, which, at some point, calls for decisions to be taken about what to do. If a therapist lays claim to expertise, she or he might have to argue a case that a certain course of action (based on her or his own understanding) is advisable. In this sense, the process can be gently adversarial as well as collaborative. There seem to be few arguments in favor of pursuing an intervention simply because a client wants it. In any case, practitioners are unlikely to be effective when they do not believe in what they are doing.

A major portion of the work of case formulation takes place at the start of therapy and sometimes in just one session. In this initial phase there are many other tasks to perform, such as getting acquainted with a client, informing him or her of what to expect, explaining the ground rules of the relationship, and providing information about the rationale of therapy. However, in order to limit the length of this book, I do not make these tasks, or the formation of a therapeutic relationship, a central theme. Aspects of the relationship will be discussed along the way but I will be concerned primarily with a therapist's conceptual understanding of a problem. This understanding typically develops within an interview assessment, supplemented by various additional means of gathering information (see Guidelines). The end result is a kind of negotiated account of the problem that satisfies both parties. However, this account should always be seen as open to revision or renegotiation. The chosen title of this book, *individual case formulation*, is intended to indicate that the process is not one of matching a client to a preconceived model of a problem. The title emphasizes the fact that no one client is identical to another and that a therapist, even when following a standard protocol, has to adjust an intervention to a client's unique circumstances. Of course, a client's problem is never entirely unique and it has to be understood within a framework of prior knowledge of effective techniques, psychological theory, and a familiarity with cultural norms and practices.

The first phase of therapy is generally known as "assessment and formulation" and something needs to be said about its defining limits. Given that the process of gathering information never really stops at any point, reformulation is the rule rather than the exception. A client may conceal crucial facts about him- or herself (not necessarily deliberately) and only reveal them six months or more into therapy. In practice, the first stage ends when a therapist feels that he or she has enough information to be going on with in order to initiate an intervention that it is believed will make a difference. If this stage is not reached, it seems best not to proceed at all, as then it would simply amount to groping around in the dark. Preliminary discussion is sometimes sufficient by itself, if only to conclude that there is nothing to be done. One criterion for proceeding is that the client has been sufficiently "educated" into the rationale of the methods employed. Reading matter, such as information leaflets or chapters from a self-help book, is often a valuable means of educating a client into the type of therapy on offer (see Guidelines).

In all styles of therapy, whether prescriptive or open-ended, a case formulation helps to match a set of interventions to the unique constellation of circumstances of a client's life. Foremost are a client's long-term and short-term objectives, the feasibility of achieving them given inevitable social constraints, the residue of historical habits that impede change, and the current factors that seem to be perpetuating a problem. Even in non-directive forms of therapy, some discipline has to be exerted over the way a client's problems are understood. The approach to formulation that I set out in the Guidelines will assume that a therapist possesses basic interviewing and counseling skills. My presentation of case formulation as a process is largely concerned with strategies for obtaining relevant information, organizing it, and submitting it to interpretation and evaluation. The approach could be described as a set of rules of sorts. However, it is not a manual that is rigidly prescriptive.

If the need for an individual formulation sounds convincing, why has so little been written about the process and why have researchers come to the conclusion that it does not really matter too much what kind of psychotherapy is offered (Wampold, 2010)? Although it is widely agreed that psychotherapy is effective, it has been much harder to demonstrate differences in outcome between different approaches to the same problem (e.g. Elkin et al., 1989; Shapiro et al., 1994). The finding of equivalent results with very different methods is a challenge to the intuition that an accurate formulation, identifying key obstacles to problem resolution, is an important determinant of success. There are common helpful elements in all types of psychotherapy, and perhaps it is these that are critical for success rather than a good analysis of the presenting problem. Another possibility is that therapists who adopt different theoretical models come up with similar useful interventions in practice. Some researchers have argued that the accuracy of a formulation may not matter as long as it is convincing and leads to changes that a client finds beneficial. Other factors to consider when accounting for equivalent results are methodological. Problems are often evaluated in a gross and standard manner rather than in terms of specific difficulties that are, or would be, responsive to a tailored intervention. In any case, given that a well-founded formulation is only one possible determinant of success, it would not be too surprising if a fog of other influential factors were to obscure its role. Whatever the eventual explanation for the finding of equivalent results with different types of therapy (and this is by no means a uniform finding), I assume that it will not diminish the important role of case formulation.

DIFFERENT MODELS OF CASE FORMULATION

There are marked differences in the way case formulation is undertaken in different forms of therapy. Some of them can be attributed to the enormous variety of clients that come to therapy. A client could be someone living in an institution, a child and his or her family, a couple, or a person with a health problem. I have restricted the scope of this book to adults who are living independently and, for the most part, are seeking one-to-one therapy over a relatively brief period of time. However, the proposed guidelines for assessing and formulating problems need not be seen as limited to this client group, or to one-to-one therapy alone. I have attempted to produce a method that can be generalized.

I have taken the interview to be the chief means through which information about clients' difficulties is collected because this reflects everyday practice. Standardized assessments may be performed as well but these cannot individualize a problem to a sufficient degree or relate it to the overall context of a client's life. Much of the information that is gleaned (and inferred) lies outside the strict content of what is said. The interview, combined with additional sources of information, enables a therapist to amass what might be called "facts" or "observations" from which inferences can be drawn. Through a process of reasoning, a therapist generates a number of "hypotheses" to explain these "facts" and how they relate to the origins of a problem and its persistence. I will take it that the making and interpretation of observations is a process common to all forms of therapy. The terms "observation" and "hypothesis" are not meant in an overly technical or scientific sense. I use the term hypothesis to include speculation, conjecture, hunch, and inference. The distinction between observation and hypothesis is a useful one, even though it may not be easy to justify philosophically. It has the advantage of making it possible to talk about a process of formulation that can be seen as applicable to all types of therapy. It is assumed that problems have causes and that it is possible to understand them theoretically. I develop this model of practice in Chapters 4 and 5.

As already noted, there is no uniform approach to case formulation. With so little research having been undertaken into formulation as a *process*, it is difficult to interpret the significance of the differences that exist. If we knew better what therapists actually do when formulating, we would probably make more progress toward a genuine integration across therapies, rather than settling for a pragmatic eclecticism. A significant aspect of all therapeutic activity is the role it plays in the life of a culture (Rose, 1998). It is possible that a better understanding of individual problems, and how they can be formulated in different ways, would suggest policy changes at a societal and political level (Rosenwald, 1988). Some light could be thrown on this if a micro-analysis were to be undertaken of moment-to-moment decision making in therapy. Research into formulation as an element of practice would very likely draw upon qualitative methods such as discourse and narrative analysis (e.g. Avdi & Georgaca, 2007). The need for this kind of analysis has become more pressing as therapy has moved away from the biomedical model and has presented itself as a practical philosophy. Psychological therapy is now seen as a sensible remedy for such disparate social problems as dependence on welfare, unemployment, the aftermath of trauma, and, more simply, raising the general level of happiness. There would be profound implications, for psychotherapy and for society, if therapists were to abandon the mission of treating problems as if these were the natural consequence of psychological disorders whose causes resided primarily within the individual.

"GOOD AND BAD" THERAPISTS

The strongest argument for the importance of professional expertise is the fact that some therapists consistently produce better results than others. This may account for more of the variation in outcome than does the choice of one therapeutic method over another. The variation due to therapists is one of the strongest predictors of success (Garske & Anderson, 2003; Wampold, 2010). In a study of 91 therapists in a university counseling center, clients assigned to the "best" therapists improved at a rate ten times faster than the rate achieved in clients seen by the "poorer" therapists (Okiishi, Lambert, Nielson, & Ogles, 2003). In fact the latter group showed an average *increase* in "symptoms" among their clients. A large variation in therapist effectiveness was also found by Kraus, Castonguay, Boswell, Nordberg, and Hayes (2011). Despite these findings on competence having been known for some time, Wampold (2010, p. 102) comments, "Depressingly, after decades of research, relatively little is known about the characteristics and actions of effective therapists."

The demonstration of differences in the success rate of different therapists leads one to believe that it would be helpful to investigate what actually takes place in therapy. According to Kazdin (2008, p. 155), "A critical deficit in our clinical training is in the evaluation of clinical cases in the context of 'real' therapy and clinical practice." At the conclusion of their edited book, *The heart and soul of change*, the editors (Hubble, Miller, Duncan, & Wampold, 2007, p. 424) look to the "next frontier" and recommend that we turn our attention "to the moment-by-moment, encounter-to-encounter processes associated with effective psychotherapy."

The chief contenders for explaining different rates of success among therapists are, first, something to do with the quality of the relationship that develops between client and therapist, and second, a therapist's ability to conceptualize a problem, and thereby do something to help resolve it. Baldwin, Wampold, and Imel (2007) found that the ability to form an alliance with a client completely accounted for differences between therapists in terms of the outcomes they achieved. However, in developing an alliance, the skills of relating to a client and formulating his or her problem are both likely to make a contribution (see Chapter 7). The relative importance of each skill may depend on the existence of interventions that can actually address the underlying causes of a difficulty. This is obvious in the case of medical treatment. If bloodletting is the only treatment on offer, it is more likely to achieve a good result if done by someone with a smile who inspires trust and generates hope. This point is underlined in a study cited by Wampold and colleagues (McKay, Zac, & Wampold, 2006) in which either an antidepressant or a placebo was prescribed. "Psychiatrists with the highest effects had better outcomes with the placebo than did the poorer psychiatrists giving the antidepressant" (Wampold, 2010, p. 101). However, in the case of a medical problem for which an accurate diagnosis is essential and for which there is a clearly effective treatment, it may not matter if the medical expert is taciturn or even downright rude. Of course, unlike medicine, where many diagnostic procedures are impersonal, in psychotherapy (and clearly in pharmacotherapy) it is necessary to have a good relationship with a client in order to achieve results and to obtain information relevant to a formulation.

CASE FORMULATION AND THE MEDICAL MODEL

By medical model I mean therapy that is styled on diagnosing a "condition" or "disorder" and then aiming to restore the client to a state of normal health. It hardly needs saying that case formulation should include the contribution of medical and biological factors but this is very different from making diagnosis a central aim of assessment. There is very little evidence for discrete biomedical causes of the common psychological problems: "psychological disorders" bear only a minor resemblance to medical disorders. In contrast to a period in the 1960s and 1970s, when there was an emphasis on "personal growth" rather than "treatment," the last 40 years has been the heyday of psychiatric diagnosis, associated with an enormous increase in the prescription of psychoactive medication designed to return clients to "normality." In the third edition of the *Diagnostic and statistical manual of mental disorders* (DSM-III), the American Psychiatric Association (1980) introduced descriptive, operational definitions of common psychological problems that proved extremely useful to academic researchers and those evaluating the new drugs and new therapies. The diagnostic approach to formulation is still the dominant one, although we are now witnessing a swing back to "positive psychology"—the aim being to promote well-being rather than to treat disorders (see Chapter 9).

Although psychiatric diagnosis plays a relatively small part in formulation as presented in this book, this is not to deny the existence of very distinctive patterns of complaint. For instance, a problem with an intrusive thought about feeling responsible for having caused harm is quite likely to coexist with other behaviors, such as seeking reassurance or checking that harm has not been caused. Phenomena that group together in this way have, of course, been labeled as disorders. Although psychiatric patterns of complaint might at times guide the direction of an assessment interview, labeling a pattern as a disorder does not amount to an explanation for it. Panic disorder is not an explanation of panic attacks any more than trichotillomania is an explanation for hair-pulling. Psychiatric diagnosis has become important because so much research into the effectiveness of therapy has been conducted on psychiatrically defined groups of participants. Individual case formulation (ICF) is bound to take note of the results of randomized control trials (RCTs) conducted on this basis, but I will argue that decision making is best guided by research evidence that points to reliable mechanisms (principles/processes) of change rather than to the success of a set of techniques with specific disorders.

However, therapy based on principles is not the prevailing view of evidence-based practice (EBP), which typically uses the RCT to pit one therapy against another, or to compare an experimental therapy with no treatment or treatment as usual. The result of an RCT, when the experimental treatment is shown to be efficacious, is called "empirically supported" treatment (EST) or "evidence-based" therapy (EBT). This kind of study is distinguished from one that shows "effectiveness" of the same "treatment" when it is evaluated in ordinary practice settings where the conditions of administration are less highly controlled. When proven successful, this is then referred to as evidence-based practice (EBP). The therapy manuals that have been developed in EBT research have been presented as the way to disseminate "scientific knowledge." I will refer to this form of science-based practice as manualized EBP or MEBP, and critically discuss the merits of this approach in Chapter 3.

REASONING ABOUT INDIVIDUAL CASES

The case study has for a long time been a feature of the therapy literature (e.g. Fishman, 1999; Stiles, 2005) but accounts of single cases are usually produced retrospectively, showing how the formulation led to a successful resolution of a client's problem. The write-up may be presented with a degree of triumphalism—the client improved even though previous techniques delivered by competitors had failed. In the Guidelines, I will attempt instead to illustrate case formulation as an evolving process, subject to all kinds of error, sometimes lacking key information, and usually needing to be constantly refreshed and renewed. In other words, formulation is not seen as a grand summing up, in the manner of a trial judge, based on an appraisal of everything that has been presented by the witnesses. It is for this reason that attempts to describe the process of formulation by asking practitioners to examine a vignette of a client, and then come to an opinion, hardly touch upon the nature of reasoning in actual situations. The actual process of formulation is one in which information is sought sequentially and for a purpose. The assessor thinks prospectively, not retrospectively, and the process may take place over an extended period of time. As Kazdin (2008, p. 149) remarks in relation to case formulation and decision making, "There are no formal or clearly replicable procedures for how to do this."

However, a great deal has been written on reasoning processes in individual case studies and various models are discussed in Chapter 4. One tradition of scientific reasoning that has influenced the author's approach to ICF goes back at least to Claude Bernard (1813–1878), the great French physiologist, who described his individual case experimental method in some detail (Bernard, 1957 [1865]). One of Bernard's chief pieces of advice was to keep a completely open mind when making observations. While his experiments were driven by specific hypotheses, he always attempted to put them aside when he confronted the "facts" revealed to him when his intervention (often surgery on a single animal) was undertaken. Bernard felt that his own field of physiology was complicated enough but in fact it was largely limited to the organism's internal environment and how it maintained itself as a stable system. It is fair to say that this system is more lawful and its behavior more closely linked to observable events than the open and indeterminate system in which clients' problems are situated. Unlike Bernard's aims, the practice of ICF is not an attempt to discover universal laws: there are far too many complicating influences to consider. The aim is to make use of nomothetic principles when constructing an idiographic understanding. There are several features of Bernard's single-case experimental method that can be usefully adapted to the formulation task. Bernard emphasized the process of reasoning about the facts of the case and this is true also of formulation. The conceptual foundations for ICF are developed in Chapters 4 and 5.

CHAPTER 2

Conceptual Frameworks for Case Formulation

The psychotherapist is a somewhat marginal figure in society. She or he claims knowledge and skills that are only partially available to people without training. The public's attitude wavers between two extremes: on the one hand, respect, gratitude, and even awe for someone who might solve a disabling problem, and on the other hand, skepticism, usually mixed with a dose of humor or disparagement. These attitudes are not infrequently expressed when therapists comment on each other's abilities. Perhaps this state of affairs will change when it becomes clearer what therapists actually do and how they reason when confronted with a client's problem. One purpose of this book is to present a method for carrying out a case formulation that should make it easier to debate the activities of therapists out in the open.

If the success of therapy is derived, at least in part, from explicit principles and methods proven to be effective, we can speak of potential advance in case formulation as a field of endeavor. It should be possible to codify the conceptual foundations and teach them. In this chapter, I will consider a number of attempts to conceptualize case formulation as a process and I will assume that progress in this area is achievable. There are widely differing views on the topic and not much sign of agreement at present. Handbooks of psychotherapy lay out the wares of the most popular models, each seeming to describe clients' problems in terms of its own theoretical assumptions. Consequently, there is little sense that the description of a problem can be separated from the proposed manner of its solution. The handbook of Dryden (2007) presents 16 models and Corey (2009) 12, but neither has an entry "formulation" in the index. Assessment and functional analysis usually get a brief mention in relation to cognitive behavioral approaches. Narrative therapists tend not to see themselves as having any special theoretical or technical expertise. For them, a therapist facilitates a process in which a client conceptualizes the source of his or her problem in a new way and considers the opportunities open to him or her to escape it (see Chapter 6).

A psychotherapist has an unusual social role in the sense of dealing with the most intimate aspects of a client's life while not normally allowing this

Individual Case Formulation
http://dx.doi.org/10.1016/B978-0-12-398269-8.00002-8

intimacy to develop into friendship. Moreover, he or she expects a salary or payment. For this reason, psychotherapy has sometimes been thought to bear comparison with prostitution. Yet trust, respect, affection, and loyalty are characteristic of many client–therapist relationships as much as they are in any friendship. I am going to assume that the relationship is a very important mediator of change, while maintaining that knowledge of psychology and the ability to formulate a problem using concepts that a client may not understand are equally important ingredients of success. There is no reason to view technical expertise as incompatible with sensitivity to social cues, empathy with cultural predicaments, and an ability to communicate in a manner that a client finds acceptable and engaging. In Chapter 7, I review research on the therapeutic relationship and attempt to unravel its relationship to formulation. In sum, I view case formulation as drawing upon expert knowledge of a conceptual and methodological kind as well as craft skills of an interpersonal nature.

RECONCILING NOMOTHETIC PRINCIPLES WITH AN IDIOGRAPHIC ANALYSIS

As this book is about *individual* case formulation, it might be assumed that attending to the features of a problem that make it unique means, inevitably, that therapy ends up being an art rather than a science. Held (1995, p. 15) poses the issue as follows: "How can the practice of therapy be individualized, and at the same time also be consistent, replicable, or generalized—that is, systematic across cases?" Held modifies her view on the art/science divide by arguing that even art follows rules. It does not seem inconsistent to maintain that therapy draws upon principles, processes, and rules while acknowledging that some problems do not have a single answer or even an answer of any kind that can be derived from a system. But a therapist can still be helpful by facilitating a creative or pragmatic rejoinder to life's seemingly unanswerable dilemmas by applying general principles.

Held expects that any self-respecting therapy should have a theory of problem causation, and this implies putting forward generalizations about clients who have problems. However, it could be argued that a theory of disorders is not needed. I do not mean to imply that psychological theory and other forms of knowledge are irrelevant; it is to maintain, rather, that they are equally relevant to "disordered" and "non-disordered" behavior. We do not need a theory that applies only to disordered people in order to help them to act normally. Put differently, it may not be necessary to have a theory of problem causation that is distinct from theory in general. Just as the random assortment of genes produces a unique biological individual, a certain combination of values on the cultural, psychosocial, and biological variables that determine behavior might produce a unique kind of problem. Its uniqueness resides in a configuration of otherwise shared characteristics. Although there are undoubtedly groups of people with similar problems, it will be argued that the creation of problem-specific causal theories is not the best way forward to provide a conceptual rationale for therapy.

One question to consider is whether progress has been, or could be, made in the "science" and methods of producing a case formulation that respects the fact that we are all unique. I take up this question in Chapter 5, where I discuss how scientific and other forms of reasoning have been applied to the single case. Although case formulation is an aspect of a relatively recent social practice found in developed societies, I reject the view that as a largely Western phenomenon, nothing of a universal nature can be said about it. If it were merely a culturally specific practice, there would be few reasons to expect any advance in the field associated with a unifying body of knowledge. However, I assume that when therapists from different schools of thought formulate, they are trying to answer similar questions from a basis in theory. Psychological science is not at present unified and that is the normal state of affairs in any academic field. The hope instilled by the idea of progress in formulation is not so much integration within the psychotherapies on the basis of an agreed model or set of techniques, but a hope that a clarification of the *process* of formulation will be recognized as such by people following different models. In other words, therapists might agree on the general nature of what they are trying to do while disagreeing on how best to do it.

IS A THERAPIST'S COMPETENCE RELATED TO THERAPEUTIC SUCCESS?

Turning to the empirical evidence, what is damaging to the hope for progress in defining case formulation and related skills is the fact that a therapist's adherence to a treatment protocol and their rated competence as a therapist seem to bear little relationship to the success of therapy (Webb, DeRubeis, & Barber, 2010), although there are some exceptions to this conclusion (Trepka, Rees, Shapiro, Hardy, & Barkham, 2004). It is possible that adherence to a method and competence as a therapist are necessary to produce good results but may not be sufficient in themselves. Trepka et al.

found that therapist competence was most strongly related to outcome when the statistical analysis was limited to clients who completed their therapy. Characteristics of the client were more likely to determine outcome for the non-completers.

Outcome is likely to be determined by a variety of factors besides a therapist's competence. One extra ingredient is the quality of the therapeutic relationship and another is an event that lies completely outside a therapist's control. For instance, adverse or beneficent influences, such as bereavement or a financial loss or the client finding a mate or a job, could determine outcome. According to Norcross and Lambert (2011), around 40% of the variance in outcome status after therapy is unexplained. They consider that 30% is related to characteristics of the client, 12% to the quality of the therapeutic relationship, 8% to the treatment method, and 7% to variation between therapists. They conclude that customizing therapy to the individual client probably adds to effectiveness through multiple pathways. In other words, it is not known whether a good formulation contributes to outcome or even whether it is important. This might come as a surprise to some prospective candidates for therapy. A popular view of psychological experts is that they can read minds and that this makes them effective.

One lesson that could be drawn from the apparent lack of relationship between competently delivered therapy and a successful outcome is that more attention needs to be paid to the uniqueness of clients' problems and to a micro-analysis of therapists' actions. This kind of analysis might reveal what is happening when a client does not appear to be responding to an intervention. As Barlow (2010) points out, the efforts to demonstrate positive effects from therapy have obscured the circumstances surrounding the production of negative effects. He advocates an idiographic analysis of these failures, not only as a way of avoiding harm but also of learning more about the processes underlying therapy. However, given the variety of theoretical models and methods employed in psychotherapy, a prerequisite for an analysis of success and failure is a common language for discussing clients and their problems (see below).

HAS PROGRESS BEEN MADE IN PSYCHOTHERAPY?

If we survey what has been taken to be progress in the field of psychotherapy over the last 100 years, we can see that it has often been driven by schism. A new therapy is a kind of revolt against an earlier one. Techniques of psychological therapy have certainly made strides since the mid-twentieth century but largely through the efforts of charismatic individuals who have followed a path of their own making. These individuals are inspirational but their claims frequently outstrip the evidence. For example, in relation to cognitive therapy, Dobson and Khatri (2000), at the turn of the millennium, looked backward and forward in their evaluation of this therapy's undoubted achievements. They sounded many cautions while at the same time regarding cognitive therapy "as enjoying unprecedented strength and popularity" (p. 920). They described it as "a complex, multi-component therapy" (p. 912) but in terms of its "effective ingredients" they concluded that the "question has no answer at present." Dobson and Khatri cited research showing that cognitive factors may not be significant in the etiology and maintenance of depression, and they wondered whether these results would be paralleled in cognitive therapy for anxiety disorder and post-traumatic stress. Seven years later, this was still a concern (Longmore & Worrall, 2007). In other words, reviewers have judged that the popularity of cognitive therapy is based on rather shaky theoretical foundations. However, this conclusion could really be drawn about any current form of psychotherapy. If in our present state of knowledge we do not really know why therapy works, it is not surprising that the skill of formulation remains obscure.

A FRAMEWORK FOR DESCRIBING PROBLEMS

The possibility of making any advance in the area of case formulation, of a kind that could be agreed across different forms of psychotherapy, would seem to depend on reaching a measure of agreement about how to describe people's problems. As noted in Chapter 1, a degree of accord has been achieved by making use of psychiatric diagnostic categories. One advantage of the definitions supplied by the American Psychiatric Association's *Diagnostic and statistical manuals* (DSM) is that they are descriptive, operational, and relatively easy to follow (American Psychiatric Association, 2002). By avoiding theoretical explanations for the presence of "disorder" in a particular form, they can be accepted by therapists holding different models. The popularity of psychiatric diagnostic systems has been consolidated by their integration into the decision making of health providers, medical insurance companies, and researchers who conduct evaluations of therapeutic outcomes. However, as descriptions they are not formulations. Researchers have attempted to understand the processes causing these "disorders" and many of their findings have been enlightening. But given the somewhat arbitrary and conventional nature of definitions of disorder, research is hampered by preconceptions. However attractive it may seem to rely on categories of disorder, it is evident that in most areas of science, researchers do not begin with operational definitions, or use them at all, until they can be justified theoretically and help to advance theory. Patterns of psychiatric phenomena may provide a source of hypotheses in individual case formulation (ICF) in the sense that an assessment might explore a correspondence between the presenting problem and psychiatric diagnostic criteria. This may allow certain inferences to be drawn but agreement with a diagnosis is not the endpoint of formulation as I intend to present it. Rather, it is more likely to be the starting point for an exploration of the determinants of a client's problem.

My adoption of a problem-solving terminology reflects the form that one-to-one therapy usually takes in Western culture. In other words, problems are presented in a certain local form, even though it is evident that some universal features of problem types can be found across cultures. Problem solving may not be a relevant framework for psychotherapy in all cultural settings. In a Western context, too, some clients may prefer to be diagnosed with a psychiatric disorder rather than consider that they have a psychological problem. A psychological formulation is not always helpful to a client in the sense that it may raise the question of blaming self or others (Leeming, Boyle, & MacDonald, 2009). The psychiatric diagnostic approach is predicated on the idea that psychiatry can be a natural science, a position I rejected in Chapter 1. Therefore, an individual case formulation is bound to take a contested form, making it possible to take several perspectives on the "same" problem.

Individual therapy primarily concerns two players who freely contract to engage in an activity that can be described in a general way as sharing a problem. The client presents a difficulty to be resolved and the therapist is assumed to possess relevant expertise. The form of their interaction is regulated socially and professionally. It is worth noting that the application of expert knowledge has strict limitations in this social context. As already noted, personal problems are open to a wide variety of solutions that may encompass hard decisions, pragmatic choices, the creation of a personal narrative, and, in fact, all of the elements to be found in a novel or soap opera. A therapist has to be aware of a client's need to weave all the different aspects of their personality and life possibilities into a meaningful whole that, barring unforeseen events, does not come apart at the seams. My use of the word "problem" therefore carries little theoretical baggage and is not meant to imply that a client "really" has a problem or that the causes of the problem lie solely within a client. Moreover, the term "individual" in ICF can be extended to mean the particular concerns of a couple, family, or group, in which case the client is not an individual person.

A problem is a product of a client's life situation, in part self-created and in part imposed. A therapist's expertise as an analyst, like that of a novelist, may lie in dissecting and unraveling the mess that conflicting stories can produce. However, expertise is not limited to a superior form of insight or empathy. A therapist is able to draw upon a body of academic knowledge about psychological processes and effective therapeutic techniques. A client in the grip of a negative emotion, a compulsive habit, or an inability to think clearly about the options for solving a problem has the right to expect a measure of expertise that derives from established theories and proven methods. In other words, a therapist draws upon causal knowledge of how particular human acts arise, are sustained, and fall out of use. The expert has to translate whatever follows from this knowledge into a credible rationale for action. The rationale must make sense within a client's understanding of her or his own life, and this is not quite the same thing as presenting it as just another kind of story.

The theories that inform case formulation belong to wider historical and philosophical movements. Therapeutic techniques have an even closer link with current fads and fashions. Psychotherapy can be analyzed as a cultural and historical practice as well as being taken at face value as a means of responding to personal problems. In many instances, a client can be helped by placing his or her problem in a social context and in this way understand how it is related to, say, gender roles, social class, racism, difficulties of cultural integration, and so forth. When the wider social context of a personal problem is clearly relevant, I will highlight it in the examples of case formulation I provide. But for many clients, social contextualization may not seem relevant to the way they rationalize what they are aiming for on a day-to-day basis. They might not seek to have their "consciousness raised" although a therapist might feel frustrated that this is not the case. The problem as presented for formulation is essentially what a client says it is, at least at the beginning of the process, and possibly throughout. This follows from the fact that psychotherapy is a voluntary activity initiated (typically) by a client.

LITERAL DESCRIPTION VERSUS INTERPRETATION/ HYPOTHESIS

There is little hope of advance in the field of case formulation until therapists of different persuasions can agree on a way of describing clients' problems. This might be possible if therapists confined themselves to a level of description that is fairly literal. By literal, I do not mean "objective" or "neutral." In other words, it is possible to produce a literal description of a client's fantasies or projected possibilities of any kind. I will take it to be the case that someone who has a fantasy or is capable of acting in a certain way (but has not yet done so) is literally describing that frame of mind or potential for action. While accepting what is literally presented as a problem, a therapist can withhold judgment on whether the state of affairs implied by a client's statement corresponds to a shared, objective view of the world. For instance, if a fantasy concerns flying to the moon, a therapist might want to assess whether this is literally possible and what the literal (objective) consequences of expressing that fantasy might be. If expressed in jest or as a metaphor, the consequences are very different from expressing the idea with a firm conviction of its possibility. The consequences are usually capable of being described literally (i.e. the actual possibility of flying to the moon or the actual consequences of expressing that belief with conviction), although the means of assessing them may have to rely on a good deal of detective work and speculation. The objection might be put forward that there is no such thing as a shared objective view of the world. Clearly, it is not always easy to establish what is "normal," "rational," "commonly believed," etc., but a psychotherapist would quickly lose a grip on reality without firmly held values and an appeal to shared assumptions about the nature of our everyday reality.

The purpose of a literal description of a client's circumstances (including his or her imagined or unrealized possibilities) is to distinguish them from interpretations that account for or explain the observations in some way. The interpretation might come from the client or from the therapist. An interpretation does not have to be framed in theoretical terms but could consist of an account that has been elaborated in ordinary language. Therapists usually prefer to interpret theoretically but as Corrie and Lane (2010, p. 37) rightly point out, a therapist's preferred conceptual model "boundaries the stories the client is encouraged to tell and, importantly, the range of reconstructions which are permitted." It is for this reason that it seems desirable to separate observation and interpretation, however difficult that may be to achieve in practice.

Clients employ all kinds of self-interpretation when trying to understand their difficulties. Most do not doubt that they possess a capacity to understand themselves or that when they express an intention to change, they actually mean it. However, I will reserve the term "case formulation" for a therapist's interpretations and regard a client's understanding of their problem as an aspect of its description. This does not mean that a therapist's formulation is necessarily "better" than the latter. In fact, the formulation may have been borrowed from the client. The difference is that therapy is not a "normal conversation" and clients do not expect it to be merely that. The suggestion I am making is that a therapist can stand back from what a client says or does and treat it in a more literal manner. A person might say that they have a good intention to change but what does that mean in context? When do they say it, why do they say it, who do they say it to, what are the consequences of saying it, and why don't they say something else instead? This amounts to taking a functional perspective on formulation. The approach is rather like that of an ethologist of human behavior who asks about the significance of gestures and vocalizations in the context in which they are expressed.

It could be argued that a psychiatrist takes a similar ethological approach when she or he records signs and symptoms of abnormality, stands back, and assigns a client to a category of disorder. The difference, though, is that this process is far less sensitive to the contextual and functional significance of the observations. For instance, the "symptoms" of major depression can also be observed in someone who has suffered bereavement and therefore the latter person might have to be assigned, on this basis, to a different category of disorder. This is a very blunt functional distinction. Is someone who is depressed by the death of a pet parrot or the death of his or her favorite celebrity suffering a normal bereavement or a major depression? The framework for case formulation that I am proposing attempts to take a much more deeply functional and contextual form.

Is everyday language adequate as the basis for problem description? Unfortunately, if we abandon the attempt to describe in a fairly literal way the circumstances that seem to surround what a client says is their problem, the alternative seems quite unclear. Sturmey (2008, p. 196) believes that a description in ordinary language can be readily translated into observable behavior. For example, he suggests that "lacks assurance" could be re-described as "low rates of public, reinforced behavior." However, the latter phrase is a theoretical explanation for something that a client says, not anything that can be observed without first defining what happens to be reinforcing to the individual in question, and without assuming a shared understanding of the rate at which a client's behavior is deserving of approval. A low rate of public reinforced behavior is not a problem for a client who is unconcerned about seeking it.

If we give up on any claim to be objective in the sense of using shared terms that have a clear meaning, the chief alternative seems to be a clash of perspectives in which the most powerful or persuasive wins out. It seems desirable to establish an agreed description of a problem in ordinary language before a process of formulating on the basis of technical terms begins. Otherwise, a therapist has no greater claim to expertise than anyone who happens to use the familiar linguistic, rhetorical, and cultural resources that can be drawn upon to influence another person. These skills and resources, when employed for a client's benefit, are essential and should not be underrated, and some therapists might suggest that this is all there is. I will argue that therapists should also appeal to theories and methods that are not employed merely as rhetorical devices. By making a therapist's theoretical inferences explicit in case formulation, and distinct from a literal description of a problem, their validity is open to public scrutiny.

WHO OWNS THE FORMULATION: THERAPIST OR CLIENT?

Despite my earlier statement that a case formulation is a therapist's construction, the simple answer to this question is that at some point both therapist and client must own a shared conceptualization, otherwise therapy would involve outright deception or manipulation. However, this might only amount to a tentative owning of the conceptualization for both parties. A picture of a problem is usually built up in a collaborative way, with an assumption of honesty on both sides. A case conceptualization is not a synthesis of two points of view or a negotiated compromise between two opposing positions. Rather, it is an agreed understanding of how to go about working on a problem jointly. This agreement might acknowledge differences of opinion. One source of disagreement might be the attribution of intent to other people in a client's life, who may be contributing to a problem. Evidence and inference have to be brought to bear on the matter and both client and therapist should undertake to consider it, even if it is not possible to reach complete agreement.

Sometimes, a therapist might not wish to challenge a client's "delusions," realizing that nothing could be achieved if this were to happen. A therapist's formulation of a problem is bound to differ in some respects from a client's, otherwise no advice would be requested, and so there is necessarily an element of challenge in the relationship. In this sense, producing a case formulation (as distinct from a literal description of a problem) is never a neutral act but is, rather, an account that is designed to encourage a client to act differently. It is presumably on the basis of *not* sharing an understanding with their client (and often on theoretical grounds unique to each type of therapy) that a therapist feels they have something to offer.

A COMMON LANGUAGE FOR PROBLEM DESCRIPTION

The idea that there is a discourse that can be shared easily between therapist and client is implicit in the recommendation to begin an assessment with a complete list of a client's problems. This has to be done in a common language. While it is obviously necessary to accept as a problem what a client says it is, this acceptance can only extend so far. In fact, many clients come for therapy expecting a therapist to clarify or identify the nature of their problems. For this reason, it is rarely possible to make a comprehensive list initially or a list that does not change later on.

A client's understanding of their own problem might be the problem needing to be tackled. If a client insists that their problem is a result of the actions of Martians, a therapist can hardly be expected to go along with it, although the belief should be treated with respect. Once a therapist has obtained a description of a client's problems, it is almost inevitable that she or he will try to identify patterns across a range of complaints. This is an exercise guided by concepts that may form no part of a client's implicit understanding of the nature of his or her problem. A therapist has to operate at a double level of understanding. He or she can imagine what it is like to be affected by powerful Martians but reserve judgment on what this signifies. A description of problems seems to be needed that allows for what is literally said or observed to be interpreted in different ways. This is needed for client/therapist communication as well as for a discussion about a client that takes place between different therapists. By sharing a literal (concrete) description, therapists holding different theories should at least be able to agree about their subject matter even if they cannot agree on its interpretation.

A literal description is not one from which all meaning has been subtracted so that it becomes merely behavior described from a third-person perspective. As noted earlier, the format is better described as ethological, applying as much to primates and newborn babies as to verbally sophisticated adults. An ethological description includes the circumstances in which behavior is expressed and also an account of other behavior that could have been expressed at the same time. It is noted what is distinctive about the environment when the particular behavior of interest occurs. The observer also speculates about (or observes) the effects of the behavior on surrounding events, including other people and their reactions.

Goldfried's CASE system (Causal Analysis and Synthesis of Events) is one of the most systematic attempts to develop a coding system that allows for a comparison of client–therapist interaction across different therapies (Jose & Goldfried, 2008). The CASE system is essentially a formal version of ordinary everyday concepts. The main categories it employs are situation, expectation, self-evaluation, self-observation, intention, other thoughts (such as attribution of intent to self and other), emotion, and action.

Although this system should facilitate communication, there is still the possibility of disagreement about the assignment of observations to categories. For instance, although a client's self-evaluation (e.g. "I am a worthless person") can be accepted as a literal expression of their problem, this might not be enough to say what kind of self-evaluation it is or even whether it is rightly categorized as a self-evaluation. Such a client would probably attribute their minor errors to deep failings but a therapist would also be interested in the literal state of affairs surrounding the statement in order to establish its meaning. Perhaps a client is simply trying to create an *impression* of worthlessness for the therapist, in which case it is not a true self-evaluation.

In other words, different therapists might disagree about the categorization of the apparently literal statement "I am a worthless person" while attempting to employ the same generic CASE concepts. The concepts do not seem easy to apply without further description of the functional context of behavior. What a client says can always be understood to carry different implications. Each categorization of behavior has to be justified and supported by further observations and reasoning. For instance, if the self-evaluation "I am a worthless person" is understood to signify an appeal to the therapist as a savior figure, this description of the statement would need to be justified by other observations about which the discussants could agree. At some basic level of description of what is said and the context for saying it, discussants must consent to agree or be accused of not playing the game. Of course, having reached this agreement, they could still disagree about the theoretical interpretation of what has been observed. The upshot of this digression is that there seems to be a level of description that involves only a low level of inference (at least when the discussants share the same cultural assumptions) and a higher level of inference that could be called theoretical. At the higher level, client and therapist, or different therapists, might disagree about the validity of the theoretical interpretation.

Goldfried writes that when other people in a client's life are involved in their problem, a therapist speculates about the determinants of the other's behavior, based on cultural experience and general knowledge. While it is certainly natural, and almost inevitable, for a therapist to do this, the grounds for doing so have to be backed up by evidence and inferential reasoning. Otherwise, a therapist might get the other person's attributions entirely wrong.

One reason for insisting on a description of the circumstances surrounding a statement or observation is that it opens up the possibility of a greater number of theoretical explanations. For instance, Jose and Goldfried state quite reasonably that not doing something can count as an action. However, without a description of the context for not acting, the act cannot be interpreted. The non-action has to be linked to the actual consequences of acting or not acting. There are many possible interpretations of inaction that rest on a theoretical interpretation. Does a therapist accept a client's remark that he or she could have performed an action if only they had wanted to? This is unlikely without further checks.

Jose and Goldfried include in the formulation a description of a client's assets and resources, which is understandably a necessary feature of the context. However, an asset or a resource only makes sense in relation to something else—a client's behavior in a particular situation or a client's life goals. It has to be made clear how an asset or a resource is integrated into the formulation. In fact, a client may not realize what assets and resources they possess and the promotion of this realization could become an objective for therapy. The rationale for formulating at all is that it is suggestive of interventions that might result in the resolution of a problem.

In the Guidelines, I develop a similar approach to CASE but one that is more explicitly functional in tying together the elements. Jose and Goldfried implicitly take a functional view when they recommend analyzing patterns of functioning across situations and "synthesizing the underlying determinants." However, there is always the risk that therapists who follow different conceptual models will be selective when choosing which features to observe. If so, it is doubtful that they would synthesize the determinants in the same way. Despite the rather intractable nature of this problem, it can be mitigated by openness to what counts as a useful observation, by a comprehensive coverage of all relevant sources of information, and by seeking contextual and inferential support for any proposed synthesis. Furthermore, a therapist can entertain different interpretations, pitting one against another, in order to counteract the tendency to be determined by one preferred model. As I intend to portray it, case formulation is an ongoing process of hypothesis testing in which a variety of interpretations, sometimes derived from very different theoretical models, are compared for their fit to the evidence.

HOW DO THERAPISTS ACQUIRE THEIR SKILLS?

There are a number of generic skills that are bound to be required in psychotherapy, such as building a relationship and engaging a client in the therapeutic process. This section is concerned with skills of observation, analysis, and formulation that go beyond these basic requirements. Most texts on therapeutic practice say surprisingly little about the methods a novice therapist has to learn in order to formulate well. In fact, experts in the field do not seem to blush at the notion that the whole process of psychotherapy lacks transparency for outsiders. Bearing in mind the needs for privacy and confidentiality, Sharpless and Barber (2009, p. 54) note that "a veil of secrecy surrounds so much of our work and the presentation of our work." Their account of the process of teaching professional expertise amounts to saying, more or less, that it is a matter of experience. Novices are seen to be applying, rather mechanically, the context-free rules that they have been required to learn; theoretical knowledge effectively distances them from truly "encountering" the client. Later on, the accounts that novices give of clients become "more organized, nuanced, contextual, and coherent." Ultimately, the expert grasps the features of situations intuitively and begins to work on automatic pilot. Experts simply immerse themselves in what experience has taught them. This description of the surface signs of developing competence may not be inaccurate, but it does not engender confidence that it corresponds to a definable learning process.

The account of developing competence given by Sharpless and Barber (2009) does not square up with the evidence, in part collected by themselves, that ratings of therapist competence do not correlate with a successful outcome of therapy (Webb, DeRubeis, & Barber, 2010). Either competence is not what it appears to be or therapists have failed to formulate and intervene on critical aspects of a problem and this leads to ultimate failure. However, the authors' recommendation to use video and audio recording, and direct observation during training, must hold out some hope (if combined with adequate analysis and discussion) that therapist competence is capable of being defined with greater precision (see also Chapter 9 for further suggestions on training).

With regard to the skills of case formulation, most accounts of therapy do not go much beyond listing aspects of a problem that need to be assessed and tasks that have to be performed (e.g. Stuart & Robinson, 2003). A transcript with a commentary, the method I adopt in the Guidelines, is probably the closest one gets to understanding how information about a client is translated into a formulation and intervention. A videotaped interview with expert commentary is also instructive (e.g. Padesky, 1997). Published case studies are not very informative unless they follow a therapist's line of thinking as it develops rather than how it is presented with hindsight.

I will now comment briefly on how formulation is understood by some of the major forms of psychotherapy. The process is likely to include helping a client to explore the questions on her or his mind, listening, empathizing, and facilitating solutions with reflective comments. However, my purpose here is to consider *proactive* attempts to analyze and interpret problems.

DIFFERENT MODELS OF FORMULATION AND THEIR RELATIONSHIP TO INTERVENTION

Integrative Therapy

Taking Norcross and Goldfried (2005, p. 443) as a guide, their account of this approach could be described as eclecticism rather than theoretical integration: "The training emphasis is placed squarely on acquiring competence in multiple methods and formats as opposed to pledging allegiance to theories, and pragmatically blending these methods and formats to suit the situation." Held (1995, p. 37), quoting Paul (1967), calls this approach technical eclecticism: "*What* treatment, by *whom*, is most effective for *this* individual with *that* specific problem, and under *which* set of circumstances." It is not clear from Norcross' statement how a therapist decides what suits the situation apart from empirical evidence, if it exists, about the effectiveness of various techniques. The implication is that there is no generic model, just an attitude of impartiality. However, there is a presumption that there exist types of clients, types of problem, and types of therapy about which something of a general nature can be stated. While this is true to some degree, it is difficult to see how a therapist, acting as a kind of omniscient observer, could impartially select a particular intervention for a particular client. In any case, what makes a client unique is not necessarily that he or she possesses the mark of "client" stamped on his or her forehead; rather, at a particular moment in time, a person is presented with a unique configuration of events or challenges (none of which is necessarily out of the ordinary) that creates a problem.

The difference between technical eclecticism and ICF is that, in the latter, a therapist attempts to be impartial when laying out the details of a problem but does interpret observations theoretically. Like an integrative therapist, she or he would entertain a range of interpretations, some of which might be borrowed from competing theoretical models or they might have little to do with psychological theory as such. The therapist is guided by, rather than relies on, generalizations about what works for whom, and an attempt is made to choose between hypotheses that best explain the problem and offer up hope of a solution. In contrast, technical eclecticism amounts to offering "what works" or "seems best" in the circumstances.

Beutler (2000) takes this empirical approach to its logical extreme by deriving guiding principles from nomothetic research into client and therapist variables that are known to influence therapy outcome. These are combined with "simple principles of relationship and interpersonal influence and applying them in creative ways that fit the endless permutations and complexities that characterize the people who seek the therapist's services" (Beutler, 2000, p. 1006). The assumption is made that all therapies share some common therapeutic change principles. However, it is doubtful that empirical evidence for general factors influencing success can provide a sufficiently rich source of ideas for formulation. Beutler has produced 18 guidelines that have rather little in the way of a unifying conceptual thread (Beutler, Moleiro, & Talebi, 2002). He argues that "Only an artist can apply these scientific principles" (Beutler, 2000, p. 1006) but here lies the problem. Something beyond the 18 guidelines seems to be needed to warrant an artistic practice.

Goldfried's view of integrative therapy seeks a richer synthesis between different theoretical models (Goldfried, 1980, 2009). He also emphasizes some common principles and strategies of the change process, such as forming an alliance with a client, attending to motivation and expectation, raising awareness of factors that contribute to a problem, and the general notion of "corrective experience." An important example of this overarching view is the idea of levels of readiness for change (Prochaska, 1979). These are all important considerations that are inseparable from the process of ICF. They will be discussed in this book in relation to specific case illustrations in the Guidelines. ICF is theoretically eclectic and therefore does not aim for integration in the sense of a brand label. However, it is not technically eclectic, given that ICF attempts to understand and explain rather than select interventions on an empirical or pragmatic basis only.

Cognitive Behavioral Therapy (CBT)

There are two major theoretical strands in cognitive behavioral therapy (CBT)—one behavioral and the other cognitive. The behavioral tradition grew out of the application of theories of conditioning and learning that were mainly developed from experimentation with animals. The influence of behaviorist philosophy and related methods began to wane in the 1970s, to be replaced by increasing interest in cognitive models that speculated about events and processes within the "mind." The most influential voice came from Aaron Beck, who introduced cognitive concepts that were loosely based on information-processing models (Beck, 1970, 1976). His cognitive therapy distanced itself from behavior therapy but, in reality, cognitive therapy retains many concepts from theories of learning. In the last 25 years, cognitive therapy has imported new ideas from a variety of other therapeutic traditions. The earlier behavioral strand of CBT has remained sufficiently distinct from cognitive therapy to be considered separately here under the label "functionalist." The defining characteristic of the latter approach is an analysis of behavior into functional units linked together into causal chains, in which there is greater emphasis on situational determinants than on internal factors. Functional approaches have changed considerably from their earlier and radical incarnation within behavior therapy. This has been necessary to accommodate the undeniable reality of cognitive mediation.

Some cognitive therapists take an idiographic approach while others subsume problems within a general model for the client's "disorder" (a nomothetic approach). The open-ended (Socratic) style of questioning that is so essential to the execution of many cognitive therapy techniques is almost bound to ensure that a therapist elicits an account that does justice to a client's unique circumstances.

Other techniques, such as homework tasks designed to test a client's specific beliefs, also ensure that the formulation is idiographic. However, the nomothetic element can loom very large when problems are matched to a psychiatric diagnosis or to a disorder-specific conceptual model. This now seems to be the mainstream approach within cognitive therapy. For example, Persons (2008), who is guided by both learning and cognitive models in her approach to formulation, suggests that a case-level formulation should be used in conjunction with a symptom-level and disorder-level formulation (Persons, 2008, p. 94). Persons argues that one reason for determining a psychiatric diagnosis is that research on treatment efficacy is geared to diagnostic entities.

Although Persons has promoted her style of CBT as based on an individual case formulation, the strategy she adopts is very much a compromise between manualized evidence-based practice (MEBP) organized around concepts of disorder, and the use of hypothesis testing that is sensitive to an individual client's circumstances. Consequently, clients are described in both psychiatric terms (as having symptoms, psychopathology, disorders) and in terms of "problems" (social isolation, work problems, etc.). The ICF approach proposed in this book avoids using medical terminology and attempts to formulate problems using general principles or processes. There are, of course, no empirically supported protocols for "problems" as such, because problems arise in a set of individual and usually idiosyncratic circumstances. Their formulation has to extend beyond any methods that have been devised to deal, say, with obsessions in general or depression in general, useful as these methods might be.

Persons' case formulation model consists of the mechanisms to account for symptoms/problems; these are chiefly the historical origins that gave rise to "maladaptive schemas" or "conditioned responses." A problem is defined partly by what a client says it is and partly by what, in the therapist's opinion, seems to be having a deleterious effect on a client's life, for example, circumstances that produce a depressed mood. Functional relationships are invoked to explain how one problem can lead to another or exacerbate it in a vicious cycle (e.g. a client's irritability might have led to marital friction). In Persons' view, the descriptive analysis of a problem is not the source of ideas for an intervention in a bottom-up manner but influences how, given that a "schema" or "a conditioned response" is viewed as the main mechanism, a top-down theoretical model is applied. In one of the case illustrations supplied (Persons, 2008, p. 141), the interventions were derived from Beck's cognitive model, Mowrer's two-factor theory of fear and avoidance learning, and Lewinsohn's operant model of depression. As Persons (p. 143) succinctly puts it: "A shorthand strategy is to simply identify the nomothetic formulation(s) the therapist is using to conceptualize the case without writing down the details that are involved in individualizing it."

The strategy Persons adopts is probably used to some degree by all therapists, in the sense that some interventions are routinized and others are flexible and creatively designed (see Chapter 5 for models of expert reasoning). At one end of the continuum a therapist follows a protocol closely, and at the opposite end decisions follow a reasoning process or simply rest on intuition. It is difficult to place Persons (or any other practitioner) in a precise position along this continuum without closer analysis of decisions made moment to moment. Persons (2005) describes her approach as "mix and match," using a disorder-specific manual when one is available, at other times selecting modules from a treatment protocol according to the causal mechanism assumed to provide the most likely explanation of a client's problem. In summary, "It is simply a systematic method for adapting EST protocols to meet the needs of the case at hand" (Persons, 2005, p. 113).

This strategy is not hypothesis-driven in the sense used in this book (see Guideline B). In Persons' words "the formulation serves as the central hypothesis about the mechanisms causing and maintaining the psychopathology" (Persons, 2005, p. 111). However, Persons also uses the term "hypothesis" in a narrower sense of trying out a particular intervention on an experimental basis. Persons regards any intervention that deviates from MEBP as an "experimental treatment" and therefore requiring informed consent from a client (Persons, 2005, p. 113). I have adopted a much looser concept of a hypothesis for ICF and assume that all therapy is "experimental," even when guided by strong evidence. This can be made clear to clients although, on the whole, they do not expect that results can be guaranteed even when officially sanctioned methods are adopted.

Another account of cognitive case conceptualization supplies many case examples and these include the therapist's reasoning process (Dudley, Kuyken, & Padesky, 2011; Kuyken, Padesky, & Dudley, 2009). Like Persons, these authors emphasize theoretical flexibility and the application of a variety of established CBT conceptual models, as well as drawing upon other sources of research evidence. They recommend both "top-down" and "bottom-up" approaches to formulation, suggesting that "therapists follow evidence-supported protocols whenever possible" (Kuyken et al., 2009, p. 45). Most of their case illustrations are in fact individual formulations that freely employ a variety of hypotheses. In other words, they are "bottom-up" in the sense that descriptive observations lead to the formation of hypotheses. Nevertheless, certain cognitive concepts are viewed as fundamental (modes of information processing, schemas, core beliefs, underlying assumptions, automatic thoughts, coping strategies, strengths, resilience). In this sense, the reasoning is "top-down" because the description of a problem is assumed to take a particular cognitive and behavioral form (Dudley et al., 2011, p. 217).

These authors also put forward a generic basis for visually representing the formulation called the crucible model. This includes five causally interrelated elements—environment, thoughts, mood, behavior, and physiological responses—that are integrated in a descriptive, cross-sectional, and longitudinal manner. Given its rather schematic nature, this model would seem to be mainly useful as a teaching aid when educating a client into their approach.

Case conceptualization (i.e. formulation) is presented by Dudley et al. (2011) as principles-based. However, the principles relate to the procedures they adopt rather than principles in the sense of generalizations about processes or therapeutic techniques. The principles are: (1) levels of conceptualization (e.g. descriptive/idiosyncratic, functional, disorder-specific, diagnostic, historical); (2) collaborative empiricism (i.e. working jointly on goals and conceptualization, and empirically testing out hypotheses); and (3) including clients' strengths in the formulation and conceptualizing their resilience (i.e. helping to create conditions for lasting recovery through positive goals and aspirations). Dudley et al. place considerable stress on the last principle, another illustration of the contemporary move away from a biomedical model of disorder toward a concept of promoting wellbeing. Nevertheless, they still advocate the employment of MEBP guided by a disorder-specific model when a problem can be subsumed within a psychiatric classification and there is an evidence base for it. Transdiagnostic models (see Chapter 3) are preferred in cases of "co-morbidity" or the lack of a strong evidence base.

The message conveyed is therefore a compromise between an individualized case formulation and MEBP. Collaboration with the client is regarded as so important that formulation is really an integral part of therapy from beginning to end. As a cognitive approach, a client's understanding ("his or her formulation") of his or her own behavior is key. A therapist might generate possible hypotheses to account for a problem and seek feedback from a client. Hypotheses can also be tested out through Socratic questioning, thought records, and behavioral experiments. Conceptualizations are written out or drawn as a diagram with a client. Simplified diagrams, using a client's preferred words, metaphors, or images, may be written onto index cards to be used as an aide-memoire or prompt.

The authors work initially with a "cross-sectional" formulation, meaning one that focuses on what it is that is maintaining a problem in its current form. This is contrasted with a "longitudinal" formulation that reviews a client's developmental and family history, explores significant events and memories, and relates all this to a client's core beliefs and underlying assumptions. This level of analysis is considered to be more inferential, and it may be reserved for a mid- or late-stage of therapy, if required at all. From a functional perspective, this cross-sectional/longitudinal distinction seems questionable. If a past event still has functional significance, its importance is likely to be recognized from the beginning of an assessment and there seem to be few arguments for setting it to one side (see Chapter 8). There may be strategic reasons for not attempting to modify a core belief that is related to historical events, given that to do so may have the potential to disrupt a client's precarious adjustment. However, this reason for staying at a "lower" level is likely to limit what can be achieved in therapy. Reasons for doing so will probably get discussed when goals are agreed with a client.

A longitudinal formulation is said to provide an opportunity to conceptualize a client's life in the round, such as long-term goals, and to identify both repeating maladaptive patterns and evidence of effective coping. Kuyken et al. (2009) also focus on how a client's strengths are employed to foster a client's resilience. Despite the importance these authors assign to cognitive concepts, their examples of analyses of clients' problems (to which they devote most space in their book) seem more closely allied to a functional approach. Elements of the problem are described as functional units (e.g. "act calm and walk out," "ignore my ideas"), and in the formulation diagram these are linked with arrows representing causality. Strengths are likewise specified in a functional form (e.g. "I come from a dignified culture and family") that, in effect, summarizes how the client would behave in specific situations. It is therefore somewhat surprising to read that, "functional analysis provides a simple model based on behavioral contingencies" (Kuyken et al., 2009, p. 144). By this is meant no more than an antecedent–behavior–consequences (ABC) analysis that is, of course, an oversimplification of functional concepts. The authors' emphasis on strengths and resilience bears a strong resemblance to the constructional approach within CBT (e.g. Evans, 1993) that in many ways is a more coherent conceptual basis for understanding how competing elements (positive and negative) in a client's repertoire interact with each other.

While the case illustrations in Kuyken et al. (2009) provide a good deal of insight into a therapist's reasoning processes when using a "bottom-up" approach, this is a feature lacking in many accounts of formulation. This is evident in a recent attempt to analyze the competencies needed to conduct cognitive therapy (Roth & Pilling, 2007). If we leave out of consideration their itemization of the *knowledge* required for formulation, Roth and Pilling's specification of competencies does not attempt to describe a *formulation process* as such. The abilities include holding a client's world-view in mind while retaining an independent perspective, eliciting information regarding problems, assessing motivation for therapy, selecting target symptoms or problems, and so forth. What is missing is any attempt to characterize a process of reasoning about the evidence. Roth and Pilling do list "an ability to implement the CBT model in a manner which is consonant with a comprehensive formulation that takes into account all relevant aspects of the client's presentation," but they do not begin to specify how this can be done. In effect, the formulation process amounts to being flexible and responsive to idiosyncratic details and ensuring that all components of a disorder-specific model are covered.

Functionalist Therapies

I will elaborate a functional/systemic framework for formulation in Chapter 8. At this point, I will compare some variations on the functional approach. The essence of a functional model is that it tries to specify how all the elements in a formulation are causally related to one another. For instance, the existence of one element might depend on a stimulus event or situation and its maintenance might depend on events that follow it. A vicious circle phenomenon is a good example of a functional explanation. Models vary in terms of how much detail is provided in specifying the elements and in showing how they are related. As in cognitive therapy, some functional approaches attempt to accommodate concepts of psychiatric disorder.

For instance, diagnosis seems to be an essential part of the process of formulation as proposed by Nezu, Nezu, and Lombardo (2004). However, their overall framework is a problem-solving one that works on "goals" rather than the reduction of "symptoms." They refer to a client's "intermediate" goals, and these are assumed to have causal links with his or her "ultimate" goals. Ultimate goals are defined, first, in the negative sense of removing psychological disorders, and second, in the positive sense of attaining something desirable, such as a new career. The selection of a technique is based on research concerning empirically based treatment (MEBP) in relation to a particular psychiatric disorder. As Nezu, Nezu, and Cos (2007, p. 351) put it, "therapists need to creatively apply evidence-based clinical protocols in a tailored fashion." In other words, an attempt is made to ensure that nomothetic research into all the interventions that could possibly be relevant to a client's presenting problem or "symptoms" have been considered and tailored in a form that matches a client's individual circumstances. This is a "top-down" strategy rather than a "bottom-up" functional analysis of the circumstances surrounding a client's problem.

Examples of formulation diagrams provided by Nezu et al. (2004) do not specify the elements very precisely, and so many are packed into the "organismic variables" that moderate or mediate the relationship between responses and their outcomes that it is not clear how this information could be used. The elements included within the "organism" are a client's social, ethnic, and cultural characteristics, level of social skills, cognitive distortions, medical illnesses, problem-solving ability, fears, and physiological arousal.

By contrast, the problem-solving strategies described by Nezu et al. (2007) do seem to represent a bottom-up idiographic approach. A client's ultimate goals may be self-defined, modified through discussion, or discarded as appropriate. A therapist might translate them into a formal diagnosis but this does not seem to be obligatory. If there are no obvious solutions to a client's problem based on general principles or research evidence, a large number of alternatives are generated in a brainstorming process. A detailed functional analysis is made of all relevant causal chains of behavior. The relationship between the elements is graphed as a "clinical pathogenesis map" that they describe as a causal modeling diagram. This is usually shared with the client and feedback is sought. There is an attempt to confirm and disconfirm testable hypotheses that are implicit in the causal model. If an intervention suggested by the model does not produce expected changes, the formulation is reconsidered and modified. The authors stress that there is no "cookbook" to follow; each client's problem is specific to them alone.

Functional analytic psychotherapy (FAP) also takes an idiographic functional approach and assumes that formulation continues throughout therapy as a client's behavior changes and its consequences outside sessions create new situations (Tsai et al., 2009). The aim is to extinguish instances of problem behavior within the one-to-one client/therapist relationship and to reinforce helpful alternatives that are compatible with a client's goals. The therapist encourages generalization of these responses to the client's daily life. This form of therapy seems to be especially suited to relationship difficulties that express themselves spontaneously in a therapy session, that is, as "transference" responses from a psychodynamic perspective. The relationship skills of the therapist are therefore paramount. The re-learning process relies on the "natural" reinforcing qualities of an intimate, emotionally expressive relationship that engenders trust. Consequently, in addition to a thorough knowledge of behavioral learning principles, a therapist has to be someone who can read interpersonal situations well, knows how to resolve conflicts, and is acutely aware of his or her own reactions to a client (i.e. his or her own "counter-transference" responses).

Given that the chief mechanism of change in FAP is moment-to-moment events in session, the process of formulation (assessment, functional analysis, hypothesis testing, etc.) is hardly distinguishable from therapy itself. The authors of FAP state that "the therapist systematically manipulates antecedent and consequential variables during interactions with clients, observes the predicted changes in behavior as they occur, and compares these changes with previous levels of responding" (Tsai et al., 2009, p. 40). An example is given of changing tone of voice and rate of speech with an emotionally reserved client. For reasons just given, case conceptualization in FAP is a fluid process and "the rapid establishment of an intense, important relationship with the client" takes precedence over it (Tsai et al., 2009, p. 43). However, life history, goals and values, and behavior outside sessions are assessed. Guidelines are offered for a "functional idiographic assessment" but it seems likely that a novice would need intensive supervision to translate them into practice. Though the process of ICF has strong parallels with FAP practice, I will attempt to provide a framework that covers a broader set of client problems. However, as in FAP, formulation is integrated with therapy and supervision. It is not a prescription that follows from an initial stage of assessment.

Acceptance and Commitment Therapy (ACT) is a very distinctive functional approach—an unusual combination of a behavioral theory of language and cognition, a practical philosophy of life, and a set of techniques to address obstacles to psychological flexibility (Hayes, Luoma, Bond, Masuda, & Lillis, 2006). One example of inflexibility is an avoidance of experiencing distressing emotion and another is a rigid adherence to unworkable solutions to a problem (Hayes & Strosahl, 2004). Case formulation in ACT is largely organized around six basic processes that promote or obstruct flexibility and a commitment to act (in a broad sense) to support the values an individual has chosen to pursue for her or himself. Like FAP, ACT does not focus on symptoms or psychological disorders. It aims to develop broad, flexible, behavioral repertoires rather than solutions to specific individual problems (Hayes et al., 2006). ACT is a major departure within CBT in the sense that it provides a different kind of rationale for conducting therapy, making it more like a form of applied positive psychology.

However, ACT has sought legitimacy by showing (1) that individuals who exemplify the six processes are less likely to demonstrate psychopathological symptoms and (2) that ACT is superior to other forms of therapy in reducing pathology (Hayes et al., 2006; Twohig et al., 2010). In practice then, ACT seeks validation by showing that it reduces signs of psychological disorder. ACT researchers also adopt the methodology of the RCT rather than attempt to demonstrate that effective interventions can be deduced from ACT's own principles. Participants in research trials have been selected on the basis that they fall into psychiatric categories and so ACT sends out a mixed message about its underlying philosophy. In a single-case study reported by Twohig (2009) assessment was largely by questionnaire and diagnostic interview, and there was no attempt to show how the intervention was based on an idiographic formulation.

The underlying theory of ACT is called contextual–functionalism and it is based on a theory of language and cognition known as relational frame theory (Blackledge, 2003; Hayes, Barnes-Holmes, & Roche, 2001). While it is clear that the techniques ACT uses attempt to change the functional consequences of beliefs and private experience in the contexts in which they have become maladaptive, language-mediated behavior is presumably just as important in the control of adaptive and flexible behavior. A judgment has to be made that a client is literally too "fused," in a linguistic and behavioral sense, with certain of his or her own beliefs and values—but what exactly is the process in making this decision and how can it be assessed? Moreover, behavior under verbal or symbolic control can often be modified directly by changing its environmental consequences rather than by attempting to modify a client's attitude toward (or way of coping with) his or her own private feelings or beliefs.

Formulation in ACT therefore seems to jettison some of the key strengths of a behavioral and functional analysis and consequently may make too many assumptions about the source of a problem. As already noted, formulation is organized around six basic processes. Few clients would object to increased flexibility as a goal, but in many cases, a client's problem relates to inflexibility in specific contexts only, and in relation to particular goals. By focusing on processes "within" the individual, such as motivation for change, fear of change, rigid strategies, avoidance of emotion, fusion with beliefs, etc., there is a risk of losing sight of the contextual determinants of problems in an approach that claims to be contextual.

Psychodynamic Case Formulation

As is generally true of the formulation literature, psychodynamic case formulation is discussed in terms of its "format and content" rather than its process (e.g. Summers, 2003). Psychodynamic researchers are also interested in whether independent judges can agree on the nature of a client's underlying pathological mechanisms when they read an interview transcript or listen to, or view, a recording (Barber & Crits-Christoph, 1993). None of this really tells us how a therapist reasons about the evidence in a *prospective* way. Wolitzky (2007), a psychoanalyst, is an exception in this respect. In line with the proposal that observation and inference should be clearly distinguished, he observes that "remarkably little has been written on the topic of clinical inference." He is concerned with how a therapist scans, selects, and organizes information, and how theory is utilized in making inferences from the information. He draws the distinction between low-inference observations (e.g. what a client says or what a therapist feels about a client in a session) and high-level inferences that clearly depend on theoretical interpretation.

Of course, the aim of psychodynamic therapy differs greatly from the aim of more directive forms of psychological therapy. Wolitsky describes it as grasping a client's "inner life" and co-authoring a story that takes account of the transference and counter-transference of feelings between client and therapist. Nevertheless, the *process* of formulation as he describes it must find echoes in other forms of therapy, focusing as it does on repetition and convergence of themes within a client's account, and applying various reasoning strategies to integrate the information. Wolitsky mentions how a therapist notices analogies or instances of the juxtaposition of ideas, and uses criteria of coherence and consistency. As he rightly says, in order to teach formulation, it is necessary for trainees to be made aware of their reasoning processes when making decisions and when drawing inferences from theory to explain observations. Only in this way can theories be compared and related to therapy outcome.

The need for low-inference description becomes obvious when reading some accounts of psychodynamic case formulation. Horowitz (2005) describes in admirable detail how he begins to formulate a case. The unit of analysis is a "state of mind" which he defines as "a recurrent pattern of experience, mood, and behavior that is both verbal and non-verbal in its manifestations." A state of mind can be recognized during interview by gesture, facial expression, expression of a self-image, empathy for others, and many other indicators. An example is "simmering vexation." States of mind may consist of oscillating or discordant elements. Horowitz recommends focusing on four to eight of the most relevant states of mind in each client.

From a behavioral and functional perspective, these units of analysis are simply too imprecise to expect any substantial level of agreement between therapists on their presence in any given individual. They do not correspond with a system of behavioral description, lay or academic, and they are too readily run together with assumptions of a psychodynamic kind, making it difficult to distinguish observation from inference.

SOME INITIAL PROPOSALS FOR ICF

The style of ICF I will put forward in later chapters can be characterized as follows. It has:

- an eclectic theoretical basis in which concepts derived from academic psychology play an important role;
- rigor in its observation and testing of ideas, which also stems from its roots in science;
- a commitment to innovation and change in underlying theory and techniques;
- a functional/systemic level of theorizing that includes the social environment in its cultural and historical aspects;
- a commitment to empirical validation, especially in terms of making a real difference to a person's life, as demonstrated by setting and accomplishing action criteria rather than simply changes in questionnaire scores; and
- a proactive, pragmatic orientation.

CHAPTER 3

Evidence-Based Practice: Diagnostic and Transdiagnostic Approaches

It seems fair to say that over the last 60 years real progress has been made in developing psychotherapeutic methods that are helpful for common psychological problems. The new methods are backed up by strong theoretical rationales, and the effectiveness of many has been convincingly demonstrated.

However, it is not so clear how this progress has actually been achieved, nor how it should be furthered. One school of thought maintains that success in psychotherapy has little to do with a therapist's preferred model of problems or the specific techniques she or he employs (Wampold, 2010). A successful outcome is attributed chiefly to qualities in the therapist, the client, and their interaction. Others point to the development of carefully constructed practice manuals based on theoretical models of specific "psychological disorders" and evidence for their efficacy in randomized control trials (RCTs). This chapter will critically examine this latter claim before moving on, in the next chapter, to approaches that apply evidence to the problems of a unique individual client. Whatever approach is taken in developing an evidence base, it involves reconciliation between idiographic and nomothetic perspectives.

The phrase "evidence-based practice" (EBP) encompasses a range of possibilities and so it is important to begin by discussing how it can be defined. Summarizing somewhat, I will consider the definition supplied by Rubin and Parrish (2007) in the context of social work. EBP can be defined as: (1) formulating an answerable question regarding practice needs; (2) tracking down the best evidence available to answer that question; (3) critically appraising the validity and usefulness of the evidence; (4) integrating the appraisal with one's own clinical expertise, client's values and circumstances, and decisions that have to be made; (5) evaluating the outcome.

Although this is a sound definition, it frames EBP in abstract terms. The process of tracking down evidence at leisure differs vastly from researching with a client, moment-to-moment, and in face-to-face contact, the possible causes of a problem. Shapiro (2009) points out that: "Clinicians are on the lookout for useful ideas that require only a few words to implement, brief techniques that can be conducted in a few minutes." Consequently, the sort of evidence that is relevant to a problem is not always immediately obvious or researchable. The skills needed for the critical appraisal of published research are different from those that are required to apply, in practice, the fruits of accumulated knowledge. A practitioner has to combine nomothetic knowledge that relates to a theory of therapeutic change with an intimate knowledge of cultural norms and social practices.

Point 4 asserts that a therapist should take account of is or her own level of expertise and translate his or her knowledge into a form that can be applied to a client's unique circumstances. These requirements seem to demand a verifiable system if they are not to degenerate into a subjective and dogmatic adherence to received wisdom. It is on this point that some commentators criticize "laissez-faire" practice and argue for the advantages of training in standardized assessment procedures and strict adherence to treatment protocols. They would favor the diagnostic approach discussed in this chapter. On the other side of the argument, sensitivity to a client's needs and circumstances is seen as incompatible with assigning a client to a limited set of categories of disorder. The protagonists in this argument would probably agree that therapy involves applying general principles to the particular case, generating a debate between "top-down" and "bottom-up" thinkers. The former reason from models and diagnoses to what a client needs, and the latter infer in the opposite direction by attending to the facts as a client presents them.

With regard to the evaluation of outcome (point 5), this can be done informally when a successful outcome is fairly obvious (e.g. a client no longer complains of being depressed), or done formally through repeated assessment using the same measure. A measure may be specially designed to assess a client's unique problem or it could consist of a standardized scale, usually of the self-report variety. Given these options, there is room for considerable disagreement between practitioners on how best to evaluate outcome. On the question of evaluating the whole exercise, Rubin and Parrish (2007) favor single-case experimental designs when feasible, and most therapists can manage pre–post measurement or some means of continuous assessment. However, any serious attempt to implement a single-case design requires considerable planning and effort, a luxury that most practitioners cannot afford.

There can be no hard and fast solution to the issues surrounding EBP because many of them, as it turns out, are pragmatic, financial, ideological, or managerial. I hope to illustrate this point in this chapter and the next. Some of the issues are given a further airing in Chapter 9.

CLIENT'S PROBLEMS AS AN EXPRESSION OF NATURAL DYSFUNCTIONS (DISORDERS)

The mainstream position on EBP maintains that evidence should be collected on the efficacy and effectiveness of well-defined procedures applied to clients who share the same problem. By the same problem is usually meant the same psychiatric diagnosis. Efficacy studies typically consist of a randomized control trial (RCT) designed to optimize the quality of the causal inferences that can be drawn from its results. In other words, is the method/technique really responsible for the changes that are observed? On the basis that each research participant shares the same diagnosis (i.e. the same "psychopathology") it is assumed that any client given the same diagnosis will respond similarly to the same intervention. This is confirmed in "effectiveness studies" when a method shown to be efficacious is tested out under field conditions.

The process of reasoning in this form of EBP rests heavily on the assumption that the causes of problems assigned to the same diagnosis or disorder are sufficiently similar to generalize across them. It is assumed that there is such a thing as a science of psychopathology and it is made up of what I will call "disorder-specific" theoretical models. In reality, there is only limited evidence for any *specific* bio-psycho-social explanation for the common psychological problems. This undermines the concept of psychopathology, although current "disorder-specific" models do attempt to show how a variety of processes typically interact. They have a multifactorial conception of causation, and the factors include perceptual, cognitive, and behavioral processes that function perfectly well in most areas of a client's life. Only rarely do they point to a specific etiology. The problem may be due to the frequency or intensity of a behavior that is otherwise normal, or its problematic nature may be due to the inappropriate circumstances in which it is elicited.

On the assumption that clients' problems have non-specific and variable causes, rather than disorder-specific causes, it would be surprising to find that a "proven intervention" for a particular disorder would meet the needs of all clients who are diagnosed with it. The results of RCT studies bear this out. According to Barlow, Allen, and Choate (2004), only 50–80% of participants in treatment studies for emotional disorders are "responders," where even a good response does not necessarily mean "cured" or "symptom-free."

I propose that the terms "psychopathology" and "psychiatric disorder" are best understood as metaphors. It is true that events such as trauma can produce pathophysiological changes in the body of an enduring kind. Here the pathology is secondary rather than the primary originating cause. It is also clear that there is a complex interaction between somatic and psychological processes, and this interaction needs to be captured in a formulation. Problems have a biological basis but so does normal behavior. The objection to the concept of psychiatric disorder is the assumption it makes about a correspondence between psychiatric criteria and a subset of natural processes. A more reasonable assumption is that normal psychological processes, in combination with events that are not necessarily out of the ordinary, can conspire together to produce problems of all kinds.

This is a minority view at present because the field of psychotherapy seems to be moving in the direction of neuroscience explanations. There is no need to deny the role of natural processes while still holding to the view that the current emphasis on biological, pathological, and genetic etiologies is unbalanced (Hallam, 2012). Moreover, an objection to seeking an evidence base centered around diagnostic groups is not an objection in principle to classification. It holds true only for generalizations about classes of problem or categories of client that wrongly presume that there is a specific underlying etiology. Psychiatric classification schemes are largely based on morphological features and so they may not assume a specific etiology. However, the effect of using them in practice is to endorse a narrow view of causality.

Quite apart from the questionable foundation of psychopathology, it can be argued that current disorder classifications are unsatisfactory from the standpoint of tools for scientific research. Diagnostic criteria are conventions designed for purposes other than research. They have arbitrary features, one of which is that diagnostic criteria can be fulfilled in ways that differ from client to client. This is bound to induce skepticism about generalizations that relate to a category of disorder—including ones that make claims about the "recommended treatment" for a disorder.

The popularity of the diagnostic approach to formulation is a relatively recent phenomenon, and several explanations can be suggested for its current prominence. Some practitioners may believe that the analogy with pathology is, in fact, valid. This cannot be said of early behavior therapists. Kanfer and Saslow (1965) remark that, in the face of criticism, "many clinicians now use diagnostic labels sparingly and apologetically." Albert Bandura (1969, p. 2), never noted for hyperbole, writes, "Many contemporary theories of psychopathology thus employ a quasi-medical model fashioned from an amalgam of the disease and demonology conceptions, which have in common the belief that deviant behavior is a function of inimical inner forces." Behavior therapists argue that "pathology" should be described and explained functionally. Kanfer and Saslow (1965) refer to "problem resolution" rather than "treatment," an objective principally achieved by changing a person's environment. However, these authors do not ignore the necessity of changing a client's way of "perceiving, classifying, and organizing sensory events, including perception of himself," nor do they exclude consideration of biological factors.

In essence, behavior therapists argue that the same learning processes underlie the acquisition and extinction of all behavior, "pathological" or normal. They also assume that some people acquire psychological problems more easily than others according to where they lie on biologically based dimensions of personality such as extraversion and neuroticism. An acceptance of biological determination is compatible with a rejection of specific biological etiologies for various kinds of psychological problem.

The anti-diagnostic attitude was reversed when behaviorism fell out of favor, and complaints were seen, once more, either as expressions of psychological disorders or as dysfunctions of inner psychological processes. It could be objected that the term "disorder-specific conceptual model" has few implications of a negative kind. Different types of problem do, of course, really exist, and researchers who investigate them understandably want to develop a generalized conception of each type. People who feel "entitled" are a distinctly different group of people to those who feel impelled to subjugate their own needs in the service of others. Research into types of problem has been productive in many ways but the point at issue is the appropriateness of the label "disorder." In other words, is entitlement a disorder? If so, what psychological processes are disordered? On the whole, people who are "entitled" consider others to be the source of their difficulties, if they identify any personal problems at all. Entitlement does not seem to be the kind of problem that can be defined in biological or psychological terms alone. Social criteria inevitably enter into the definition of disorders.

A more plausible account of the boundary between normal and abnormal is not dysfunction but the crossing of a threshold that relates to degree of "tolerable suffering" as judged personally or socially. This criterion applies also to medical disorders, although for a disorder to be "genuine" a somatic cause of suffering has to be identified. It is almost a certainty that thorough medical screening would reveal some abnormality or defect in the healthiest of persons. In other words, genuine medical illness is an internal dysfunction that also happens to cause intolerable suffering (or portends future suffering). However, suffering associated with psychological problems typically does not have specific causes analogous to an internal dysfunction of a bodily system. It has to be explained in other ways. In some instances, suffering is clearly social in origin, that is, related to the way in which a person makes an unfavorable social comparison between themselves and the advantages that others are perceived to possess.

Another explanation for the reversal of the anti-diagnostic trend in the 1970s was the arrival of new editions of the American Psychiatric Association's *Diagnostic and statistical manual of mental disorders* (DSM), which provided operational definitions of disorder (American Psychiatric Association, 1980). By avoiding any concept of pathology that could be proved wrong, these definitions sanitized concepts of disorder, thereby encouraging the development of a hybrid psychological/psychiatric approach to research and practice.

THE EFFECT OF DISORDER-SPECIFIC MODELS ON PRACTICE

The popularity of the concept of psychological disorder has meant that treatment manuals have been devised to translate each model of disorder into an effective therapeutic procedure. In summary, a diagnostic approach to formulation follows this line of reasoning: (1) First establish that you have a type X disorder. (2) Consider how all the potential components of the disorder-specific theoretical model for X are expressed or interrelate (or do not apply) in a particular client. (3) Follow a set of procedures, as successfully trialed in RCT studies, and do this in the optimal order to produce change Y. (The treatment manuals are not necessarily over-prescriptive because they allow for some flexibility when the model is translated into practice.)

The essence of the diagnostic approach to formulation is analogous to the model employed by a dentist. Is there infection, is a cap needed, is the client making the problem worse by grinding his or her teeth? A body of knowledge will have accrued as to the range of problems normally seen and there will be evidence for the efficacy of a number of solutions. Once the problem has been identified as being of a certain type, the reasoning process is inductive. If B is the problem, the client who has B should be offered the most effective solution according to the proven response of B to techniques X, Y, and Z in clinical trials. A dentist might lay out the advantages and disadvantages of each one so that a client can either choose between them or be helped to understand the option the dentist recommends.

So much has been invested in the diagnostic approach that the bulk of research evidence concerning psychotherapy relates to psychiatric disorders. It is therefore not surprising to find 13 of the world's leading cognitive behavioral therapy (CBT) researchers recommending that "clinicians should have easy access to training in diagnostic assessments" (Shafran et al., 2009). As these authors state in the opening sentence of their article, "considerable progress has been made in developing effective psychological treatments for a wide range of psychiatric disorders." The authors acknowledge that "many clinicians are reluctant to use diagnostic labels" but imply that any deviation away from a recommended protocol will lead to a drift away from the effectiveness of therapy. They feel it might be necessary "to allow for the local modification of protocols to facilitate dissemination" as this might "increase their willingness to change their habits."

The slight impatience expressed here reflects a not unfounded concern that practitioners are failing to take up effective forms of therapy when the evidence for them is good (see also Weisz, Weersing, & Henggeler, 2005). However, the diagnostic approach is presented as if there were no alternative. As I hope to show in the next two chapters, it is possible to draw from academic knowledge in general, and from studies of the effectiveness of therapy, the value of certain principles, processes, and techniques that are applicable in the individual case. This can be done without having to view a client's putative disorder as determining what is offered. The choice of a therapeutic method can be grounded in a general conceptual understanding, in conjunction with an idiographic analysis, rather than "what has been shown to work" for a particular diagnostic group.

In an eloquent defense of the disorder-specific/manualized approach, Wilson (2007, p. 120) nevertheless makes the point that "we need to move beyond the atheoretical and heterogeneous categories of DSM-IV." He also notes that many manuals are comprehensive and flexible, and that their effectiveness "is contingent on therapist expertise." He suggests that the latter might entail a detailed functional analysis of the variables that maintain the problem behavior in question. The further manualized therapy moves away from diagnosis and adherence to a protocol, the more it approaches an individualized formulation. However, Wilson argues that,

"There is little evidence to indicate that routine clinical practice is self-correcting" (Wilson, 2007, p. 122). This is not quite the same as arguing that it can never be self-correcting. In fact, there would be no grounds for appealing to a detailed functional analysis if it was not. Wilson accepts that principles-driven individualized approaches have much to recommend them but he argues that what may be needed are specific instructions for translating a principle into an effective technique. This is probably true in all applications of science—the expert has to turn to tables, devices, instruments, protocols, etc., when applying a general principle. However, when the technique alone dictates action (as in many bureaucratic organizations) the point of using it is lost. Manuals are useful servants but poor masters.

A CRITIQUE OF RANDOMIZED CONTROL TRIALS AND MANUALS AS THE BASIS FOR PRACTICE

The popularity of the RCT is understandable. Clients' problems do fall into recognizable patterns that respond to similar techniques. Obsessing about sinning is unlike obsessing about winning. The RCT strategy involves studying well-defined groups of clients who are then administered a standardized form of therapy. The RCT was first borrowed from the field of medicine, where the intention was to test experimental hypotheses, not to prove that a package of techniques was effective for a particular disorder (Westen, Novotny, & Thompson-Brenner, 2004). These authors argue (p. 658) that the RCT strategy is only really suited to problems characterized by "readily identifiable, maladaptive links between specific stimuli or representations and specific responses" in which there is "dissociation between symptoms and personality dispositions." They maintain that any therapy that needs to be principle-based, where choices must be made on the basis of the material that clients present, will introduce too much variability to permit optimal use of an RCT design. For example, a comparison between a complex therapy and an equally complex "treatment as usual" could be seen as a blunderbuss evaluation that reveals little about why one turns out better (or equivalent) to another. There are simply too many variables in the therapeutic situation to tease them apart by the RCT method when a problem is complex. Differences between groups become impossibly difficult to interpret.

It is worth summarizing the essence of an RCT evaluation of therapy in order to see its drawbacks. One major weakness is the impossibility of a double-blind control (Wampold & Bhati, 2004). In a drug study it can be ensured that the clinician is unaware of whether she or he is administering an active drug or an inactive placebo. In contrast, therapists are bound to know what they are doing and may be influenced by that knowledge to conduct themselves with more (or less) enthusiasm. This problem of a therapist's allegiance to a particular method is not an easy one to control for.

At its simplest, the RCT method involves identifying a group of participants who share the same problem. They are then divided at random into one group given one method of treatment and another group given a different treatment or no treatment at all. A standard way of measuring the problem has to be devised—a measure that can show whether the problem has got worse or better as a result of therapy. This measure is given before and after treatment and the average change in each group is compared. The results are bound to differ by chance to some degree but if neither treatment were superior to the other, the results would eventually average out to be the same if the experiment were to be repeated many times. In the statistical evaluation of an actual experiment, the size of the difference between the average results for each group is compared with an estimate of the variation that would be found by chance in repetitions of the experiment. The range of this variation can be estimated by statistical methods, taking into account how accurate the measure is in detecting change, the size of the sample of participants, and so forth. If one treatment produces a larger improvement than another, the size of this difference is compared with the range of differences that would be found according to chance. When the difference is large enough, it is concluded that it is statistically unlikely (i.e. likely to be due to chance in, say, only one in 20 or one in a 100 repeats) and it is accepted as indicating a genuine superiority of one treatment over another. This conclusion must take into account the fact that it is more likely to find statistical differences in very large samples because the error of estimating variation is then much reduced. A "significant" finding may in fact represent too small an actual difference between groups to be meaningful in practice. Large changes in a small number of cases are usually more convincing than small changes in a large number of cases.

There are several points to note about a study of this kind. Suppose we use the hypothetical example of research to show that aspirin cures headaches. First, if aspirin works, the study does not tell you why. Second, the experimenter needs a standard measure of headache, one that is not all that easy to devise. Third, the study must recruit participants with standard headaches. This raises the issue of setting criteria for, say, the seriousness of the problem (e.g. a frequency of headache greater than once per month). It is only by means of standardizing the participants, selecting highly reliable measures, and routinizing the treatment that chance variation can be reduced to an acceptable level, making it more likely that a difference between groups will be found after treatment. Ideally, the participants should be selected as "uncomplicated" cases, otherwise other life difficulties (substance abuse, other illnesses, life crises due to homelessness, unemployment, relationship break-up, etc.) would introduce an unacceptably high degree of variation in outcome, masking the effect of the therapeutic method that is being evaluated.

Another issue is whether there is such a thing as a standard headache. Perhaps, as in fact we know, there are different kinds of headache with different causes and perhaps they do not all respond to aspirin. Can it be ensured that the groups being compared contain the same number of participants with different types of headache? Another complicating factor is that many participants drop out of treatment trials for reasons that cannot always be determined—30% is not uncommon. If it is assumed that they were not going to benefit, the success of a treatment should be estimated as a proportion of everyone who started it, regardless of whether they later dropped out. Results are not always reported in this way. Moreover, given that the criteria for admission are tightly drawn, a considerable number of potential clients are refused an offer of therapy in the first place. Evaluative research on highly selected participants can therefore give an illusory estimate of success. In routine practice, therapists are not usually in a position to pick and choose their clients.

All of the aforementioned difficulties are not a reason for abandoning the RCT to evaluate therapeutic techniques, especially when the experimental design is good enough to tease apart the effect of different variables. The tight control of procedures is essential and, in fact, an asset in drawing causal inferences, whether or not the experimental treatment mimics routine practice. It is just that when we are dealing with psychological therapies designed to solve client's problems, rather than aspirin for headache, the difficulties encountered with an RCT design are multiplied tenfold. It is far more difficult to recruit participants uncomplicated by additional problems, not easy to ensure that therapy is delivered in a standard way, not easy to find a standard measure of outcome that is suitable for all participants, and not always easy to ensure that results are evaluated by "blind" independent assessors who have no stake in the outcome. Despite these reservations, any therapist would be foolish not to be influenced by the findings of an RCT. I have also underplayed the possibility of varying the experimental design to reveal something about the underlying mechanisms of change through which a therapy may be effective.

The RCT is much less illuminating when it is simply a way of globally assessing the impact of treatment package A versus package B in a routine practice setting. This may be an important practical concern but this kind of "effectiveness" study does not usually cast much light on why one therapy is more helpful than another.

Wilson (2007) believes that the RCT method has greatly advanced theory and practice. Although it has undoubtedly made a contribution, it can hardly be claimed that evidence gained in this way has been the most important source of innovation. Wilson cites "dismantling studies" in which a complex package of therapy is broken down into its components, which are then pitted against each other in an RCT. The dismantling strategy can be highly informative, especially when debunking over-elaborate theoretical rationales or techniques. This approach was famously employed by Paul (1966) in his investigation of Wolpe's method of systematic desensitization for phobias. It was eventually shown (after many years and studies) that the mechanism of reciprocal inhibition proposed by Wolpe was an unnecessary component of desensitization. Exposure was sufficient to produce change. However, the exposure principle itself was hardly an innovation. It had been used before (Donley, 1911) and its truth is enshrined in many proverbs. Rousseau, in his book *Émile* (1762), wrote as follows:

> *Therefore do not argue with any one whom you want to cure of the fear of darkness; take him often into dark places and be assured this practice will be of more avail than all the arguments of philosophy. The tiler on the roof does not know what it is to be dizzy, and those who are used to the dark will not be afraid.*

The RCT has, of course, proved useful as a way of investigating parameters of the exposure principle but a recent review of the underlying mechanism of action does not point to what has been learned from therapy studies. Instead, it recommends an inhibitory learning-based approach that is derived from "basic sciences of extinction learning and memory" (Craske et al., 2008).

Another example of dismantling that Wilson (2007) offers is more convincing, and memorable, because the results were unexpected. In a treatment trial conducted on clients suffering from depression, a form of cognitive therapy that omitted the key component of cognitive restructuring and focused instead on the behavioral activation component proved to be as effective as the full package (Jacobson et al., 1996). "Behavioral activation" is now seen as a powerful intervention in its own right (Martell, Dimidjian, & Hepman-Dunn, 2010). Dismantling studies help to identify the components of a therapy that produce change but they do not necessarily help to identify the mechanism of change (Doss, 2004). Cognitive restructuring could still be the theoretical mechanism through which behavioral activation operates. In other words, instructing a person to be more active could convey a powerful cognitive message. Despite considerable efforts, it has proved very difficult to demonstrate the mediating processes that underlie effective cognitive therapy. After about 15 years of published research, Whisman (1993, p. 260) concludes that "many of the theoretical viewpoints regarding the effective ingredients in cognitive therapy have yet to be tested." He recommends that investigators move toward "multidimensional, interactive models," such as developing "models or micro-theories that describe the process of change for specific individuals in specific situations" (Whisman, 1993, p. 260). The process of therapy may simply be too complex to research by means of dismantling studies. Hollon and DeRubeis (2009) also state that efforts to determine whether cognitive change mediates the effects of cognitive therapy "are far from conclusive." Watkins (2009) provides evidence to show that a potential mediating mechanism in cognitive therapy for reducing depressive rumination is simply to train individuals to think more specifically and concretely.

An RCT treatment comparison that is focused only on change in terms of the reduction of "symptoms" may therefore reveal little about causally effective mechanisms. Another weakness is that a therapist's adherence to the standard protocol used in an RCT can only be approximate. Weisz, Weersing, and Henggeler (2005, p. 421) adopt the RCT method but argue that a core element of EBP is "individualizing treatment procedures to fit each individual's personality and situation." Accordingly, they recommend that treatment should be "formulation-driven" and "principle-based." But these recommendations are not really consistent with RCT methodology. Weisz et al. believe that an RCT is the best available method to develop practice but if this is designed around a psychiatric diagnosis, it is not driven by a formulation as recommended. However, Weisz et al. also acknowledge a need for triangulation with the results of other methods. One such method would be to study how therapists who are considered to be experts construct formulations and apply principles. In fact, Weisz et al. work closely with clinicians in developing "practice-ready treatments," and so the RCT seems to be employed here as a form of quality control rather than innovation.

The efficiency of the RCT as a source of innovation has been questioned by Barlow and Nock (2009), who remark that "Scientifically, relying on a relatively small group of researchers requiring enormous amounts of time and resources to perform a single treatment trial can be seen as an inefficient method of advancing knowledge." As Hayes (2011) remarks, if research was confined to comparing all techniques for all disorders "it would take 500 years to do one study that compared every possible pairing." Therefore, despite the RCT having been the preferred method of evaluation for around 50 years, its value is now being questioned by some of the leading researchers who have adopted it. And looking back, it is not obvious that advances in actual practice have come about in this way (Salkovskis, 2002).

MANUALS AS A MODEL FOR ROUTINE PRACTICE (MEBP)

The therapy protocols used in efficacy trials cannot possibly specify rules for all contingencies and so there must be a continuum between principles-based and techniques-based interventions. Psychotherapy is simply too complex to be purely techniques-based. Treatment manuals allow for flexibility of approach and include decision trees to take account of exceptional circumstances such as risk of suicide (Addis, Wade, & Hatgis, 1999; Wilson, 1998). There is nothing in principle to object to in a manual when it adequately encompasses all the variables relevant to practice in a sufficiently flexible form. The Guidelines in this book could be seen as a manual of sorts for individual case formulation (ICF). A therapist's manual that specifies how a technique should be applied can be extremely useful to a therapist who has already developed an individual formulation and wishes to implement a certain strategy. It is also clear that clients themselves can benefit from a self-help manual, with or without some additional advice from an expert (Rosen, Glasgow, & Moore, 2003). In fact, a self-help book is often the most efficient way of introducing therapeutic concepts to a client.

What then is the objection to using a manual as a model for routine practice? If it embodies rules that are only somewhat more concrete than principles, and efficacy studies have shown that a method is ripe for dissemination, there would appear to be no objection to practitioners working with a manual. A research environment, however, differs greatly from a routine practice setting. When used in research, a manual must be capable of being taught to therapists in a manner that allows for adherence to its rules to be assessed. This is the only means of ensuring that an experimental hypothesis can be tested properly. Therapists in an RCT efficacy trial are therefore highly trained and supervised. When manuals are evaluated in practice settings (i.e. in an "effectiveness trial") the leeway given to therapists to adapt the manual to individual circumstances is likely to be considerably greater. In fact, without close monitoring, it is difficult to know whether or not a therapist is applying his or her independent "expertise" or following rules derived from a theoretical model of the disorder for which the manual was designed (Gifford et al., 2012). This is not an argument against the flexible adaptation of a manual but a recognition that a manual is unlikely to incorporate all of the variables and circumstances that it is necessary to consider. However, without knowing whether an adaptation is done well or badly, the use of manualized procedures may inspire a false confidence in their effectiveness. If shown to be effective, it is not really known how much a therapist's independent judgment (or other characteristic) has made a contribution.

When MEBP is intimately tied to a psychiatric diagnosis, its generalizability is put into question. Teachman and Clerkin (2010) acknowledge that a disorder-specific theoretical model may not offer much more than an educated guess at the first intervention to apply, and that unique features of a client may have to be assessed individually. For instance, in cognitive therapy, the origin and type of an anxious client's particular "catastrophic thoughts" have to be determined. In practice, it is far from obvious that an individual case formulation can be dispensed with at any level of expertise. Opinion to the contrary does not ring true, such as the following statement from Wright and Truax (2008, p. 65): "For beginning clinicians, the specificity provided by protocols creates easy-to-implement interventions." Therapy is almost never easy and it always demands an attitude of moment-to-moment alertness. In any case, formulation should be an ongoing process; it is not a stage that is completed when therapy begins. The phased procedures that are now commonly recommended do not reflect the reality of practice. According to Wright and Truax (2008, p. 62), "After collecting information in the observation phase, in next phase hypotheses are developed about cause, maintenance, and treatment of the client's presenting problem." However, to suppose that there is a phase of collecting information which is not already driven by ideas about the formulation does not, I think, match any therapist's method of working. The concept of an initial diagnostic phase applies more to medical treatment where a series of tests may have to be performed before their joint implications can be inferred.

DOES MEBP SERVE BEST PRACTICE OR OTHER PURPOSES?

Arguments for and against manualized therapy persist without a clear reso-lution (Emmelkamp, Ehring, & Powers, 2010; Westen & Weinberger, 2005). The *de facto* outcome has been the development of disorder-specific theo-retical models and the adoption of manualized approaches when services are planned on a large scale. This seems to be the case in both the USA and in the UK (APA Presidential Task Force on evidence-based practice, EBPP, 2006, and the "Increasing access to psychological therapy," IAPT, program, Clark et al., 2009). The key part of the argument for the wide-scale adop-tion of MEBP is that results achieved in efficacy studies in a research setting generalize well to practice settings where there is less control over selection of clients and over the level of therapist competence. In other words, evidence-based treatments (EBTs) are said to provide a good foundation for evidence-based practice (EBP) under field conditions (Hunsley, 2007; Wilson, 2007). However, as pointed out above, the extent to which indi-vidual professional judgment has to be employed additionally, and *how* it is employed, is difficult to estimate. If the success of therapy relies considerably on additional skills, advocates of MEBP would be guilty of demoting their importance. As Hunsley (2007, p. 114) states "evidence hierarchies place expert opinion on the lowest level of the hierarchy."

The alternative to MEBP is seen by Ruscio and Holohan (2006) as "implementing an entirely novel treatment with no empirical support," and deviation from a protocol means that "the personal beliefs or preferences of the therapist will again predominate." Ruscio and Holohan admit that complex cases present a problem for MEBP, that novel strategies may be needed, and that clinicians familiar with complex cases might have some-thing to offer. As a solution, these authors suggest adjusting the design of RCTs by stratifying clients according to a "complexity variable," such as problem severity. But given the wide range of complexity factors, and their potential interactions, this solution is not feasible. Ruscio and Holohan's advice is to persist with a proven protocol regardless of complexity, citing the example of therapists who deviate from an exposure protocol (e.g. one that is designed to reduce fears or post-traumatic stress), thereby producing poorer outcomes, when compared with those therapists who diligently follow it. However, the tendency to want to avoid distressing clients with exposure tasks is not a defining feature of non-manualized therapy. Exposure causes distress, and just as medical staff have to get used to the sight of blood, novices using exposure therapy have to develop confidence that the end justifies the means, even if it involves distressing a client. Ruscio and Holohan seem to imply that a protocol is necessary to force adherence. Knowing when to "push" a client or hold back is often a fine judgment, and various considerations of an individual nature apply to it (Hallam, 1992). The failure to use exposure appropriately is a sign of ignorance or incompetence and says nothing about the merits of manualized procedures.

When expected change does not occur with exposure techniques, this could indicate either poor application of technique or a need to reformulate. In the Guidelines, I give an example of an attempt to reformulate in these circumstances. In many cases, a relevant protocol does not exist. For example, when working with an adolescent girl residing in a hospital ward, exposure to obsessional thoughts (by preventing her seeking relief through verbal reassurance) was achieved by placing her in a locked section of the ward where she was isolated from others, apart from staff who were under strict instructions not to respond to her attempts to seek reassurance (Hallam, 1974). This decision was guided by theoretical considerations, not by a protocol. Initially, the intervention proved highly upsetting both to the girl and to staff, but it was ultimately so successful that other residents requested to be "locked up." If Ruscio's advice had been followed, the action taken (given the state of knowledge at that time) would have amounted to relying on "personal beliefs" and implementing an entirely novel treatment with no empirical support.

A cynical view is that the move toward employing staff guided by manualized protocols is driven by considerations that have little to do with the effectiveness of therapy. Progress on a large scale in any technical field usually requires a specialized vocabulary and routinized procedures. Health management systems demand this in order to make them compatible with requirements for regulation and financial accounting (Cushman & Gilford, 2000). No large commercial organization could function easily if all of its products and services had to be individually specified. Health insurance companies need a system of reimbursement that is simple to operate. There may also be a managerial desire to use a one-size-fits-all measure of outcome, an attempt to ensure "quality control." A technical vocabulary also assists in marketing. Types of disorder are each associated with an etiology for which a company has a remedy. In fact, disorders may be created with the explicit purpose of supplying the remedy.

A major disadvantage of defining problems as disorders and working to manuals is that it encourages procrustean solutions. It should not be considered the only model for routine practice. For example, the commercial artist who supplies a unique product is an exception to this style of working. The value of the product depends on the established reputation of the artist as someone who produces something to a certain quality but within self-chosen artistic rules. To an extent, the privately practicing psychotherapist falls within this model, with standards in part guaranteed by reputation or professional accreditation. However, it seems to be the case that in large organizations employing therapists, it is preferred that clients are identified in standard ways and are offered standard treatments by therapists who have a nationally approved qualification. Employees exercising independent professional judgment do not fit easily into this structure. In this sense, the tail has wagged the dog with respect to models for the delivery of therapy. Nevertheless, it should be possible to deliver services without the stock-in-trade of standardization. In fact, insurance companies often commission specific pieces of work from an independent practitioner on the model of the commercial artist.

Fixed categories and measures rarely capture the precise nature of a client's problem. Success in dealing with the primary problem might be handicapped by an additional medical condition or other circumstances that, for administrative purposes (or lack of insurance cover), have to be ignored. Advocates of MEBP implicitly recognize this state of affairs when they betray their allegiance to a "gold standard" of higher expertise. Wilson (1998, p. 371) writes that "for complex or treatment resistant cases there can be no substitute for appropriate therapeutic expertise." Teachman and Clerkin (2010, p. 11), who advise a staged approach to therapy, write "In the case of complications due to disagreement about the appropriate diagnostic focus, we recommend a careful functional analysis for the client and therapist to evaluate how the different problems are related." This is really an admission that manualized therapy is "second best" even though its adoption can be justified on other grounds. Another potential disadvantage of a manualized approach is that it can lead to trying treatment B (and then C) when A does not work, assuming that the client stays the course. It seems safer for all therapists to aspire to the gold standard. A few judicious decisions made early on might forestall a misdirected intervention or even harm.

Just because standardization is required in an RCT (with good grounds for doing so), this is no basis to argue that routine practice should mimic a clinical trial. Dobson and Khatri (2000) believe that therapies that are scientifically evaluated, replicable, and shown to be safe and effective are less likely to lead to civil claims against therapists for causing harm. This fails to consider that an inadequate formulation could also constitute a reason for making a claim, equivalent to the accusation of medical negligence against a doctor who misses the diagnosis of a significant symptom and therefore applies the wrong treatment. In any case, effectiveness is not the only consideration because it is important to know why a therapy works well so that it can be applied intelligently. It is partly for this reason that researchers have argued for the importance of establishing empirically supported principles rather than empirically supported therapies (Beutler, 2000; Kazdin, 2008; Rosen & Davison, 2003). It may turn out that quite different techniques are successful because they share effective processes in common and it would be nice to know what these are.

Advocates of MEBP who bemoan its poor uptake by practitioners (e.g. Shafran et al., 2009) seem to be unaware how this message comes across. On the one hand, these authors stress the serious implications for research of failing to employ "intensively trained therapists who are also supervised throughout a trial" and, on the other hand, note the poor delivery of MEBP by therapists who may be working in unsupported clinical environments with few opportunities for expert supervision. An experienced supervisor presumably has to play several roles: to select clients who are suitable for an intervention provided by a therapist lower down the ladder, to trouble-shoot when obstacles to progress are encountered, and to act as a back-stop by taking on those clients who have not responded to manualized procedures. In the latter case, does the supervisor possess "meta-manual" skills or is it always the case that lack of success is due to poor execution of proven methods? Shafran and colleagues remark that many studies have shown that level of therapist training is a vitally important determinant of success. At the same time, the authors admit that it is not really known what constitutes therapeutic expertise or how best to teach it. With respect to CBT, they also acknowledge the difficulty of measuring the quality of therapy, and the fact that "very little is known about whether these factors [i.e. those assumed to underlie the treatment] are actually the mechanism of action"(Shafran et al., 2009, p. 906). Given this level of skepticism about their own position, it is not clear why they should be surprised at the absence of a full embrace of MEBP.

The choice between manualized and individualized EBP does not have be framed as an either/or one for health providers. Different considerations will come into play according to the complexity of a problem and the level of skill it requires from a practitioner. From the perspective of the author, all clients should be offered a principle-based case formulation and, in many cases, a principle-based therapy. This does not mean that manuals have no value within therapy guided by ICF.

Summary

Evidence-based practice centered around disorders has become the main influence on the provision of psychotherapy services. In order to introduce rigor into its experimental methods, therapy has been operationalized in the RCT in the form of strict protocols (manuals) that have become the model to follow for routine practice. While manuals undoubtedly have some valuable uses, when translated wholesale from an RCT into practice they have led to a situation in which alternative forms of EBP are regarded as inferior. EBP based on an individualized approach has been viewed as unproven or simply as too costly to implement when it requires a more highly trained workforce. However, most advocates of MEBP still seem to hold on to a "gold standard" of expertise when MEBP fails. On the assumption that disorders do not represent a sufficiently distinctive set of causal factors and do not take account of a sufficiently wide range of contextual circumstances, individualized therapy is regarded as the more promising approach. So far, there has been no move in this direction. Instead, researchers have adopted transdiagnostic models.

THE MOVE TOWARD TRANSDIAGNOSTIC MODELS

It is little surprise that researchers have begun to question whether each "disorder" has to be explained by its own specific theoretical model—a model for obsessions, a model for social phobia, a model for trauma, etc. (Barlow et al., 2004; Mansell, Harvey, Watkins, & Shafran, 2009). Barlow et al. point to considerable overlap between the phenomenology of "emotional disorders" and to evidence that therapy directed at one disorder has effects that generalize to others (i.e. a reduction in anxiety may also improve depressed mood). The transdiagnostic approach to theory-building assumes that there are common causal mechanisms across different "disorders." These theorists still believe that there is an etiological divide between normal and abnormal behavior but they have shifted their ground to a broader based set of causes. Barlow et al. (2004) pin their account on the biological substrate of different emotions, harking back to Darwin's description of species–specific patterns of emotional behavior that have evolved over the course of human evolution. The twist to their argument is that people prone to emotional disorder (now called "emotion dysregulation") end up in a vicious cycle of distress by trying to control or suppress their emotions rather than accept them. This maladaptive coping strategy is said to be a common feature of emotional disorders that were previously considered to be distinct (e.g. major depression, generalized anxiety, post-traumatic stress, obsessions, and panic). In their model, Barlow et al. assume that there is causal interaction between several determinants, namely, (1) a genetic/constitutional predisposition, (2) adverse events in early childhood (producing a generalized psychological vulnerability), and (3) stressful life events. They also assume that the interaction is mediated by an additional "specific" psychological vulnerability that results from perceiving events (e.g. sensations, thoughts, social evaluations) as uncontrollable. A perception of lack of control may relate to a client's prediction of a catastrophic consequence of their distress in a certain situation or, alternatively, to an unrealistically high estimate of the probability of something unpleasant happening to them in the future. Specific vulnerabilities may be the outcome of a specific learning history, such as a road traffic accident.

The transdiagnostic model of Barlow and colleagues has the advantage of dispensing with an over-large number of disorder categories, each with its own theoretical explanation. These are replaced by a "negative affect syndrome," the remedy for which is some general strategies for healthy emotional regulation. The focus shifts from a meaningful (reality-based) interpretation of the contextual precipitants of distress to a client's manner of dealing with negative emotions (e.g. suppressing, avoiding, ignoring, distracting, or catastrophizing). The reality content of a particular threat therefore becomes less significant than a client's general attitude to threat and his or her manner of dealing with his or her own emotional responses. Barlow et al. use the term "action tendencies" rather than "habits" or "learned responses," presumably to emphasize the biological underpinnings of their approach. For instance, it is suggested that distress can be countered by encouraging the action tendencies and motoric components of other emotions (e.g. adopting the facial expression of a competing emotion, approaching instead of withdrawing).

In contrast, the transdiagnostic model of Mansell et al. (2009, p. 9) "focuses uniquely on the mental processes that have predominated research since the late 1970s beyond earlier work on conditioning and thinking errors." These mental processes include attentional bias, selective recall, thought suppression, reasoning biases, and avoidance/safety behaviors. The authors argue that science is normally advanced by studying universal principles and processes, and their transdiagnostic model is an attempt in this direction. Therefore, they seek a universal theory of emotional distress, by which they seem to mean a theory of psychiatrically defined disorders. This is a forlorn hope if the biological dispositions toward developing problems are distributed throughout the general population. If disorders are not "natural kinds," their explanation cannot be sought in distinctive natural processes alone. The processes that Mansell et al. identify are of course involved, but the divide between people with and without problems is not primarily a natural one.

The emergence of the transdiagnostic approach has led to a suggestion to replace the categorical system of diagnosis in the DSM with a dimensional system (Brown & Barlow, 2009). This latter system is linked to a "unified protocol" for therapy, a modular set of largely CBT techniques that are adapted for each individual client. Although any module can, in a sense, stand alone, its selection is based on a prior assessment and formulation (Ellard, Fairholme, Boisseau, Farchione, & Barlow, 2010). The principal assessment for emotional problems consists of a profile of scores on a number of dimensions that comprise temperament, mood, focus of anxiety, and avoidance (Brown & Barlow, 2009).

Research on the existence of two higher order traits of temperament is strong, going back to the work of Eysenck in the 1960s (Eysenck, 1981). These traits are labeled by Brown and Barlow (2009) as A/N (anxiety/neuroticism/behavioral inhibition) and BA/P (behavioral activation/positive affectivity). The overall tenor of the model is biological because Brown and Barlow (2009, p. 264) argue that the psychological vulnerabilities (mentioned above) in combination with a biological predisposition "could be considered more accurately as temperament." It is accepted that temperament is only one causal factor that must be supplemented by an analysis of specific cues for emotion (both external and interoceptive), as well as life stressors and avoidance behavior. Nevertheless, this still leaves a rather diminished role for learning and functional analysis in formulation.

The proposed diagnostic model is therefore essentially a biological one. Brown and Barlow (2009, p. 267) argue that it facilitates "a more comprehensive conceptualization and assessment of temperaments and associated foci of A/N" but they also cite evidence that changes in A/N can be substantial after successful therapy (Brown, 2007). An inference that can be drawn from change in scores on measures of temperament after therapy is that the scores also reflect life experience (Ormel, Riese, & Rosmalen, 2012). For instance, Hallam (1976a) found, in a mixed anxiety/phobic sample, that neuroticism reduced and introversion increased in proportion to the degree of success of therapy. Both scales demonstrated reasonably high test–retest reliability but neither predicted therapeutic change. The Eysenck personality scales have been widely employed in research for over 50 years, but it seems worth pointing out that they have played almost no role in case formulation over this period.

One of the consequences of giving prominence to general biological factors in assessment is an under-emphasis on an idiographic formulation of a client's overall life situation, and its dilemmas and conflicts. In fact, the distress and physiological arousal created by conflict between habitual behaviors seems to be neglected in this particular biological view. Transdiagnostic perspectives do not dispense with functional analysis and concepts of learning altogether but the situations that occasion distress are primarily significant in the sense that they are triggers for an emotional response (or "symptom") to which a client's response is maladaptive. The "problem" the client has to solve is to understand the adaptive nature of emotions, to accept them, and, where distress arises, to understand how this is a result of their malappraisal of the situations that gave rise to it. Clients are exposed to cues that elicit distress, following the learning theory rationale that extinction will occur, but the notion of intervening to change the situational determinants of a problem, in a wider sense, seems to be given less attention (e.g. Ellard et al., 2010). Consequently, there is no real need for an individual case formulation apart from giving a battery of diagnostic and symptomatic assessments.

Barlow and his colleagues do assume that learning plays a major role in the conditioning of threat to internal sensations, and in mediating the effect of adverse early childhood experience, but the significance of a client's learning history is conceived in terms of lowering the threshold for a maladaptive style of coping. Therapists have for many years been in broad agreement that there are common processes in emotional problems, such as maladaptive coping strategies, and would also acknowledge processes of the kind identified by Mansell et al. (2009). Research into coping has identified several styles that are known to be unhelpful (e.g. the Ways of Coping Checklist developed by Vitaliano, Russo, Carr, Maiuro, & Becker, 1985). Nevertheless, it is difficult to understand how the real-world context of a problem can be seen as less significant than a "dysfunctional" personality characteristic. Change has to begin in a concrete situation, normally one with a specific learning history, even when the overall aim is broader and designed to encourage, say, a general tendency to approach rather than avoid. The content of a catastrophic worry typically relates to believable (if unrealistic) consequences in real situations. Worries might be driven by meta-worries (worry about the effects of worry), but the latter, too, have content and a source in ways of thinking that are shared in the general population. Of course, a therapist cannot afford to get bogged down in specific content when the target in therapy is a general response class. For instance, the focus of an intrusive rumination might change from month to month.

Transdiagnostic theorists have pointed to psychological processes that are clearly important in generating problems, but their centrality seems exaggerated. There is a risk that clients will be stigmatized as constitutionally "neurotic," and real-life contextual determinants will be seen as less important. In many cases, what makes something into a problem is related to an unfortunate and unique combination of circumstances, rather than any intrinsic vulnerability or cognitive characteristic of the person concerned.

CHAPTER 4

Theory and Evidence in Individual Case Formulation

In earlier chapters I argued that an ability to produce an individual case formulation (ICF) combines various reasoning skills. It is necessary to reason from scientific principles and technical knowledge but there is also a need to think systematically and reflectively when helping a client to solve problems and make decisions. In an activity that combines art and science, it is bound to be difficult to separate out the employment of theory, evidence, and craft. There is general agreement that research feeds into practice and vice versa, but authors have conceptualized this relationship differently. Advocates of the approach to evidence-based practice (EBP) I critiqued in the last chapter assume that the most relevant form of evidence concerns a theoretical understanding of specific psychological disorders and generalizations about the best way to treat them. I argued that extending this diagnostic approach in a transdiagnostic direction (by theorizing "psychopathological processes" at a broader level) does little to address the idiographic (contextual) nature of problems. In this chapter, I examine alternative ways of understanding how knowledge feeds into and guides psychotherapy.

There are psychotherapists of a humanistic persuasion who emphasize moral reasoning and may not see any role for science. Miller (2009, p. 104) claims that scientific theories "are of no use to an applied field like psychotherapy" and similarly, Yanchar (2009) argues that case studies "could begin and end in the world of lived experience" and need not involve a "set of abstractions" taken to be the root cause of a phenomenon. This position is at least plausible; a therapist could be helpful without drawing on theoretical knowledge of any kind, just as a friend might supply valuable support and advice. Training in psychotherapy would amount to a honing of skills that everyone possesses in some degree. However, it is equally plausible to suggest that scientific and technical knowledge also have something to offer in addition to wise counsel. Those psychotherapists who endorse the application of theory can be divided into two broad camps, one that emphasizes general or "common" processes that are seen as the primary vehicle of change in all forms of therapy, and another camp that sees a role for specific theories of psychological change, depending on the problem presented.

Individual Case Formulation
http://dx.doi.org/10.1016/B978-0-12-398269-8.00004-1

65

The first camp is based on the view that human beings are problem-solvers by nature and do not need their therapist to provide specific techniques to overcome their difficulties. The role of the therapist is to facilitate change by coaching, nudging, enlightening, challenging, and advising a client to bring this about in him- or herself. This method is predominantly conversational, although other means can also be adopted to bring about insight and increased awareness. Theory in the common factors camp focuses on the attributes of the client, the therapist, and the quality of the therapeutic relationship (see Chapter 7). Viewing psychotherapy in this way—as an activity that is essentially one of mutual influence—it seems rather unlikely that the psychotherapeutic implementation of common processes requires its own unique theory. The elements common to all forms of therapy are probably shared in some respects with the techniques of door-to-door selling or the methods of a team coach in sport. However, psychotherapy is imbued with a set of values that uniquely shape its practices. One of these is that a client should experience change as authentic, in other words, as consistent with their core notion of self. Another is that change is freely undertaken, as if a therapist must refrain from offering direct advice and avoid being seen as an obvious source of influence of any kind. There is an expectation that a client will develop insight in the course of a therapeutic conversation, and responsibility for change is placed squarely on her or his shoulders. These values do not sit easily with a concept of psychotherapy as a technology or treatment that draws on scientific evidence and sets out to produce change. This view of therapy may be seen as mechanistic or coercive. In this respect, some forms of psychotherapy stand in sharp contrast to medicine, where advances in scientific and technical knowledge are generally welcomed.

GROUNDS FOR EMPHASIZING COMMON FACTORS IN THERAPY

As just noted, the application of any specific technology of change runs the risk of being interpreted as coercive and therefore incompatible with the value that Western societies place on freedom, authenticity, and choice. Consequently, there may a strong ideological preference for the common factors approach. This observation is not meant as a criticism. There are, of course, solid reasons for investigating common factors and theorizing about them (e.g. Prochaska, 1979; Stiles, 2002).

A second reason for interest in common factors is that the employment of specific techniques, unique to each form of therapy, seems to play such a small part in contributing to the overall success of therapy (Wampold, 2010). On the face of it, one might have expected that a therapist's ability to analyze the causes of a client's problem and integrate them into an overall formulation would be a common factor. However, there is no widely accepted terminology for problem analysis and no means currently available for quantifying the formulation process for research purposes. The most recent edition of *The history of psychotherapy* (Norcross, Vandenbos, & Freedheim, 2011), an encyclopedic work, does not contain an entry in the index for assessment or formulation. Without a common conceptual model or methodological approach, there seems to be little possibility of creating an evidence base for case formulation as a generic process. Some forms of therapy do, of course, pay considerable attention to problem analysis and interpretation, but case formulation is then viewed as a specific factor and treated as an aspect of the theory of change that a school of psychotherapy happens to endorse.

The failure to identify formulation as a common process may be a consequence of the employment of quantitative research methods. Wampold, Hollon, and Hill (2011) admit that these methods (e.g. correlation, analysis of variance in factorial group designs) have little chance of elucidating the process of psychotherapy because important variables cannot be experimentally manipulated. Their summing up of the state of the field could be interpreted as a negative verdict on decades of research: "What remains unclear . . . is whether different kinds of patients respond best to different therapies and the process through which each intervention works" (Wampold et al., 2011, p. 339). The field seems to be hampered not only by an excessive reliance on quantitative methods but also by the terminology of patient, disorder, and treatment that holds out the promise of discovering causal processes analogous to those in physical medicine.

A quite different avenue of investigation into the role of formulation as a common factor is to ask highly experienced therapists what they think about its place in their work. The research that bears on this issue has not brought problem analysis to the fore. Based on interviews with 14 highly eminent psychotherapists, Leavitt and Williams (2010) extracted the principle of "developing client awareness" as the therapist's primary intention when conducting therapy. Given that this entails "stimulating self-curiosity," "emotionally engaged exploration," "challenging ideas that block growth," and "integrating new symbolization," it would have been reasonable to expect that this style of expert therapy would have included a therapist's ability to analyze and formulate problems. Leavitt and Williams (2010, p. 344) note that therapists use the method of challenging and interpreting when a client's "growth" is obstructed. In other words, this method is employed when clients "were trapped in one way of making sense of their experience and lacked the ability to find the solution themselves." The clear implication here is that the therapist either knew of a solution or a better way of thinking about the problem. However, in the midst of a therapy session, experienced therapists probably operate on "automatic pilot" and only later, given time to reflect, are they able to analyze (if at all) what they are doing and why (see Chapter 6). In an earlier qualitative study of "master therapists" (Jennings & Skovholt, 1999), the participants stressed the importance of knowledge and the cognitive complexity of human problems but they did not (apparently) describe how they applied their knowledge to solve clients' problems.

Three of the 14 therapists (two cognitive behavior therapists and one constructivist) interviewed by Leavitt and Williams (2010, p. 347) emphasized the importance of utilizing their scientific knowledge and skills, suggesting that they belonged to a group of therapists who saw themselves as applied scientists. They would presumably place more emphasis on a theory-informed analysis of a client's problem. One interpretation of the finding that a majority of eminent therapists do not refer to a knowledge base (at least of a scientific/technical kind) is that they do not believe it has much to offer, and another is that it is inconsistent with their set of personal values. A further possibility, noted earlier, is that experienced therapists are actually unaware of the basis of their expertise.

ARGUMENTS FOR CHANGE METHODS BASED ON SPECIFIC THEORETICAL PRINCIPLES

The general argument put forward in this section is that not all similar problems have the same causes—some may be due to rather specific obstacles to optimal adjustment—and that a variety of theoretical hypotheses could be relevant to understanding a client's problem. Rather than relying on strategies and processes that are common to all therapies, the aim is to apply theory and techniques flexibly and individually. This style of therapy also avoids the tendency to subsume a problem within a type of disorder. For this reason it does not model therapy on the treatment protocols developed for evaluative research.

When reviewing the progress that has been made over the last half century, it seems clear that much of it has not stemmed from the style of evidence-based research described in Chapter 3. Disorder-specific theoretical models and manualized techniques grew out of experimentation and experience with the problems of individual clients. For instance, all of the recently introduced "brands" of cognitive behavioral therapy (CBT) had their origins in direct work with clients, helped along by a speculative application of theory. This was the initial impetus for cognitive therapy, dialectical behavior therapy, schema-focused therapy, and Acceptance and Commitment Therapy. All of our present well-known techniques began life as a case study or series of case studies grounded in a practitioner's familiarity with a category of problems. Meyer's paper on his method of "modification of expectations" described only two clients with compulsive washing rituals (Meyer, 1966). This study, which led to the method of "exposure and response prevention," heralded a revolution in therapy for obsessions. However, Meyer was not following a protocol but creatively applying his clinical skills and academic knowledge.

I will leave it to Chapter 5 to describe the reasoning skills that underpin an individualized approach to formulation and therapy. At this point I will trace some of its historical roots and consider conflicting opinions on the relationship between research and practice.

Early Application of Scientific Method to Case Formulation

Meyer's formative experience was at the Institute of Psychiatry in London, where a new style of experimental investigation of clients' problems was beginning to be developed in the 1950s and 1960s. This was part of a general move to re-position the profession of clinical psychology as a branch of applied science (Raimy, 1950). Therapists saw themselves as both scientists and practitioners and used experimental methods to investigate a client's problem in order to develop a theoretically based intervention. For instance, Yates (1958) experimented with methods of massed practice to eliminate muscular tics, and Gwynne Jones (1961) investigated a bell and pad method for treating bedwetting in children. The general approach is described by Shapiro (1961) who underlined the importance of (1) devising measures that are geared to the unique nature of a client's problem; (2) establishing experimental control over a phenomenon of interest, meaning that a therapist comes to understand what produces it or removes it; and (3) ensuring that relationships observed between variables found in a single client can be replicated again in the same client or in other clients with a similar problem. An early text was called *Experiments in behaviour therapy* (Eysenck, 1964). The underlying rationale of the approach was to work out the parameters and determinants of a problem with the aim of finding an individually tailored solution. A somewhat different style of single-case investigation was adopted in America, influenced by B. F. Skinner's methods and concepts. The origins of this method were not therapeutic although they came to be applied in clinical settings (e.g. Lindsley, 1959). Over time, a subfield of research methodology developed, now known as single-case experimental design (Barlow et al., 2008; Morgan & Morgan, 2001).

When applied in routine practice environments, most therapists found the high-minded aims of this early experimental approach too demanding. It proved time-consuming to carry out thoroughly, even assuming that the parameters of a problem could be identified with the level of precision required. Nevertheless, it created a new emphasis on causal relationships and it exerted a strong influence in a less rigorous form, shaping the style of work of some of the early pioneers of behavior therapy, such as Joseph Wolpe and Victor Meyer (Bruch & Bond, 1998). These pioneers focused on the concrete details of a problem and their interview method involved a process of testing hypotheses about its underlying causal determinants. They demonstrated that even without the benefit of precise measurement and the experimental manipulation of conditions, a practitioner could reach sound conclusions with implications for selecting a successful intervention. A similar style of interviewing guided by hypotheses is described in the Guidelines (Section B), and my case illustrations also demonstrate how competing hypotheses are evaluated.

Further Development of the Applied Scientist Model

The history of research into psychotherapy since attempts were first made to marry scientists with practitioners has tended to bear out Frank's (1984) view that these kinds of people do not interbreed. If they do, they cannot agree on how the ceremony should be performed. One member of the new clan, Orlinsky (2006), really does not like the form of EBP pursued by some researchers and prefers not to read their articles. My critique of MEBP in Chapter 3 is another example of disagreement. However, some form of relationship between science and practice has to be established. There is no need to presuppose that a practitioner who attempts to apply science should have the credentials of an academic position or have published in clinical journals.

I simply hope to show in this book how scientific reasoning can enter into the process of conceptualizing a client's problem. The method described in the Guidelines is intended to aid a therapist in his or her deliberations and to expose the whole process to greater public scrutiny. In other words, the overall aim is to make the optimum use of evidence and to reason clearly about it. It is not the aim of this style of practice to convert a therapist into a scientist who necessarily contributes to the general stock of knowledge. Rather, the purpose is to facilitate the process of learning by experience so that, ultimately, clients are more likely to benefit. While not amounting to a form of science, the process of formulation should be designed to generate information reliably and to maximize the validity of any inferences that are constructed within it.

At the very least, a therapist can adopt some of the following practices when investigating a client's problems: to avoid bias when collecting and interpreting observations; to consider whether aspects of a problem can be explained in terms of psychological principles/processes for which there is strong evidence; to generalize carefully from published evidence, taking note of its underlying research methodology and whether its validity can be extended to different circumstances; to reason about the evidence in accordance with standard philosophical and scientific criteria; to be systematic when seeking evidence for causal relationships between the elements of a problem; to seek out a means of validating (or invalidating) hypotheses about the causes of a problem (see Chapter 5 and the Guidelines).

These commitments do bear some resemblance to the model of an applied psychologist as a scientist–practitioner. As Shakow (1976) portrays it, this role combines a humanistic and scientific outlook, with an emphasis on research undertaken in community or clinic. The proposed model is perhaps closer to that of the "local scientist" (Stricker & Trierweiler, 1995) or "scholar–practitioner" (Peterson & Trieweiler, 1999). These authors are concerned that academic research is often too far removed from the complexities of an individual or local context. There is a desire for a broader, critical and reflective vision. According to Stricker and Trierweiler (1995, p. 998), "The clinical setting can be regarded as the laboratory for the clinician and it must be approached with the same discipline, critical thinking, imagination, openness to falsification, and rigor, that characterizes the scientist in the traditional laboratory." They stress the importance of the general skills of critical reasoning and problem solving rather than an in-depth knowledge of research methodology. The local scientist should also be skilled in empathic observation, intuition, and self-examination.

Consequently, in the local scientist model, academic knowledge is considered essential but not sufficient; the practitioner also needs to exercise critical judgment.

McFall (2007, p. 377) dismisses this approach to practice as "scientism," arguing that it does not represent the "traditional science model." In his opinion, practitioners should apply "predetermined nomothetic analyses and solutions." He sums up the opposing method as "teaching clinicians to start from scratch, with no preconceptions, when formulating and treating each case." Stricker and Trierweiler (1995, p. 997) express their position rather differently: "A major task for the local clinical scientist is to generate evidence that either supports or questions the applicability of scientific conclusions in particular cases." As I hope to show in the next chapter and elsewhere, we do not have to suppose that a creative application of scientific knowledge means abandoning checks on reliability and validity. For McFall, it is better to appeal to therapies that have been given a stamp of approval for safety and effectiveness, provided by managed-care systems that ensure quality control. But as we saw in the previous chapter, this style of EBP has weaknesses and carries its own risks. McFall is mainly concerned with applying what he calls "basic science." The dispute between this philosophy and the one described above became so severe that eventually one group of clinical psychologists involved in academic research broke away from the American Psychological Association to form an organization that is now known as the Association for Psychological Science.

As I pointed out in Chapter 3, for many psychotherapists, MEBP (manualized EBP) is a sticking point. In order to achieve a successful dissemination of MEBP to routine practice settings, practitioners need to be convinced by the research evidence and feel that their expertise is respected (see Chapter 9). Some have been vehemently opposed to standardized protocols and uniform outcome measures that prejudge the nature of the therapeutic task (e.g. Bohart & House, 2008; Marzillier & Hall, 2009). Concern grows when even the advocates of a careful appraisal and synthesis of the findings of randomized control trials (RCTs) are not happy with the way this task has been performed. Littell (2010, p. 187) is highly critical of the conclusions these appraisals have reached and believes that the widescale adoption of EBP is premature. The beliefs and ways of thinking of some researchers and ordinary practitioners have diverged so markedly as to represent virtually two different cultures. Kazdin (2008), an outstanding contributor to quantitative methodology in the field of evaluation, is clearly aware that there is a gulf between research and practice that needs to be bridged. He also worries that the accumulated wisdom of highly experienced practitioners will disappear when they die. He suggests using qualitative methods of research to study therapy as it is ordinarily practiced, just as an anthropologist might be called in to study a threatened indigenous society.

The research/practice divide is not helped by the fact that there are few rewards and career advantages in a self-critical and research-oriented style of practice. Health providers rarely allow time for experimentation. Moreover, as the quality standards of publishable research have risen, the necessary skills have moved beyond the capabilities of the jobbing therapist. The chief concern of the latter is to make sure that he or she is up to speed with the latest therapeutic techniques and to ally him- or herself with whatever movement or dictate is likely to ensure career advancement or security of employment. Despite these undeniable barriers to the exercise of independent judgment, the fundamental importance of good case formulation continues to be promoted by the professions (e.g. British Psychological Society, 2011). It is assumed that the ability to formulate means more than the application of "validated techniques" and that a critical research attitude in part defines the role of an applied psychologist.

There is a risk that too great a reliance on pre-validated therapeutic interventions will inhibit the development of new ideas. The history of psychotherapy reveals a rather capricious relationship between theory, techniques, and trial-and-error thinking. Take, for instance, the "running treatment" for agoraphobia described by Orwin (1973). It was based on the theory that "relief" after breath-holding, and also vigorous physical exertion, caused "inhibition of anxiety." A further justification was that physiological arousal associated with fear would be reattributed by the client to exercise. Orwin's therapy was conducted by regular nursing staff, a welfare officer, and spouses. Success was reported in all eight individuals in this uncontrolled trial. However, Orwin's use of theory was approximate, he regarded physical exercise as just an old technique reapplied to a new problem, and something must have prompted him to break with established practice in his hospital in order to try his method out. Since 1973, the field has clearly moved on; agoraphobia now tends to be seen as a feature associated with panic attacks, the relevance of hyperventilation and the importance of exposure to interoceptive sensations is now well-established, physical exercise is now widely employed for emotional problems including panic (Smits, Powers, Berry, & Otto, 2007), and research on anxiety sensitivity has become a minor industry. Orwin was not, of course, perceptive in foreseeing all these developments, but his general intuition was correct and he added to a growing awareness of the efficacy of new methods. The lesson seems to be that a certain combination of reasoning styles happened to be productive in this case. It would be undesirable to inhibit a spirit of experimentation that seems to be so essential in advancing any field.

CURRENT STATUS OF INDIVIDUALIZED APPROACHES TO THERAPY

It is really too early to say what level of expertise is needed to deliver therapy effectively. Success also depends on clients' abilities to solve problems by themselves. Some will pick up a self-help manual and will not need a therapist. Training for therapy based on ICF is probably more demanding than that needed for learning a manual but it does not require a doctorate in psychology. It is an approach to EBP based on principles rather than techniques, and for this reason might be considered over-ambitious as a training aim. However, if the nature of the work actually demands it, the routine practitioner should aim at the highest level of expertise—even to the extent of assuming, like a surgeon, that success is possible in every operation. In any case, access to more highly trained practitioners has been made easier through widespread use of the internet, making this mode of delivery a less costly option. Communication can be face-to-face when needed (via interlinked computers) and advice can also be delivered by email or text message (see Chapter 9).

It is important to recognize that therapy based on ICF is a form of evidence-based practice. There is a prevailing opinion (e.g. Spring & Neville, 2009) that "evidence" has to concern disorders, and that the only compelling method to obtain it is by means of an RCT with disordered groups. From this it follows that efficacy is demonstrated by a reduction in "symptoms." Therapy grounded in ICF aims for a much broader concept of an evidence base and what it is that constitutes success. A depressed or anxious mood may be a good marker that a person is becoming aware of the need to make adjustments to their life, but the ultimate test of success is that life becomes more meaningful and full of possibility. The kinds of problem that a person may need to resolve are quite variable and therefore inadequately captured by measures of symptoms. In other words, clients typically suffer from symptoms of a failure of adjustment, not symptoms of a disorder. Consider the analogy of a crime investigator—here, success is measured in terms of solving a crime, not in reducing the frustration and perhaps depressed mood of the investigator who fails to solve it.

A problem-solving perspective is, in fact, implicit in most programs designed to prevent or treat the disorders of "depression" and "anxiety." Prevention programs are psycho-educational and teach skills such as good parenting, challenging a negative outlook, becoming more active and involved in life, coping with daily stress, interacting more effectively with others, etc. (Dozois, Seeds, & Collins, 2009). The justification of programs of prevention is to reduce the incidence of future "mental disorders" but the benefits must spread wider than this. However, the positive outcomes tend not to be measured because the concept of mental health is overly narrow.

In a service with limited financial resources, it may make sense to offer time-limited group therapy that is primarily educational in function and excludes only those clients who have severe or complex difficulties (Erickson, Janeck, & Tallman, 2009). The aim is to teach general strategies that, it is hoped, will benefit enough clients on average. There is no real attempt at case formulation and outcome is assessed with standardized measures such as the Beck Anxiety Inventory (Beck & Steer, 1993). This cost-cutting approach is offset by clear disadvantages. As pointed out by Ericksen et al., these include a high attrition rate and, in an anxiety group, an inability to work effectively with obsessions and post-traumatic stress. For instance, participants who "re-experienced" their memories during group sessions distracted others from their exercises. The authors portray their method as disseminating empirically supported treatment but it is hard not to see it as other than a bargain-basement choice whose chief merit is that it can be afforded. These authors also point out that for staff who have little background in EBP, training in their transdiagnostic protocol is a more practical (and less costly) option than training in up to half a dozen different diagnosis-specific CBT manuals. An ICF approach to therapy holds out the possibility of a different option.

It is natural to ask whether a more expensive formulation-driven individual approach produces better outcomes, but this question cannot be answered without more research. Eells et al. (2011) feel that the evidence is too weak to come to any definite conclusions concerning the contribution of ICF skills to the success of therapy. However, they believe that expertise in formulation might mediate the relationship between a therapist's competence and his or her success. They also suggest that a good case formulation might prove to be a moderating variable in the success of therapy with clients who have more complex problems.

The choice between individualized and manualized EBP has to be guided by effectiveness in the longer term. Ideally, a comparison should be made between a generous allocation of therapy conducted by ICF practitioners who use their independent judgment, and therapy conducted according to a protocol. There should also be a lengthy post-therapy follow-up period. However, little research of this kind exists. Individualized therapy has been compared with manualized therapy in a small number of studies. There has been some support for an individualized approach in social skills training in children (Schneider & Byrne, 1987), in behavioral marital therapy (Jacobson et al., 1989), and when working with bulimia (Ghaderi, 2006). However, in an outcome study of obsessive-compulsive problems (OCD), no difference was found between standardized "exposure and response prevention" (ERP) and a range of CBT interventions selected on the basis of a detailed behavioral and functional analysis (Emmelkamp, Bouman, & Blaaw, 1994). Participants were assessed at the end of therapy and at two months follow-up on a range of measures that related to obsessions, mood, and interpersonal anxieties. The authors mention in passing that two thirds of clients given standardized ERP in previous studies had subsequently needed individualized therapy. Presumably, the same would hold true for their clients in the ERP group in their 1994 study. The follow-up period was too short to evaluate any possible long-term benefits of individualized therapy compared to standardized ERP. Given that the former did not focus only on obsessions, one might have expected that it would have led to less change in measures of OCD, which was not the case. From these authors' observations about previous clients receiving ERP, it would seem that people with OCD typically have a range of problems. The fact that the individualized therapy group clearly had additional problems, yet still benefited in terms of OCD, suggests that there are merits in carrying out an ICF.

Schulte and colleagues found that manualized therapy based on "exposure principles" produced better results in clients with phobias (including those with panic attacks) than a treatment in which therapists offered their own tailor-made interventions (Schulte & Eifert, 2002; Schulte, Kunzel, Pepping, & Schulte-Bahrenberg, 1992). In fact, clients in a yoked control group in which therapy mechanically followed decisions made in the individualized sessions improved even more than clients in the individually tailored therapy. Therapists given the freedom to adapt therapy deviated more from the exposure principles that underlay the manualized approach; this was true for both experienced therapists and novices. Since exposure therapy provokes distress in clients, it would be natural to want to avoid discomforting a client, and this may explain the findings (see also Becker, Zayfert, & Anderson, 2004). A reluctance to cause distress would apply particularly to therapists relatively unfamiliar with the exposure method. Therapists who changed methods or treatment goals rather than sticking with prolonged *in vivo* exposure produced poorer therapy outcomes (Schulte & Eifert, 2002, p. 322). Knowing the good record of exposure therapy with phobias, the results are not particularly surprising. The freedom to use individual judgment should not be a license to choose ineffective interventions or to chop and change methods and goals.

The research conducted by Schulte and colleagues on therapist decision making is detailed and illuminating, and has the advantage of being based on observations conducted in a naturalistic setting (a university clinic). All sessions are videotaped, and session-by-session questionnaires are completed by therapists and clients. Therapy is conducted by trainees whose level of skill is more likely to vary than would be the case with more experienced therapists. Schulte and Eifert (2002) maintain that therapist decision making is directed toward two different ends. The first is to ensure "positive patient behavior," by which is meant all the behaviors necessary to be in place in order for a client to benefit from an intervention (e.g. actively seeking therapy, being cooperative, self-disclosing, and exploring/testing out new behaviors). A therapist will normally act so as to inspire confidence and promote an expectation of ultimate benefit. One type of formulation skill is therefore directed toward identifying any aspect of the client, or the relationship, that is likely to impede the chance of success. The second end to which decision making is attuned is that of choosing and implementing a *method* to achieve behavioral change. Schulte and Eifert name the two therapist strategies "method-oriented" and "process- and patient-oriented." Of some interest, decisions that are process-oriented occur more frequently within sessions (55%) than method-oriented decisions (19%). (The remaining decisions are focused on therapists themselves.) The more frequently process-oriented decisions are made, the poorer the ultimate outcome, presumably reflecting the fact that client motivation is a more prominent concern. Conversely, the frequency of method-oriented decisions correlates positively with outcome.

Clients who lack signs of "positive patient behavior" (e.g. by not cooperating or "resisting" therapy) achieve a poorer outcome, although the direction of causality in this correlation could be questioned; a client's impression of his or her own progress (especially a lack of it) might influence his or her motivation. Schulte and Eifert (2002) discuss at length therapists' reasons for deciding to change their methods, such as perceiving that therapy is not going well or acting in response to new information. However, they maintain that therapists usually perceive these shortcomings too early, too often, and at the wrong times, and this is because they have largely invalid negative outcome predictions. On balance, these authors recommend that a therapist should adhere to a manual derived from trusted empirical research, except when clients are perceived as failing to cooperate.

What this body of research shows with considerable clarity is that therapists make frequent decisions within sessions that relate to an awareness of signs of a lack of client motivation/cooperation and also when it is thought necessary to make adjustments to the active intervention method. However, it is rather doubtful that these findings can be generalized beyond the heavily scrutinized and inexperienced trainees employed in this research. Nevertheless, they illustrate the importance of a detailed session–by–session analysis of client and therapist behavior, without which the advantages and disadvantages of ICF and manualized approaches are unlikely ever to be discovered.

In the next chapter I describe the various reasoning processes that enter into the process of ICF that help to ensure that it is not a purely "subjective" process as sometimes claimed.

CHAPTER 5

The Process of Reasoning in Individual Case Formulation

Chapter 3 has been critical of an approach to therapy that fits problems into diagnostic categories and offers standardized or modular protocols as their solution. There are other reasons for being skeptical about over-prescriptive solutions to personal problems. A person's life is a kind of balancing act between a variety of influences, including the actual realities a person faces and a range of potential future scenarios. A change in any direction is likely to have consequences that require careful forethought. A client's difficulties are likely to be an adjustment, however unsatisfactory, to circumstances that still call for a response. Put differently, a person's life cannot easily be compartmentalized into two parts—a well-adjusted part and a "disordered" part. For example, helping someone to overcome social fears has to be accompanied by a program of changed activity that allows anxiety-free behavior to be expressed. This may mean taking up new hobbies, breaking old patterns of avoidance, making new friends, and so forth. A more expansive social life might signal the end of a significant relationship. A therapist's remit is not just to facilitate change but to help a client manage change in the context of a life that is bound together by a set of values and a sense of direction. Given that peoples' lives and their opportunities are so different, there are bound to be severe limits on what can be achieved with a manualized approach. In this chapter I will discuss some issues that have to be faced when therapy is individually tailored to a client. How, for instance, should problems be investigated and what kind of reasoning processes are involved?

I will first consider why practitioners have sometimes been regarded as hopelessly incapable of thinking objectively about what they are doing. This is followed by a discussion of retrospective and prospective ways of thinking about, and learning from, case studies. These sections are followed by a summary of the biases that commonly affect the process of drawing inferences from evidence gathered during an assessment. Finally, I explain the role of deductive, inductive, and abductive reasoning when arriving at a formulation.

Individual Case Formulation
http://dx.doi.org/10.1016/B978-0-12-398269-8.00005-3

ARE PRACTITIONERS ABLE TO THINK OBJECTIVELY?

Over many years, there has been a sustained questioning of the ability of practitioners to make decisions that stand up to empirical scrutiny. In other words, their decisions have been regarded as subjective, unreliable, and probably invalid. For instance, Bickman (1999) states that there are six myths about mental health services:

1. The myth that practitioners get better with experience. In fact they do not get better for the following reasons: (a) they are unaware of their own therapeutic outcomes, (b) they do not respond to feedback, (c) they cannot remember what they have done in therapy, (d) they cannot link process to outcome, (e) they have difficulty in adapting general principles to the individual case and in learning from individual cases.
2. The myth that advanced degrees produce better practitioners.
3. The myth that continuing education improves competence.
4. The myth that professional licensing is a guarantee of effectiveness.
5. The myth that accredited health delivery organizations perform better than non-accredited.
6. The myth that clinical supervision improves practitioner effectiveness.

Bickman certainly points to aspects of practice that must be questioned very thoroughly. His observation that "I know of no instrument that can describe what clinicians do in usual care settings" is accurate, but his remarks seem to be premised on the assumption that there should be (or could be) some rapid, sure-fire method of ensuring quality control. There is, of course, the instrument of the video recorder as a reasonably adequate document of what a practitioner does. The problem is that of interpreting what is done without background knowledge of a client's typically complex life circumstances, which remain unseen. Bickman's solution for ensuring quality improvement is to recommend adherence to manualized treatments, teaching practitioners general skills known to be associated with a good outcome, and adopting comprehensive data systems that utilize standardized measures. These solutions are ideal for systems of production in which process and product really can be standardized. Unfortunately, people and their problems cannot readily be compared to faulty plumbing systems. Although it is understandable that attempts have been made to create the style of service delivery that Bickman advocates, the results so far have not been very encouraging or convincing (see Chapter 9).

Skepticism about the independent practitioner's skills stems, in part, from the influence of Meehl's book (Meehl, 1954) demonstrating the superiority of predictions made statistically (i.e. from objective test data) over a clinician's own appraisal of relevant information. Westen and Weinberger (2004, 2005) make the point that there has been confusion between a method of aggregating information (i.e. the sort of intuitive consideration sometimes given to information collected for a case formulation) and the fact that this typically happens to be done by practitioners. Their own research demonstrates that carefully constructed measures based on practitioners' judgments can be reliable and perform well when used to make predictions about future outcomes. In other words, before being too critical of judgments made in practice settings, attention must be paid to what a practitioner is being asked to do and the means of doing it.

Some of the tasks used in laboratory simulations of clinical judgment betray a narrow, and to some extent outdated, conception of actual practice. In some studies, the assumption was made that practitioners were using observations, or interpreting psychometric test scores, in order to make predictions about such matters as diagnosis, personality traits, and therapeutic outcome. The criterion for prediction was therefore far removed from the context of moment-to-moment decision making. The prediction was deemed correct if it matched the results of other assessments that were regarded as valid indicators of the "true" state of affairs. Practitioners generally performed poorly in these kinds of task when compared with the success of actuarial methods that relied on objective data (Garb & Boyle, 2003).

In retrospect, we can see that many of the prediction tasks would now be considered of little interest or relevance. The process of assessment and formulation is more likely to rely on face-to-face interviews than reactions to ink blots or cartoons of cute dogs. Some of the experimental tasks *did* involve "listening to segments of an assessment interview" or "reading a short description of a case history," but it is hard to imagine that anything of much significance could be reliably inferred from these brief extracts, even in the best of circumstances. Decontextualized information is simply too impoverished. With regard to the determination of a psychiatric diagnosis or personality type, this is at best a secondary consideration in individual case formulation (ICF), if considered at all.

Given the influence of chance in human affairs, it is very difficult to predict the future status of a particular person over an extended period of time. Even with group studies that utilize numerous objective measures, the accuracy of predicting the outcome of psychotherapy is, on average, rather low. Forty per cent of the variance is "unexplained" (Norcross, 2011). Thirty per cent *can* be explained by "client factors" but we are not referring here to a subtle formulation of problems but, rather, to gross demographic and personality characteristics, factors that are unlikely to determine the choice of an intervention. What is a therapist expected to do when faced with a client whose personality and demographic characteristics predict a poor outcome? The information is only of value if it can be acted upon to increase the probability of a successful intervention. Rather than refuse to take on this sort of client (which might be the rational decision), a therapist might simply try, as in the case of heroic surgery, to do his or her best in the circumstances. This optimistic stance could indeed bias the accuracy of their judgment.

These remarks do not dispute the fact that when practitioners are confronted with ambiguous information and complex decision making tasks, they are susceptible to numerous cognitive biases and environmental influences that can result in poor judgment (see below). The potential for error increases when the practitioner does not seek, or does not receive, corrective feedback. Garb and Boyle (2003, p. 31) argue that practitioners should wait until their "assessment instrument or treatment method is supported by empirical research," but this assumes that all of the factors that influence decision making in individual therapy can be subsumed under general principles discoverable through nomothetic research. This view seems unrealistic.

In order to validate the outcome of an assessment procedure, such as a case formulation, it would be necessary to reach agreement on the criteria that constitute validation, and this is not easy. Benchmarking criteria can always be questioned. For instance, cognitive therapists have investigated the reliability and validity of their cognitive formulations. Kuyken, Fothergill, Musa, and Chadwick (2004) assessed the formulations produced by attendees at workshops designed to teach the skill of producing one. The "valid" formulation was benchmarked by an expert (Judith Beck). This formulation referred to significant childhood data, and predisposing characteristics, such as core beliefs, conditional assumptions/beliefs/rules, and compensatory strategies. This method of validation is limited because it already presupposes what a good causal explanation should look like. Moreover, the correct identification of a cognitive construct, such as a core belief, is only one possible component of an adequate formulation. It would be important to explore the extent to which significant others (e.g. a family member or partner) reinforce the core belief. A client's willingness to change this state of affairs, perhaps by exiting an unhealthy relationship, could also be relevant. To be really convincing, the validation of a case formulation needs to assess its usefulness in practice.

One criterion for a valid formulation is that it is productive in the sense of generating potential solutions that lead to interventions that are effective in terms of their intended short-term outcome. However, if an intervention based on a formulation fails, it may do so for a variety of reasons. An example is provided in the Guidelines (Section E). A valid formulation is one that allows for failure to be explained and is sufficiently flexible to suggest an alternative strategy that might prove successful. As already noted, in relation to future states of affairs, such as a client's status 12 months following therapy, there is no reason to expect that a therapist's predictions from a formulation would be especially accurate. It is still reasonable to expect that, on average, a therapist's clients would continue to benefit over the longer term and so some means for obtaining this feedback should be sought. This raises the difficulty of aggregating and averaging changes in clients who may have presented with very different types of problem initially.

In the initial assessment stage, the adequacy and validity of a formulation are put in jeopardy if a client is not an honest informant or if she or he deliberately undermines the aims of therapy. A therapist should strive to be sensitive to a client's defensiveness about revealing information, or her or his inability to access relevant information, but this difficulty cannot easily be remedied by even the most astute and experienced practitioner.

When actually conducting an assessment, there are several factors that protect against unreliable and invalid judgment. First, clients often repeat themselves or say the same thing in different ways. Second, they are typically quick to correct factual inaccuracies or inappropriate interpretations when a therapist misunderstands. Third, it may be possible to use multiple sources of information (e.g. speak to different informants) to increase confidence in a judgment. This is the strategy of triangulation, whereby it is expected that the results of different modes of assessment should converge on the same conclusion, and that if there are discrepancies, these can be explained. Fourth, regarding validity, opportunities usually do exist to obtain corrective feedback. A therapist is not a passive processor of information but attends to inconsistencies in the information and employs investigative questioning as well as, where possible, actual hypothesis testing. If therapists do not make use of these strategies, this is a criticism of professional competence rather than an indictment of judgment in practice situations.

Once therapy has started in earnest, there is an opportunity to compare and contrast information obtained over a number of encounters with the same person. Clients do, of course, frequently surprise a therapist. Unforeseen events can lead to major revisions in a formulation. Surprising information can also be a form of corrective feedback leading to a revision of the formulation or intervention strategy.

Garb and Boyle (2003) rightly point out that a client may be unaware of, or unable to articulate, information that is relevant to his or her problem. A client may be deferential to a therapist and too easily convinced by his or her interpretations. It would helpful to be in possession of objective tests that could overcome these obstacles to assessment but attempts in this direction (e.g. projective tests, social desirability scales, lie detectors) seem to have gone out of fashion, presumably because they have not been very helpful. It seems best to adopt a strategy of self-critical thinking at all stages—when gathering the evidence, when weighing it up in light of hypotheses, and when reaching a conclusion about the best way to proceed (see Bromley, 1986, and Gambrill, 2005). Faust (1991) contrasts science as a public, self-correcting enterprise with a reliance on personal experience that he considers to be more typical of the practitioner. Faust's emphasis on science as self-correcting not only exaggerates the extent to which scientists are unprejudiced but also underestimates the checks and balances in practice situations introduced by supervision and team meetings. However, while stressing the importance of scientific validation, Faust also notes that "Experience has no peer or substitute in the formation of ideas and hypotheses." This is precisely a central feature of case formulation.

WAYS OF LEARNING ABOUT SINGLE INDIVIDUALS
Retrospective Learning

The careful description of individual cases has been persuasive in the history of all types of psychological therapy (Fishman, 1999; McLeod, 2010; Stiles, 2005). A single case often sheds light on prior assumptions and new possibilities. The generalizations that can be shown to apply in a single individual might be true only for that individual but very often they can be shown to be true of successive clients with a similar problem. The purpose here is to reason *from* a case in order to establish a general principle or prove a theoretical point. A conclusion is reached *retrospectively* and is instructive for future cases. ICF is essentially concerned with reasoning *prospectively about* an individual case rather than *from* it (see below). I will therefore give only brief consideration to retrospective case research.

One approach to learning from cases aims to build up a body of "case law" over time (Bromley, 1986). Each case is a "one-off" but is sufficiently similar to previous cases to generate an accumulating body of rules. In one example of this method, a "jury" evaluated the evidence relating to a single case, and the whole procedure was modeled on practices in civil law (Miller, 2011). Up till now, the reasoning that goes into case law in psychotherapy has remained at a rather informal level, although this may change if the method is systematically adopted. A jury of experts is unlikely to agree about the formulation of a case unless they have been trained in a similar way, as in the "plan formulation method" of Curtis and Silberschatz (2007). The relevant assessment information would simply take a different form for a psychodynamic and cognitive behavioral therapist.

Prospective Reasoning about a Case

I have conceptualized therapy as problem solving and this is a form of prospective reasoning. Typically, a client has hit some kind of obstacle to a "normal" way of proceeding. Habitual methods of coping no longer work. This situation can be compared with other forms of trouble-shooting in society. One example would be the investigation of a railway accident and another the detective work needed to solve a crime in the style of Sherlock Holmes. The task requires an ongoing appraisal of the facts of a single case, analyzing and explaining them, and then offering up a solution or judgment.

Each "case" is the outcome of a unique set of circumstances, although a seasoned investigator like Sherlock Holmes would draw on previous experience, aided by his keen observation, deductions from the facts, and probably an appeal to a little science. Today, the crime investigator has access to vastly more sophisticated forensic science techniques. From the combined evidence, certain inferences can be drawn, even though each criminal investigation is unique.

A reliance on past experience is rarely sufficient by itself to solve a new case, and specific investigations may need to be undertaken. For instance, the investigator of a railway accident might attempt to simulate the conditions that could have caused it and thereby generate hypotheses about what has happened. In a similar way, a therapist might role-play a client's problem and draw certain conclusions from aspects of the problem that this exercise reveals. The logic of investigation does not follow an inference from an empirical generalization of the kind "lethargy is a sign of depression." There may be some truth in this generalization but we can go much further in the individual case and collect evidence to support a variety of hypotheses about a client's lethargy and depressed mood.

In other words, a therapist is forearmed with a range of possible interpretations, each of which has a greater or lesser probability of being true for a given individual. Has the client recently suffered a loss, such as a bereavement, or been made redundant? Has the client been let down by a friend? Does the client have a physical illness that produces fatigue, which accounts for inactivity? A therapist already knows a great deal about why people sometimes sink into lethargy and much of that has little to do with psychological theory or clinical outcome studies. It might be necessary to call upon a therapist's knowledge of medicine, physiology, or the cultural practices of a minority group, all of which could be supplemented by a search for reliable sources of relevant information. From the point of view of manualized evidence-based practice (MEBP), the suggestion that a therapist should take into account prior expectations about a client might be viewed as a subjective bias. It could be dismissed as a personal opinion that should be ignored in favor of an appeal to evidence about the "best treatment for clients who show the classic signs of depression." Although a therapist has to guard against prior expectations that are based on prejudice or ignorance, it would be silly (if not impossible) to ignore a common pool of knowledge, especially when it is enhanced by a therapist's long experience with a particular type of problem.

Evidence from trials of therapeutic methods may provide some sound guidelines, but beyond that a therapist has to generate a variety of hypotheses to account for the unique features of a problem. As in a police investigation, the formulator must make observations with care in order to restrain any tendency to assume the obvious, must consider all possible explanations, and must work out a means of testing which explanation best fits the facts. The problem presented by each client is treated as a unique puzzle to be solved. Therapist and client collaborate together—the very opposite of a criminal investigation. The formulation is laid out quite explicitly, and is sometimes presented in written form or as a diagram. The facts are identified and any inferences that can be drawn from them are stated. Not only does this minimize the risk of poor judgment, it also allows others to criticize and debate the formulation. This is clearly necessary because an individual formulation stands or falls on a therapist's ability to reason coherently and justify the intervention it suggests.

Reasoning in ICF is therefore *prospective* rather than being a retrospective summation of the evidence that has been gathered. The opportunity to reason prospectively during formulation allows for the testing of hypotheses as assessment proceeds. In other words, if a hypothesis has any validity, certain questions, tests, or interventions will yield predicted answers or consequences. Of course, information has to be gathered in such a way that the refutation of a hypothesis is also possible. An interview question can be asked in order to confirm or disconfirm a hypothesis. Godoy and Gavino (2003) studied information–gathering strategies in behavioral assessment when trainees attempted to detect functionally significant relationships between stimulus antecedents and stimulus consequences. They found that trainees in equal proportions used a verificationist strategy and one that permitted refutation of a hypothesis. Only 8% collected comprehensive information from all four cells of a contingency table, that is, events A and B jointly present, jointly absent, A present, B absent, and A absent, B present. One implication of this study is that trainees need to be taught how to collect information systematically and comprehensively.

Hypotheses are based on different kinds of inference and are not limited to functional relationships. I will adopt the term hypothesis for whatever kind of speculative reasoning is involved. A hypothesis is based on induction when it is inferred that an observation is an instance of an empirical generalization thought to be generally true. For instance, it might be predicted that if a client has a fear of X, she or he will show some of the well-known signs of fear when exposed to X. The results of a test trial (if properly appraised) may or may not support the prediction. It is possible that an observation made during the test favors an alternative hypothesis. A formulation is not built out of one hypothesis but at some stage hypotheses considered to be credible will have to be brought together and integrated. The purpose then is to develop a good "general formulation" to bring together what usually amounts to a rather disparate set of observations. This reasoning process has been called "abduction" (see below).

A different kind of hypothesis relates to moral reasoning, which takes a hermeneutic form (Seale, 1999). Here, the criteria are chiefly consistency and interconnectedness (coherence). Conclusions reached in this way can be highly relevant to the origins of a problem, to current moral dilemmas, or to a client's future goals. In fact, a "problem" only arises as such in the context of a life that is interpreted from the point of view of its meaning and values. The results of moral reasoning may be relevant to the choice of an intervention but the judgment that is made may not have any obvious relationship to academic theory or an evidence base. For instance, predicting whether a client who is looking for a new partner would be better off circulating with like-minded people, enlisting the help of an online dating service, or contacting friends made in the distant past, is not a prediction that can be derived from psychological processes. A therapist can only make a reasonable guess based on life experience and knowledge of a client's personality and preferences. In other words, is the judgment consistent with previous choices and coherent with the client's values? This guess is likely to be closer to the mark when therapist and client share the same social and cultural background. Where these differ, a therapist should explore the issue with the client in greater depth, or perhaps do some background research. For instance, when finding a partner implies only marriage, there are likely to be culture-specific practices to follow.

To sum up, ICF is the best account that can be given of a client's problem, having gathered evidence that is sufficiently comprehensive, and having discounted all feasible alternative explanations of the problem as unlikely to be true. Weighing up the truth of a hypothesis to account for any given observation requires that the facts be considered in light of the context in which they are found. To return to the earlier example of lethargy, a client referred to a clinic on account of low mood might be highly likely to feel lethargic. Stated technically, lethargy has a high base rate of occurrence in a sample of people reporting low mood in a clinic. A probable interpretation of lethargy in this clinical context is that it is an indicator of low mood, in other words part of a cluster of complaints that lies at the extreme end of the normal range. If instead, a friend says they are lethargic, the probability of this being similarly a part of an extreme mood is much lower given that friends (i.e. people in general) are not, on the whole, that severely depressed (the base rate is lower). The significance of lethargy is assessed in relation to a range of other hypotheses that might be more likely to be true (the friend stayed up all night at a party, the friend is trying to get out of a commitment to go running, etc.). The facts of the case, jointly considered, might narrow down the hypothesis about lethargy to just one credible explanation. In another investigative strategy (counterfactual reasoning), a therapist speculates that if a hypothesis about the cause of lethargy as a sign of depressed mood were to be true, is it possible that the client would still be lethargic if she or he were not depressed? In fact, lethargy might have been typical of the person prior to any complaint of low mood. The person has always been a couch potato. In general, it is necessary to cross-check by considering evidence from different sources. A therapist may then be prompted to collect additional evidence to confirm a hypothesis, and this would be the case whether the facts concern a client or a friend.

An important source of information for a formulation is the relationship that develops between therapist and client. This will influence the quality and type of evidence obtained, and not always in the sense that a "good" relationship yields better information. A pleasant and jocular assessment style might not supply the right opportunity for a client to talk about a deep level of despair. The quality and course of the relationship provides a rich source of information. For instance, there might be something about a client that leads a therapist to feel a certain way, perhaps cautious, sucked dry of energy, optimistic, or worried. Reflection on this feeling, combined with an inference as to the reason for its presence, might add weight to one hypothesis over another. The process of case formulation is closely integrated with other aspects of the therapeutic process. As Dudley, Kuyken, and Padesky (2011, p. 222) maintain:

> the relationship between the formulation and outcome needs to be understood in terms of a fine-grained analysis . . . . How the formulation is built with the client, how this engenders hope and optimism for change, how it impacts on the therapeutic alliance and confidence in the therapist, and how this together leads to a rationale for the selection of an intervention strategy.

Experienced supervisors will appreciate that an hour-long audio-recording of a trainee's therapy session can lead to several hours of analysis, discussion, and sometimes heated debate. Decision making in therapy cannot be reduced to a small set of general principles.

I will now summarize some common biases in information processing that research into the nature of judgment in everyday situations has rightly brought to everyone's attention.

COMMON ERRORS IN PROCESSING INFORMATION ABOUT CLIENTS

A topic of considerable importance in social psychology is the way people make decisions under conditions of uncertainty or when they have a limited amount of information available to them (Kahneman & Tversky, 1973; Ross, 1977; Turk & Salovey, 1988). Social psychologists have investigated how lay people make judgments, express preferences, weigh up positive and negative information, or attribute causes to events. One focus of interest has been whether people judge an action as caused by something "inside" a person (e.g. he is a "naturally nasty" individual) or something in the external situation (e.g. "the company was losing money and so he was forced to sack him"). How such judgments are made often depends on where a person's sympathies lie. Ideally, when assessing a client, a therapist should aim to be objective and even-handed. A client might bring misfortune on themselves by their own hand but the role of external events, forcing unwise decisions, could be equally important.

Typically, assessment produces a mass of information of uncertain significance. There is always an unknown number of potential facts to be discovered, sometimes hidden by the client or never envisaged by the therapist. When faced with this kind of situation, social psychologists have identified a number of shortcuts (or heuristics) in thinking that people commonly employ when they make sense of the significance of the information presented. These are best illustrated by posing a purely fanciful example. Let us imagine a client who is wearing a sober grey suit but happens to be sporting fluorescent pink socks. How might a therapist make sense of this? The socks immediately attract attention, just as they would outside the consulting room. One possible bias is to think that anything that stands out vividly should be given attention on the assumption that it must be important. A therapist may feel inclined to invent a complicated story around the socks that has no evidence to support it. Perhaps greater objectivity would be demonstrated by simply ignoring them. The socks might have been the client's only clean pair to wear that morning.

Another possible thinking bias is to assimilate the pink socks into a favorite theory. The therapist in question is always looking for signs of psychiatric disorder and infers that the socks are typical of the attention-getting ploy of the narcissist. A "confirmation" bias leads a therapist to use information to confirm a hypothesis while ignoring or discounting anything that might disconfirm it. One effect of this bias is to perceive correlations between events that are purely illusory. Put differently, a therapist reasons that everyone in his or her previous experience wearing pink socks has been a narcissist, while forgetting everyone who has been a narcissist wearing grey or brown socks, and everyone wearing pink socks who has *not* been a narcissist. The association between colorful clothing and narcissism does not exist in reality.

Another way of characterizing this bias is to think of it as a false stereotype. Wearing pink socks is not (yet) a cardinal symptom of any DSM disorder (in the American Psychiatric Association's *Diagnostic and statistical manual of mental disorders*) but it may be indicative of one of the therapist's favorite categories for describing clients. For example, the socks may be seen as typical of one of "Dr Brown's weird referrals." Any feature of a client that does not fit the stereotype is ignored but other features (e.g. weirdness) are ascribed without justification.

Another possibility is that a therapist might pay attention to fluorescent pink socks and interpret them in a certain manner because a way of thinking concerning the clothing of clients has been activated by recent events (the "availability" heuristic). Perhaps a therapist has just attended a lecture on "The role of luminosity in modern art." Or, closer to home, one of his or her clients who wears exotic hats of a pink hue attempted suicide the previous week.

How then should a therapist interpret the fluorescent pink socks, if at all? They are surely only relevant in the light of other sources of information. A therapist considers a range of possible hypotheses and by deduction or by testing out their validity, eventually settles on the best interpretation available. A therapist could, of course, say to a client directly: "Fetching socks you are wearing …," hoping to elicit some clues. Perhaps the socks really are a sign of a rebellious attitude toward the kind of boring office job he is doing and his desire to go to art school and work within a medium of fluorescent paint. If so, there will be other evidence to support this interpretation.

I will now give a brief explanation of deductive, inductive, and abductive reasoning and show how they are relevant to formulation. The reasoning involved in the practice of psychological therapy is probably about as complex as it gets for any craft skill that has to tailor general principles to meet the needs of a unique situation.

DIFFERENT TYPES OF LOGICAL REASONING

Deductive Reasoning

When we make a correct deduction from a starting point, we do not discover anything new but simply express what was logically implied by the statement of facts in the first place. If a client has immigrated into the country, there must have been at least one date on which this first occurred because this is part of the meaning of immigration. This may not sound like a very exciting deduction but it may be important in relation to other facts. For instance, did some variation in the client's problem relate to the timing of this event? The reasoning skill is not simply a matter of paying attention to observations from which deductions can be made but to combine these with other inferences. Care must be taken when the initial starting point has a rather fuzzy meaning. It is actually quite rare for the premises to be unambiguous. For example, when a client claims to have "retired," we cannot deduce an age, because she or he may have taken early retirement at 50 or been medically retired at 30. Does retirement mean retired from longstanding employment but continuation in other paid activities? From a client's use of the word "retirement," we can probably deduce correctly that she or he has worked at some point in her or his life. The example I have just provided does not stretch our powers of reasoning. However, when making an assessment, there is often little time to think through the implications of what has been said. Consequently, it is easy to jump to conclusions and make an invalid deduction or simply to fail to realize the implications of what has been said. Deductive reasoning takes the following general form:

A person who has "retired" has at one time been engaged in "work" (typically, but not always, gainful employment).

X has "retired."

Therefore X worked at some point in his or her life.

Of course, a client could have lied about the facts. It is possible to make a correct deduction from false premises. The potential to be misled lies in this case with the client.

While a therapist needs to be mindful of his or her own deductive reasoning, it is also important not be led astray by the logical inferences that a client makes. O'Connor, Aardema, and Pélissier (2005, p. 19) give some instructive examples of plausible but false reasoning: "If I am first in everything, then I am perfect. I am first in everything, therefore I am perfect." The reasoning is correct here but only if the client's premise that "being first" implies "being perfect" is accepted. In a related example, the following deduction from the premise would be an incorrect form of argument: "I am not first in everything, therefore I am not perfect." Even if the premise were to be true, it does not follow that anything can be deduced from reversing it because there could be other conditions that make a person perfect.

I am mainly concerned here with whether a therapist reasons correctly, and it does not necessarily help, from a therapeutic point of view, to point out that a client is making illogical statements. For example, one of my clients was convinced that had she not decided to make an extra shopping trip, her automobile accident would not have happened. The therapist may correctly infer, along with the client, that had she stayed at home, she would not have been on the road in her vehicle at the time. However, the therapist might deny the implication that her decision to go shopping could be interpreted to mean that she was responsible for causing the accident. How this contrary argument is conveyed (verbally or through experiential learning) is a matter of some subtlety.

Inductive Reasoning

Much of our knowledge of the world consists of general conclusions built up on the basis of many specific examples that follow the same rule or pattern. One example is: "Driving on a freeway is usually safe." The "usually" implies that we could be proved wrong but experience up till now tells us that driving on a freeway is safe. Knowledge from some kinds of evidence-based therapy is of this kind. "Treatment X reliably produces benefits in condition Y." Inductive generalizations apply to specific situations and therefore they are always limited in scope. In other words, it cannot be known for sure that they are universally true. It is possible to misapply them by forgetting about those specific conditions. Driving on a freeway in fog is not safe. Treatment X will not produce expected results if it is not applied as recommended and if a client does not really have condition Y as specified in the original treatment trial. One of the arguments for favoring ICF is that MEBP, although providing reasonable guidelines, may not actually apply to the client in question. When a therapist is mindful of the ways in which a client is unique, rather than representative of a class of clients, he or she has to apply a variety of arguments to support an intervention. Inductive generalizations taken from the research literature or common knowledge may not be sufficient to guarantee good judgment.

It is usual for a therapist to think inductively when gathering information about how a client's problem is expressed in a variety of different circumstances. The inductive rule applies uniquely to the client. It might be labeled as a pattern, theme, or schema—in essence an inductive rule that a client seems to be following. An example of a rule of this sort is: "Be polite to people in authority but be rude to people perceived as your inferiors." This could be a rule that a therapist has inferred from a number of examples supplied by a client or one that a client has stated in various ways as a guiding principle. In either case, a therapist might wish to draw a client's attention to patterns that have been observed so that a rule can be made explicit and questioned. Induction is one means of reducing a mass of information to a manageable level, and it is an essential part of formulation. However, there are risks to inductive inference. Let us suppose that all of a client's reported partners have been female, and from this it is inferred that the client's next partner will be female or that all previous partners have been female.

There are several potential weaknesses when using this kind of reasoning. First, the similarity that a therapist draws between different observations might have been imposed on the evidence by a rule that a therapist simply assumes without question. Information that does not fit the rule is ignored or not noticed. Second, a therapist might have adopted a strategy of seeking to confirm a generalization and might not have requested information that has the potential to contradict it. Third, an assumption about the underlying basis of a similarity between different pieces of evidence might simply be false. A therapist might have correctly identified a pattern but this pattern could be compatible with a number of different explanations.

Returning to the example of the gender of a client's partners, what can be deduced? A therapist might infer on the basis that all of a client's partners are of the same sex that his or her sexual orientation is fixed. In reality, a client might later come to revise their sexual preference or may have changed it in the past but not reported this. These possibilities are discounted if it is assumed that a client's sexual orientation is obvious from the available evidence or if the idea of a fixed sexual orientation is already part of a therapist's mindset. When interpreting the evidence, it has also to be considered that a partner may have been selected for reasons other than a compatible sexual orientation.

Abductive Reasoning

This is the kind of reasoning we are forced to resort to in many everyday situations. It means making a best guess at the most likely explanation given all the facts under consideration. Evers and Wu (2006) define it as "inference to the best explanation" or justifying a generalization by relying on "the fact that it explains the observed empirical data and no other alternative hypothesis offers a better explanation of what has been observed." They state the general form of inference as follows:

D is a collection of data (facts, observations, givens).

H explains D (or would, if true, explain D).

No other hypothesis can explain D as well as H does.

Therefore, H is probably true.

This kind of reasoning is typical of case formulation where information is often incomplete and highly contextual in nature. There may be no immediately obvious way of integrating it into one conceptualization. The data may relate to a single case or to a subset of the data that has been collected on that case. The latter point is important because it is very unlikely that a single explanatory hypothesis could explain all of the facts about a person's life. In fact, abductive reasoning in everyday situations is rarely so ambitious. The definition supplied by Evers and Wu implies that there is a choice between several possible explanations. The facts "do not speak for themselves" and, indeed, the facts may look very different from the perspective of different explanations. For this reason it seems best to start out with low-inference observations that do not prejudge the final synthesis.

It is always possible to add to the stock of facts that relate to a problem, perhaps guided by an initial hypothesis, but at some point a decision or judgment has to be made. In a scientific context, abductive reasoning can be highly creative—a leap from the facts to a completely new interpretation of why they hang together as they do. The new speculative theory leads to predictions that can then be tested out rigorously through experiment. The therapeutic situation is not unlike this. A case formulation that does not seem to lead anywhere might be completely replaced by a new way of integrating the facts. It then becomes obvious what further data collection (or intervention) will prove or disprove the new explanatory hypothesis.

Evers and Wu (2006) point out that the particulars of a case can only be identified in terms of general concepts. The specification of a local particular is achieved in ordinary language by an intersection of universals, for example, "the man to the left of the door." It is perhaps for this reason that Vertue and Haig (2008), in their account of abductive reasoning about cases, suggest that specific (contextual) data should be assimilated into "phenomena" that are stable recurrent features of a client's functioning. However, the examples they provide of "phenomena," such as DSM diagnoses or "relationship dysfunction," are already highly conditioned by theoretical assumptions and processes of prior data-reduction or interpretation. In their case illustration, the phenomena to be explained included social withdrawal, separation anxiety, aggression, attentional problems, impulsivity, and several more. The causal mechanisms given to explain these phenomena are grouped into distal causal, proximal causal, learning and environmental factors, psychological causes, and maintaining factors. It is not clear whether this division into types of causal explanation implies that there is one or more valid hypotheses. Vertue and Haig acknowledge that the process of abductive reasoning is shaped by orienting frameworks but these do not seem to be viewed as alternative and competing ways of understanding the facts. As they write,

> the purpose of this second phase [of abductive reasoning] is to identify and group the relevant plausible causal factors and suggest how they might be related to the

various clinical phenomena. It is only in the third phase that the interrelationships between the various causal mechanisms are depicted, at which point it becomes clearer how these mechanisms interact to generate and maintain the various clinical phenomena.

There is no sense here of how the phenomena could be made compatible with competing hypotheses, nor how "it becomes clearer" that the mechanisms interact. For instance, one of the possible causes they suggest is "hearing problems," and this would presumably lead to a different integration of the facts than "insecure attachment style," another of their possible causes.

My understanding of abductive reasoning therefore differs from that of Vertue and Haig (2008). Abductive reasoning is productive when a conceptualization fits the facts (or a subset of related facts) better than any alternative. Evers and Wu (2006, p. 523) portray the process as follows. A favored theory implies more than a single observation outcome; it implies instead a pattern of expectations or, over time, a succession of patterns. An exact matching of patterns and theory is unlikely so there has to be a persistent matching of feedforward patterns of expectation with feedback patterns of experience. In the case of inevitable mismatches, the theory can either be amended or the investigator looks to the next most favored theory as a source of feedforward patterns. Both strategies can be pursued simultaneously and "through the process of iterated theory revision and theory competition, the task is to come up with the most coherent theory that can account for the case, subject to the pattern matching constraint" (Evers & Wu, 2006, p. 524).

The risks to this process are ad hoc adjustments to theory and selective attention to confirmatory evidence. However, Evers and Wu point out that an appeal to the simplicity of an explanation, and its comprehensiveness, explanatory unity, fecundity, and coherence with other established bodies of knowledge, can help to reduce these risks.

Abductive inference may combine different types of reasoning, such as deduction, finding a correspondence between an observation about a client and a psychological principle, inductive generalization about patterns in a client's behavior, and more creative leaps that involve argument by analogy. Many of the concepts that we employ in explanation have rich implications and on this basis all kinds of fruitful analogies can suggest themselves. For example, even the concept "water" brings to mind its properties and behavior—that it freezes or evaporates at certain temperatures, that it is composed of hydrogen and oxygen, that there is such a thing as "heavy water," that water dissolves some solids and not others, etc. Even though a concept might not be applied to understand a client's problem in a strictly "scientific" manner, a therapist can speculate that the concept could be applied by analogy on the basis of just some of its known properties.

The metaphors that a client uses to describe their own situation might also suggest that certain psychological concepts are relevant to the formulation. "Feeling cornered" suggests a restriction of choice or an ineffectual behavioral repertoire. "Being on the brink of an abyss" suggests immediate danger or suicidal thinking. The specific usefulness of metaphor is to refer to features of things that would be difficult or impossible to refer to otherwise. A client discusses their life situation but is unable to pin down some feature of it that seems important. However, this feature is captured by a metaphorical word or phrase in which the feature is more obviously present. It is clear from the context of the conversation that the metaphor or analogy is not to be taken literally. The therapist grasps that a client is trying to express something that is only vaguely formulated. The client is not literally cornered or standing next to an abyss. Sometimes, a therapist might hardly be aware of taking take note of the figurative language that a client employs, just as a client may use this form of language unwittingly. In combination with other evidence, figurative terms may add together to produce a hunch about the way a client views self or world. This hunch could be one piece of a jigsaw that contributes to the therapist's conceptualization that best fits the facts.

Meyer's original paper concerning his therapeutic approach to compulsive rituals illustrates very clearly the kind of reasoning that enters into a creative adaptation of theory to a real-world problem (Meyer, 1966). The important point to note is the variety of evidential sources (academic literature, previous therapeutic success, self-report from clients, informal clinical observations, and behavioral monitoring) that contributed toward building up an argument for the selected intervention. Meyer attempted to account for inconsistencies in the evidence and alternative hypotheses were considered, sometimes only to be discounted. The conceptual model that Meyer developed allows a therapist to generate testable predictions about any particular client who complains of compulsive rituals. In justifying his technique, and when reflecting on its impact, he drew upon several lines of argument that can be grouped together as follows.

Concepts/Principles Drawn from the Academic Literature
- A suggestion that rituals are analogous to learned avoidance responses, originally evoked in traumatic situations.
- That there is resistance to extinction of the former (in animals) under conditions of repeated presentation of the conditioned stimulus (CS) when further punishment of the response renders it "unsuccessful."
- The opinion expressed in an earlier paper (by other authors) that it is necessary to extinguish both the conditioned emotional reaction *and* motor responses.
- That there is evidence from animal studies that preventing an avoidance response hastens its extinction.

Argument by Analogy with, or Speculative Extension of, Research Findings
- Rituals may persist if they eliminate the original aversive stimulus but, in the case of obsessional clients, this may only be a predicted (and, by implication, an uncertain/unknowable) disaster.
- An avoidance response may be unsuccessful if a CS is not under the client's control (e.g. the CS is an uncontrollable impulse or idea).
- There are good theoretical reasons for preventing the client carrying out the ritual—in this way the client learns that the feared consequences do not take place, leading to the elimination of the (avoidance) motivation to perform it.
- It may be difficult to achieve complete success when predicted disasters are vague and distant (e.g. the idea of eternal damnation).

Personal Clinical Experience and Clients' Reports
- Clients sometimes report reduction of anxiety after performing a ritual and an increase if they are prevented from carrying it out.
- Some clients found it noteworthy that the distress they predicted would get out of control after stopping a ritual failed to materialize. Predicted disasters did not occur.

Accounting for Potential Contradictions/Anomalies in the Evidence
- Some reason needs to be offered for why systematic desensitization is successful for most phobias but not for obsessions. Perhaps in the former, it is easy to prevent provocation of the phobia between sessions but this is not the case with obsessions. Clients may simply be unwilling to stop performing the ritual between sessions.

- It needs to be explained why performance of a ritual can sometimes lead to an elevation in anxiety rather than a reduction, as is more usual.

Significant Observations Made during the Treatment

- One of the clients who benefited from Meyer's technique (called "modification of expectations") had previously failed to respond to systematic desensitization, but both clients treated with his new technique showed evidence of improvement according to their daily records of rituals and intrusive thoughts.
- It is highly unlikely that spontaneous recovery or inpatient care per se could account for the improvement he observed (given the chronicity of the problem and previous unsuccessful therapy).
- There was anecdotal evidence that control of compulsive acts between sessions was important in maintaining progress, as might be predicted if it was important to extinguish an avoidance response on a strict schedule (N.B. therapy took place as an inpatient).

It is quite apparent that Meyer used a variety of forms of reasoning to build up his conceptual formulation of compulsions and devise an intervention based upon it. The academic literature was suggestive, but his own clinical experience and clients' self-reports were used to bolster up his argument. Deductions were made from general principles and observations of clients. Inconsistencies in the evidence were considered and answered. The evidence was appraised as a whole and fitted together using different types of argument. This is what makes it an abductive process and why it is essentially idiographic in nature. The important point is that Meyer's conceptual model led to testable predictions, not only in relation to each of his individual clients, but to hypotheses that future researchers could investigate under more controlled experimental conditions. The technique of "exposure and response prevention" has, of course, been subjected to many randomized control trials (RCTs). Now that we are assured that his method is often successful, we do not have to rehearse all of his arguments. Nevertheless, we cannot simply apply the method in a mechanical fashion.

Long ago, Sarbin, Taft, and Bailey (1960, p. 256) pointed out the idiographic nature of clinical reasoning when they contrasted statistical prediction (that is, using data to predict a future state of affairs, such as therapy outcome) with judgments about how best to make sense of a set of observations. Kazdin (2008, p. 150) drew an analogy between deciding what to do with a client in a practice setting and predicting from a multiple regression equation with many variables to consider. However, Meyer, as an experienced therapist, had not aggregated data from a large number of cases and analyzed them in a manner that is comparable with the statistical technique of linear regression. Data supplied by one person are instead analyzed as a configuration of elements. It is their logical coherence and "fit" that becomes the criterion of truth under these conditions.

The value of Meyer's two case studies can be attributed to the fact that they violated prior expectations. In the 1960s, psychodynamic therapists had virtually given up any hope of helping people with severe obsessive-compulsive problems. For this reason, they were sometimes referred for surgery (leucotomy) in order to sever the frontal lobes of the brain from the emotion centers. Meyer's success with only two cases was noteworthy in light of general low expectations and poor base rate of improvement with alternative therapies. An interpretation of the significance of any fact is therefore dependent on its relationship to the credibility of alternative interpretations. This is known as thinking in accordance with Bayes' rule, which takes account of conditional probabilities (Westbury, 2010). In case formulation there is an attempt to assess the probability of a hypothesis being true against a background of a diverse set of facts about the person. The value assigned to one probability is conditioned by the value of another. We cannot always be as creative as Meyer in our therapeutic practice but we can at least aspire to follow a style of therapy that allows for an argument to be built up out of a variety of different lines of reasoning.

CHAPTER 6

Narrative and Textual Analysis in Formulation

One of the messages of this book is that formulation serves the interests of a therapist who has some expertise to offer. To formulate means to clarify the reasoning underlying any approach that is undertaken, to point to further information that is needed, to guide an intervention, and to indicate which options are open or closed. Language is central to this process. It is the medium through which information is obtained, discussed, and represented. This chapter examines how a client's account of his or her problem is absorbed into a formulation and how the latter is often an attempt, through language, to bring about a change in the client's account. Although the functional/systemic framework of concepts outlined in Chapter 8 is not a form of textual analysis, yet language is also behavior, and an understanding of systems of behavior has to be symbolized through verbal concepts. The rationale of a behavioral intervention is communicated in words to a client in a form that can be understood.

This topic raises complex issues that can only be examined briefly in this chapter. There are many forms of textual analysis and I cannot provide more than a few examples of their application to therapy. Text always implies context—the system of personal interactions, situations, gestures, and signs from which a communication derives its meaning. In positioning theory (Harré & van Langenhove, 1999), the subjects of a discourse (persons, speakers, etc.) are identified by the vocabulary, grammar, and rhetorical strategies they employ. Narrative, a different kind of textual analysis, goes beyond an identification of the kinds of person and how they are "positioned" by their social interactions, and it focuses more on the story-like structure of what the actors are doing together. The metaphor of "story" implies a somewhat broader conception of language as a resource, drawing upon shared meanings embodied in sayings, myths, and ideologies. A good place to start this chapter is therefore "narrative therapy," which is closely related to the philosophical movement of social constructionism. In the more extreme relativist versions of constructionism, any theory of the natural causation of "disorders" or "problems" is regarded as just another persuasive narrative. Consequently, from this perspective, case formulation

Individual Case Formulation
http://dx.doi.org/10.1016/B978-0-12-398269-8.00006-5

should not claim to have a "scientific" or "objective" foundation that applies universally. Textual analysis need not take this extreme relativist position, and there are examples of textual and narrative analysis that undoubtedly *do* require their own brand of technical expertise. Two examples are given toward the end of the chapter.

SOCIAL CONSTRUCTIONIST NARRATIVE THERAPY

It follows from a relativist standpoint that it is necessary to conduct therapy in an essentially "non-expert" manner. The guiding metaphor is narrative, and according to Morgan (2000), this form of therapy "centres people as the experts in their own lives." Similarly, Anderson and Goolishian (1992) call it a "not knowing" approach. Given that it is not easy to resist giving advice, narrative therapists probably need to be expert at not playing the expert.

The views of those who advocate a non-expert approach to therapy raise two questions for the functional/systemic approach outlined in Chapter 8. First, does a formulation need to analyze a person's life "as a whole" and, second, what stance should be taken when a client questions the central story of his or her life, especially its values and purpose? After all, a therapist is not normally expected to be a moral philosopher or guru. How are a client's moral and existential issues to be handled in formulation?

Morgan (2000, p. 9) points out that lives are multistoried: "the act of living requires that we are engaged in the mediation between the dominant stories and the alternative stories of our lives. We are always negotiating and interpreting our experiences." The transcripts of assessment interviews in the Guidelines illustrate the truth that clients question themselves about the direction their lives are taking and whether there are different paths to follow (see especially Section D). A therapist acknowledges this fact and may contribute to these reflections, but when the problem is a fear of spiders, the moral and existential questions may be rather minor. Some clients do not perceive that their difficulties entail any need to undergo a major reappraisal of their lives or values, although their therapist might see things differently. In these circumstances, a therapist has little scope, or right, to suggest what choices a client should make. Consequently, a therapist may have rather little influence over a client's overall direction in life unless this is done by subtly drawing attention to the implications of continuing with the status quo. One of the strengths of narrative therapy is that it combines a respect for what a client's past experience has taught her or him with a strategy of placing her or him firmly in the position of re-making her or his own life.

Clients who have had especially abusive or deprived childhoods may say that they do not really know themselves at all, have little sense of direction, and little ability to make autonomous decisions. Clients in this position may be more receptive to suggestions (or actively seek advice) than someone whose life has gone smoothly until hitting an obstacle he or she had not anticipated. So in contrast to someone who feels generally at sea, a client who simply finds him- or herself in a tight spot might be looking for an escape route rather than an opportunity to question life deeply. Of course, the client may not continue to feel that way over the course of therapy. On the other hand, wider issues might never get discussed.

In brief, to a greater or lesser extent, a therapist is drawn in to discussing the big questions in life. By accepting this challenge, narrative therapy has confronted, in the most direct manner possible, the construction of alternative ways of thinking and acting, and does so without imposing a theory of "normality." Held (1995) has criticized this lack of any theory of problem causation, apart from a notion of being caught up in a narrative that creates distress. Held is concerned on a number of grounds but chiefly because the alleged antirealist philosophical underpinnings of narrative therapy are untenable. She argues that narrative therapists must assume (as most of them implicitly do) that stories refer to real events with real consequences and that the development through therapy of alternative "non-problematic" stories usually leads them to be performed with real beneficial consequences. For those theorists who take the position that problems only exist within language, Held's criticism is irrefutable. It is not enough to create a new and convincing "useful" story instead of altering the actual conditions of a person's life.

Language is nevertheless central to therapy because it is the medium through which it is, in the main, conducted. The relationship between language and reality is an enduring problem for philosophy and I will do no more than sketch out a realist position that may suffice at a practitioner level. For a functionalist, words and stories have real causal effects in the sense that they cue behavior in both an immediate and long-term sense. It is obvious, then, that the stories people tell themselves, including their reasons for having problems, are vitally important elements in a formulation. However, unlike the narrative therapist who focuses chiefly on the content of stories, functionalists emphasize the fact that language also plays a role in the formation of habits in which words lose their ability to refer to the "real world." This can happen in the sense that others do not share whatever "meaning" they contain, and even the person, him- or herself, may fail to fully comprehend the significance of his or her own thoughts. In some instances, such as obsessions, intrusive memories, or delusions, the normal functions of language seem to be appropriated by alien processes of which a client is only dimly aware, if at all. However, it need not be concluded that these phenomena have to be classed as symptoms of a disorder. It is possible that meaning can be restored, or found, through a verbal form of therapy. From the point of view that speech and also subvocalization are functional behaviors, it could be argued that some problems represent the loss of a normally flexible and adaptive linguistic ability.

A further distinction between narrative and functional perspectives is that, in the latter, verbal mediation is seen as a semi-autonomous process, in fact, one that is reciprocally related to non-verbal behavior, emotion, and environmental conditions in general. For a functionalist, it may be considered as easy to modify a client's account of him- or herself by changing behavior or its environmental consequences as it is through verbal means. A client's self-narrative is as much a response to the environment (including a biography that others routinely demand from a person) as it is a guide for living or an instrument of change in itself.

Held (1995) maintains that narrative therapy does not have a theory (of an expert kind) to explain why problems arise. This seems to imply that little can be said about it as a systematic enterprise—each client is different and therapy amounts to an art or craft. The questioning techniques employed by narrative therapists are related to theories of discourse but, nevertheless, their employment does not seem to have an explicit theoretical basis. Held (1995, p. 200) argues that the fruits of academic research on narrative processes could yield a systematic form of therapy that is more closely related to theory. This is indeed already the case. My earlier remarks that some problems arise because language-mediated behavior ceases to function as it should is one example of a theory of the causes of a problem that a client expresses in a story-like form (such as a conviction that door knobs are covered in germs). Techniques derived from theories of dialog and narrative can help to change the linguistically fixed and compulsive quality of an obsession (Davies, Thomas, & Leudar, 1999; Hallam & O'Connor, 2002; O'Connor, Aardema, & Pélissier, 2005). These techniques have also been applied to psychosis (Dannahy et al., 2011).

Narrative therapists might argue that a theory of "disorder" is not needed, a position I supported in Chapter 2. The move toward a non-theoretical narrative approach is a quite understandable reaction to a bio-medical tendency to label problems as disorders or pathologies. It seems clear that the language of disorder—and some of the remedies it proposes—often creates as many problems as it solves (Whitaker, 2010). For instance, to label behavior that falls short of social expectations as pathology may add to the stigma that the behavior attracts. Although there now seems to be greater tolerance of certain departures from the norm, this is not true for overt madness, where stigma has remained constant or even increased (Department of Health, 2010a). A focus on deconstructing narratives of mental illness is therefore understandable in this social context. A person's problem can justifiably be seen as a consequence of the exercise of societal practices as much as it is a consequence of causes lying within the individual. For instance, in an attempt to undo the harmful effect of labeling, I have on a number of occasions discussed with a client what it means to be given a diagnosis of "personality disorder." One client, on her way to see me, thought it wise to discuss this with her taxi driver who, perhaps in the manner of a narrative therapist, persuaded her of the alternative story that she was merely eccentric. For this kind of intervention, a theory of the causes of problems within the individual is not needed.

To speak even of a "problem" leads to the suspicion that something has become a problem or has been labeled as a problem because this reflects the social context and power relations in which a client is entwined. Narrative therapy responds with the following strategies: being curious rather than goal-directed, being permissive about the direction of therapy, encouraging the client to dig into his or her own resources to find an answer, creating distance for a client between him- or herself and his or her problem (e.g. externalizing it by giving it a name as an entity with intentions of its own), tracing the history of a problem's development, and contextualizing a problem in terms of background assumptions and commonly held beliefs. In large part, these aims can be achieved by asking "deconstructive" questions (Freedman & Combs, 1996; Morgan, 2000).

While these questioning strategies are likely to play a part in formulation and therapy, encouraging a client to find an autonomous voice, it is argued here that additional theoretical resources are needed for case formulation. In other words, problems do not reside only in stories, and any attempt to reduce therapy to re-storying is as narrow as reducing it to Pavlovian conditioning. In the remainder of this chapter, I discuss how meaning can be explored in assessment and suggest ways of reconciling the metaphor of narrative with a functional/systemic framework for formulation.

DISCOURSE: A DIFFERENT PARADIGM FOR FORMULATION?

The disciplines of discourse are concerned with language, meaning, and symbolic expression in all its forms. A discursive analysis of therapeutic conversations can therefore form a bridge between therapy and wider society. This kind of analysis emphasizes that people converse from "positions" (social, historical, mythological, political, ideological, etc.) that have their source in the history of a culture, its social practices, and its power relationships. A rather minor example of social power is the granting of accredited status to a therapist by a professional or legislative body, giving her or him greater opportunities to practice. On this basis, members of the public may assign greater credibility to the words of an accredited therapist than to one who is not, with the result that certain solutions to problems are favored over other (perhaps more radical) solutions.

In a social constructionist perspective, social interactions constitute social practices, and so a conversation in therapy contributes, in however small a way, to the reproduction of society in its contemporary form. In overtly political forms of therapy, there is an intention to change the way society functions through promoting different ways of dealing with what conventionally is viewed as a problem or disorder. As already noted, central to the concept of discourse is the idea that language does not merely name reality but helps to constitute it (Mair, 2000). I have used the word "helps" here because I reject a full-blown relativist position in which meaning exists only in relation to the conceptual framework of the speaker. Like Held (1995, p. 94), I would want to distinguish the extra-linguistic "facts" of the case from their interpretation. This position has been called critical realism (Bhaskar, 1979) in recognition of the fact that reality is always perceived through the eyes of a subject who lives in a particular time and place. A scientific theory might posit purely hypothetical realities, but the assumption is made that these theoretical constructs could help to explain reality as experienced. It is groups of scientists who construct and share their hypothetical explanatory mechanisms, but the latter do not construct the scientists' everyday reality. In this sense, scientific constructs differ from any of the socially constructed realities of "mental illness." The concept of mental illness is not a scientific concept; the idea of being mentally ill constitutes reality and, if taken to be something "real," a person may look to science to explain it.

An important issue in a narrative or discursive analysis is reconciling the biological reality of a "person" with the largely linguistically mediated notion of his or her "self." Harré and van Langenhove (1999) distinguish between the self-referential pronoun "I" that marks out to others which unique (biological) speaker is uttering a statement, and "self" as a socially constructed entity that is spoken about (Hallam, 2009). The construction of this self varies according to context, mode of address, gender, choice of words, etc. In addition to having a biography that in some sense is public property, people also talk and write autobiographically, subject to somewhat different constraints. As Mair (2000) colorfully sums it up: "words and syntactical structures throw their weight around, they push speakers towards saying and recognizing what the language structures imply. They are resistant to individual use and have to be wrestled with if anything other than the most conventional local ways of putting words together is to be achieved."

If Mair is correct about the resistance that must be wrestled with, a therapist cannot rely solely on a client's ability to do this alone. As Morgan (2000, p. 14), a narrative therapist, writes: "The therapist is interested to seek out, and create in conversation, stories of identity that will assist people to break from the influence of the problems they are facing." To view this as a non-expert role cannot be quite right. In the first place, the interpretation of texts is a complex discipline. The transcripts of client interviews to which I refer below (McLeod & Lynch, 2000) were read in the first stage by multiple independent readers in order to reach a consensus on the main themes, and in later stages they were subjected to intensive interpretation by the two authors of the article. We have to bear in mind that a therapist has to react moment-to-moment to what happens in a session and so any in-depth textual analysis has to wait until later.

Narrative therapists necessarily have to get around this by exploring textual meaning at the time. For instance, Freedman and Combs (1996, p. 56) use a style of "deconstructive questioning" that "invites people to see their stories from different perspectives, to notice how they are constructed (or *that* they are constructed), to note their limits, and to discover that there are other possible narratives." It is hard to imagine doing this without formulating why it is important for a client to follow a certain line of thinking. Textual meaning lies largely hidden and a decision has to be made to unpack it. A related decision has to be made about how far to unpack it. Textual interpretation can be made explicit or left as an implicit context for what is said. As McLeod and Lynch (2000) note in relation to their analysis of the therapy transcripts of a woman who was depressed, "nowhere in this case did either therapist (or client) refer to moral issues or develop a shared language for talking about such issues." Consequently, "the moral dilemma 'is it necessary to abandon any notion of the good life?' remained implicit and unstated." Nevertheless, this was the interpretation that McLeod and Lynch fastened upon in order to make sense of the transcripts.

Clients will, of course, spontaneously draw their own conclusions from what has been said in a session and they may discuss it with others. However, the idea that a person acts reflexively, as if in the position of an author creating a story from moment to moment, is more an attractive myth than an accurate representation of life as lived. MacIntyre (1981) argues that human life is only intelligible as narrative but recognizes that a person is, at best, a co-author, often entering a drama not of his or her own making. A story is always co-produced because "a person is emplotted by the stage on which he or she is placed, the dramas that others have written, and the typecasting produced by age, biological sex and other characteristics" (Hallam, 2009, p. 140). Experts on narrative are much exercised by whether human life is narratively structured by forms of social life of which a person is unaware or by a deliberate attempt to shape a life in a desired direction (or, as is more likely, by a combination of the two). Historians have questioned whether their narrative histories are simply fictions imposed on intrinsically unknowable mechanistic processes and events (Carr, 1997).

THE INADEQUACY OF TEXTUAL ANALYSIS ALONE

Despite the complexity of discourse, a therapist is safe in assuming that clients, as real-life actors, have to do the best they can to piece together the fragments of different stories into a credible whole. An individual case formulation (ICF) could not possibly encompass all aspects of a client's life, with all its dilemmas and conflicting choices. A typical assessment, lasting only a few hours in total, is bound to be limited and miss out on important facets of life. This need not be a significant worry if the changes a client makes can be viewed as experimental explorations of the options available. In this sense, they are self-correcting. Moreover, any omissions in the initial formulation will, it is hoped, become apparent over time. It is rare that a client seeks advice about a decision that has to be made within a very small time frame of opportunity. In any case, as already noted, the idea of the person as sole author of his or her life rarely rises above the level of a comforting myth. The patterns of behavior that therapists typically work with are more likely to be changed in the nitty-gritty details of everyday situations over an extended period of time. This seems to be the approach taken by schema-focused therapists who deal with deep-seated stories originating in childhoods of abuse and emotional deprivation (Young, Klosko, & Weishaar, 2003). Even though these therapists may attempt to "re-story" ingrained narratives using dialog and related techniques that involve the restructuring of memories, it is generally accepted that the maintenance of any change produced in this way depends on small daily acts of resistance and self-assertion.

To illustrate this point, consider a young man in therapy with the author, who for many years complained of incapacitating worry when anticipating almost any task, appointment, or new challenge. Midway through therapy, he was asked how he accounted for his increasing ability to overcome this problem. He replied that purchasing a tin of sardines in a supermarket was the turning point. He had been sent there with a shopping list on a mission to deal with any anxiety-provoking situation that arose, to tolerate discomfort, and to deal with difficulties rather than running out. This included seeking help when he was unable to find an item (sardines as it happened) on the list. Clearly, the lesson he learned here (and from similar tasks) was a general one—that coping positively leads to greater self-esteem, and that avoidance leads to greater anxiety and self-doubt. He began to apply this lesson spontaneously to other situations. This client could be viewed as having developed a neglected side of his identity, with important implications for the kind of story he would follow in his future life. As a working-class male, his dependency on his mother's company in a variety of minor situations did not bode well for his success in being seen as a potential partner (a matter of some importance to him). As time went on, he was able to articulate a story about the mutual dependency existing between himself and his mother, and by doing so, his options for escaping its grip became more obvious to him.

A textual analysis of this man's situation could be extended much further but, as in the case discussed by McLeod and Lynch (2000), much of the social context for his problems remained implicit. A functional analysis of his behavior in specific situations, with relative simple strategies for changing their outcome, was the initial point of entry into his problem. The background story of this young man was taken for granted as shared cultural knowledge. Clearly, this passive stance is not recommended when matters of class, gender, ethnicity, stigma, and similar issues cannot be ignored. The strategies employed by narrative therapists, mentioned above, are valuable in these circumstances.

A further examination of the therapy transcripts analyzed by McLeod and Lynch (2000) points to the need for an explicit case formulation to guide the direction of therapy. The woman described in this analysis had reached a point in her life when its central plot "living a good life" was in danger of non-fulfillment. Her children had left home, her son's girlfriend was the object of disapproval, her husband had taken on more responsibility at work and was unsupportive, along with her siblings, when she took care of her aging parents. The marital relationship had deteriorated. She, herself, was sensitive to her obligations and tended to sacrifice her own interests to fulfill them. Has enough already been said to formulate this woman's situation? The authors' analysis of the textual material cannot be faulted but they could only analyze what they were presented with. As they state, "hermeneutic inquiry of this kind can never hope to achieve a 'factual' or 'objective' explanation of a phenomenon" but just a new way of seeing it.

Nevertheless, perhaps it is important in a therapeutic context that all "objective facts" of potential relevance be considered. This really depends on whether the assessment interviews have comprehensively covered all aspects of a client's circumstances. Clients often keep quiet about significant topics out of shame or embarrassment. For instance, had the woman described above been offered antidepressants, and if so, had she taken them and with what effect? Were there any aspects of her general health that needed to be considered? Was there any sexual intimacy between herself and her husband? Had all aspects of their deteriorating relationship been covered? Was she suspicious that he had started an affair with another woman? There are strong arguments for being proactive when assessing and formulating. A client will not necessarily come up with their own alternative story and may need prodding into revealing important aspects of their situation.

Singer and Bonalume (2010) argue that the exploration of autobiographical memories and their re-examination, and possible revision, is one of the major tasks of therapy. Their system of coding narrative memories is put forward as a useful approach to case conceptualization. While this may be so, it cannot be considered sufficiently comprehensive to act as a basis for formulation. In part, their own operational definition of an autobiographical memory as one that must refer back to events of at least 12 months standing leaves more recent events to be formulated in other ways. They also decide to exclude from consideration memories that do not have a sufficiently strong narrative structure. In their case example of a client with pervasive life problems, this included her description of her mother's character and life circumstances. Given that this client's problems related to her "repetitive struggle with her confusing and at times frightening mother" it is just not clear what the authors might mean by case conceptualization. The criticism is the same as the one made in the previous example—a formulation must be comprehensive and integrate narrative and non-narrative elements.

CONSTRUCTING NEW NARRATIVES AND THE PROCESS OF FORMULATION

One of the main characteristics of a story, at least one that expresses a human life, is that it extends from the past into the future and therefore over a long period of time. Even when a problem is dissolved, a client may still have difficulty in confronting a problem-free future. Held (1995) notes that any complete system of psychotherapy should possess a causal theory of problems, but removing a problem may not be enough. For this reason, many therapies are constructional—they actively seek to assist a client in finding an alternative vision, and to build necessary resources for the future. Some clients do not need assistance in this regard, but for those who do, therapy has to delve into the possible, the hypothetical, and the imaginary. In this respect, therapy is an art rather than a science because confronting the future is an existential task, not a question of accurate prediction.

A story (or project) is a way of referring to behavior that is linked across time and represented through language as continuing into the future. Formulation is a collaborative activity and so a client will naturally get to know how their therapist thinks about him or her including the broader question of how to lead a life worth living. This is made more or less explicit, depending on the style of therapy. Most clients have already reflected on their difficulties before seeking out therapy and so they are likely to be in a receptive mode. The "work" of change has already begun and anything a therapist has to say is likely to be of interest. In turn, a therapist responds to interest shown in their observations. A formulation diagram will have implications for the future even if these are not explicitly stated. It cannot be compared to a diagnosis or an architect's drawings—it is more like a set of ideas in progress. One reason for sharing the formulation with a client is to ensure that these ideas make sense in relation to other plans, choices, or external constraints.

All theoretical models of the person accept that human life has to be comprehended in both a temporal and spatial sense. A distinguishing feature of narrative is that time and space are represented in speech or writing. However, as noted earlier, human life is probably also more deeply and unwittingly structured in a discursive form in a manner that has to be unpacked. The important point about a story is that it has a structure and endpoint. In order to have human interest, a narrative requires settings, characters, and a storyline with progressions, setbacks, and a final denouement. Our interest is absorbed and we are transported into the action. If this is what gives life its point, we can formulate a person's problems as in part a response to unfulfilled stories, conflicting stories, or the lack of a good story. However promising a life project might look at the outset, there are bound to be later revisions, reassessments, and unforeseen obstacles.

Clients are normally seen as the ultimate experts in the design of their own lives because this is a foundation assumption of the Western self. To be more correct, this is an assumption about the adult self, because parents do not usually hold back from shaping the lives of their children. The therapist's role is therefore a delicate one that cannot tread too firmly on a client's autonomy. There is an attempt to facilitate an awareness of past influences, present constraints, and future choices, and to treat a client as an adult rather than a child. Narrative therapists can give the impression that their touch is so delicate as to be invisible. Or, as it has been phrased, the therapist "unveils" and the client "discovers" his or her own concealed richness of experience (Payne, p. 418). According to Payne: "Narrative therapy does not aim to produce change in the person, if by this is meant cure, improvement, fixing of problems, personal growth or alterations of identity." I am not convinced that clients want their therapist to be quite so squeamish about influencing them.

One way of accommodating narrative with a functional approach is simply to extend the idea of a behavioral episode in time and space. Rather than story, we can refer to a person's "projects," each involving behavioral, cognitive, and emotional elements. Projects are broader than, say, a routine for dealing with an everyday situation because a project cannot anticipate all contingencies or even the final outcome in detail. In other words, situations are approached with a range of possible responses (in behavioral terms, a repertoire) or, in more cognitive terms, a range of imagined scenarios. But like a story, a project has an endpoint whether the project is of short or long duration. Stories are represented through language, and projects, too, need the support of verbal or symbolic representation. As narrative and schema therapists point out, clients may not be aware of the recurring threads that run through their life history and it may be necessary to work hard at identifying them. Giving them a label is often a useful way of placing a problematic theme at a distance, making it easier for a client to identify its influence, and reflect on other possibilities. I will now provide a couple of examples of the way textual and narrative analysis has been incorporated into case formulation.

DIALOGICAL SEQUENCE ANALYSIS (STILES et al., 2006)

As was true in the case of McLeod and Lynch (2000), the concepts employed in the textual analysis described by Stiles et al. (2006) were not explicitly employed by the therapist when conducting a session. This is not a criticism because retrospective textual analysis might contribute to a therapist's future effectiveness. However, it demonstrates that analysis requires hard work and expertise. Dialogical sequence analysis has been inspired by Bakhtin's theory of utterance (Bakhtin, 1981) and involves making sense of patterns embedded in dialogical exchanges between client and therapist. It aims to identify what is talked about and from what "positions" (e.g. in the case of a client, being, say, needy or vulnerable), bearing in mind who is the author of the utterance and who is the addressee. Another way to typify a position is to call it a "voice" within a person's self, and the aim of therapy might be to assimilate voices, grounded in past experience, that remain problematic because they have been warded off and therefore intrude in ways that cause distress. In other words, they cannot be accommodated into a client's preferred identity.

The analysis of problematic voices is represented by Stiles et al. (2006) as a collaborative activity that must, in some sense, involve conjecture and testing of ideas. With the luxury of retrospective analysis, the authors describe it as the formulation of explicit hypotheses, checking their validity, and revising them in light of later observations. This is the essence of the formulation process as recommended in this book, except that it was earlier proposed, not as a retrospective activity, but as a process that takes place moment-to-moment, and oriented toward prediction. Stiles et al. (2006, p. 411) describe their approach as one of "systematizing clinical inference." Perhaps the most important message here is that therapeutic conversation can generate a great deal of analysis and debate. The first two authors read and discussed patterns identified in the first three sessions and wrote a draft that was circulated among all seven authors. After much interpretation, elaboration, skepticism, alteration, and justification, this and subsequent drafts went through several iterations. The final summation is illustrated with textual extracts in the published article. It is noteworthy that the client reaches a point where she seems to state the essence of a formulation in narrative form that (presumably) agrees with the therapist's analysis, although at the time, this was recorded only in the form of brief session notes.

I draw from this example of textual analysis the following conclusions: (1) that experienced therapists are not fully aware of what they are doing; (2) that, in fact, they are doing something complex and meaningful when analyzed in depth; (3) that therapy involves expertise rather than simply engendering hope or convincing a client to adopt a new story, using any rhetorical device a therapist can muster; and (4) that therapy relates in a meaningful way to life as lived.

The identification of patterns of behavior, though not necessarily of dialogical sequences of the kind described above, is a ubiquitous feature of case formulation. Although questionnaires and checklists have a role in pointing to areas that should be explored, it is recommended that an idiographic, hypothesis-testing style of interviewing is the best method for making sound inferences, especially when the opportunity for consensual validation is available (see Guidelines, Section B).

A NARRATIVE APPROACH TO THE FORMULATION OF OBSESSIONS (O'CONNOR, AARDEMA, & PÉLISSIER, 2005)

This approach is based on the premise that a client complaining of an obsession is troubled by doubt, believing that his or her disastrous interpretation of an event could be true and therefore should be acted upon. However, whatever is done to relieve the doubt is typically ineffective and acts, in the end, to reinforce it. O'Connor and his colleagues formulate the problem in terms of "doubting stories" in competition with "reality-based stories." In the latter case, doubt can be relieved by sensory information to which everyone has access. With a doubt-based story, the best that can be obtained is some reassurance because incontrovertible evidence is unavailable. For example, it is not clear how the following doubt could be convincingly resolved: "Because I have had this thought, I am damned and will go to Hell." A doubting story usually trumps any sensory evidence that can be produced. For instance, reassurance from a priest could be dismissed for a variety of reasons and, in the case of a doubt about germs, cleanliness is unconvincing because germs are invisible.

Formulation is directed toward identifying doubt stories and potentially convincing reality-based stories that might act as replacements. The reasoning process employed in doubt stories is usually faulty and so this must be identified as well. It is not assumed that doubt stories are evidence of pathology—after all, how many advertisements for household cleaners encourage the belief in dangerous invisible germs? In the case of doubt about being damned, it is likely that stories of this nature relate to childhood rearing practices. Contextualizing the doubt story is therefore part of the assessment, enabling a client to trace its origins. The doubt story begins to be seen *as* a story rather than a description of reality in which a client is heavily invested and involved. Detailed analysis of the story helps a client to realize that his or her obsessional inferences do indeed come from a story and not from "facts."

It is not necessary here to provide details of the assessment procedure and all the various factors that have to be considered in the formulation (e.g. triggers, mood, primary and secondary inferences, neutralization of doubt, avoidance, etc.). The essential point is that formulation requires expertise based on a strong rationale and practical experience. The theoretical basis draws upon research into everyday reasoning, the structure of narrative, and its relationship to belief and imagination. The formulation is the idiographic expression of general principles established on theoretical grounds.

CHAPTER 7

Formulation Skills and the Therapeutic Relationship

Texts on counseling and therapy take it for granted that trust and mutual regard in the therapeutic relationship are essential for success. Clients expect to be listened to and understood, and if this happens, a therapist's ability to formulate while conversing cannot easily be distinguished from other relationship skills. This chapter speculates about a therapist's ability to formulate as one component in the complex mix of influences that contribute toward creating a productive therapeutic relationship.

The importance assigned to the therapeutic relationship should not be overrated because self-help (Gellatley et al., 2007) and computerized interactive programs dealing with psychological problems (Carlbring, Ekselius, & Anderson, 2003; Greist et al., 2002) can provide substantial benefit, sometimes equaling that of face-to-face therapy. As Peck (2010) points out, it is unclear how rather limited contact with a therapist (typically 10–20 hours) by itself could bring about major change in a client's quality of life. It seems implausible to him that mere contact with a therapist is causally effective; it must be something that is done specifically within sessions. Peck (2010, p. 148) notes that the best computer-based programs allow for "detailed problem formulation and individual tailoring of treatment plans." He argues that the client/therapist relationship "does not directly produce clinical improvements; rather, it may set the occasion for the active therapeutic ingredients, both common and specific, to come into operation." He also suggests that untrained therapists and computerized therapy can act as an effective medium for these active ingredients.

Before proceeding further, I will argue against one popular account of the nature of therapeutic influence that implicitly ties together the separate factors of formulation and the quality of the relationship. This is the idea of a psychotherapist as healer or shaman. This account denies a role for formulation in the sense of a rationale for resolving a real-life problem rationally and pragmatically. Instead, a client has to be sold a convincing story to be "cured."

Individual Case Formulation
http://dx.doi.org/10.1016/B978-0-12-398269-8.00007-7

THE THERAPIST AS HEALER OR SHAMAN

The concept of therapist as healer elevates the therapeutic relationship into a pivotal position. It assumes that there are disordered people in society who seek a healer in much the same way as people have been observed to do in many of the cultures studied by anthropologists. The healer's formulation of a problem is seen as an acceptable version of events, and this is accompanied by a ritual enactment of techniques that strengthen its credibility, thereby promoting an expectation of benefit (Frank & Frank, 1991; Wampold, 2007). In other words, it is argued that it is not what a therapist does specifically to address a client's concern but, instead, it is a client's acceptance of an "adaptive explanation that is critical rather than the absolute truthfulness of the psychological explanation" (Wampold, 2007, p. 866).

This conclusion has been driven by the dearth of evidence from randomized control trials (RCTs) that their outcome relates to the type of (credible) therapy administered. Consequently, theorists have focused on factors common to all of them, especially the quality of the therapeutic relationship. Features of the relationship do predict outcome to a modest degree (see below). However, correlational evidence is open to different interpretations. I will assume (without much evidence) that the therapist's contribution includes a formulation that points to interventions that help a client in *specific* ways. In other words, a therapist's rationale for what he or she does is not merely *convincing* to a client but is attuned to the constraints that typically operate in any situation that calls for a pragmatic response. In other words, the rationale is rational rather than merely acceptable. This interpretation of the contribution of formulation to the creation of a good working alliance does not imply that there is only one *true* formulation but it does assume that the relationship mediates a response that helps to resolve specific difficulties. The alliance would constitute a "common factor" in the sense that solving a problem is a component of any credible therapy and the relationship is geared toward this outcome.

The "therapy as healing ritual" account is, instead, a rather cynical view, placing the therapist in the position of a charismatic salesperson. As Wampold writes, each and every therapeutic practice constitutes "convincing narratives that persuasively influence patients to accept more adaptive explanations for their disorders and take ameliorative actions" (Wampold, 2007, p. 864). An assumption quietly built into this argument is that clients are suffering from mental disorders. In fact, this assumption is already part of the sales talk. Wampold maintains that the causes of any disorder are not known for sure and that remediation based on assumed causes is not specifically effective. It follows that one "acceptable" account is as good as another. However, if the concept of mental disorder is an example of mystification, the analogy between therapy and a healing ritual applies only to mystified clients. Moreover, it is inconsistent with Wampold's opinion that the healing role should be reserved for psychotherapists whose methods are based on "sound psychological principles." There really should be no objection to any healing effort, such as the laying on of hands, if it has been shown to work empirically.

Of course, the argument that a case formulation should include a considered attempt to understand the causes of a problem does not mean that this process is always guided by a conceptual model, psychological theory, or an evidence base. Empathy and common sense must also play their part. Clients sometimes come seeking a psychological explanation for their "disorder" but this interpretation of their situation, even if consistent with received psychiatric opinion, often constitutes a barrier to assisting them. If the disorder concept is dispensed with, it opens the way to viewing a client's dilemmas, conflicts, and distress as not a world apart from problems encountered by anyone in their everyday life. Problems require considerable analysis, reflection, and hard decisions. Solutions are hard fought, not just "accepted." As Garfield (1997) notes, "helping patients to face or confront a problem they have been avoiding" is likely to be one of the common factors in psychotherapy. If Garfield is right, the therapeutic relationship may be important to the extent that it is seen to facilitate the solution of specific problems. This is also the opinion of Westra, Constantino, Arkowitz, and Dozois (2011), even though they fit their views into the common factors model of change put forward by Frank and Frank (1991). They speculate that the competent delivery of therapy provides a client "with the sense that (a) the clinician has the requisite expertise to help, (b) the treatment has a believable rationale, and (c) the proposed tasks of therapy fit the rationale." Stated in this way, therapeutic tasks do not sound like rituals.

Consistent with the therapist–as–healer analogy, the specific techniques employed in therapy have sometimes been viewed as "stand-alone" rituals, rather like a magic pill. Duncan (2002, p. 41) writes that, "they may all be understood as healing rituals." In therapy guided by a case formulation, an intervention can only be viewed as a ritual when it is delivered without a considered rationale (i.e. it is actually nothing more than a display of shamanistic powers). It may be true that much of psychotherapy is snake oil, but Duncan's view of the role of specific techniques surely underestimates their rational basis. If accepted at face value, the assumption he makes would amount to a therapist acting in the role of conjuror or magician. All that would be needed is that both client and therapist believe in a technique's potency. Although there are many examples of therapeutic fads with instant appeal, most clients adopt a more considered attitude than Duncan implies. In fact, Duncan admits that clients seek therapy for "relational difficulties, unrealized potential, and the struggles of everyday existence" (Duncan, 2002, p. 46). He cannot really be suggesting that these problems do not need to be formulated in a specific way, informed by theory, and addressed by specific solutions. A set of exercises is needed to develop new habits or unlearn old ones just as it would be for someone aspiring to be a good musician or an accomplished actor.

Duncan views psychotherapy as primarily a humanistic, not a medical, activity, but this need not amount to denying a role to science or technology. If recently developed therapies had nothing specific to offer, it is difficult to explain how a generation of people diagnosed with "agoraphobia" or "compulsive rituals" 50 years ago usually failed to respond to the credible therapies available at that time. It would also be difficult to explain what motivates so many contemporary researchers to search for techniques that are specifically effective. They are not all trying to invent "designer explanations and brand name miracles" (Duncan, 2002, p. 43).

CORRELATIONAL RESEARCH ON PREDICTORS OF OUTCOME

In a meta-analytic review of studies largely relating to adult outpatients, Martin, Garske, and Davis (2000) concluded that measures of the therapeutic alliance are positively correlated with outcome, on average, at a level of 0.22. This obviously leaves most of the variance unexplained but the result is reliably observed. A number of authors question whether the therapeutic relationship can be set apart from other components of therapy. Goldfried and Davila (2005) review evidence from various sources to show convincingly that there are complex interactions between features of the relationship, a client's characteristics and preferences, and therapeutic techniques. Geller (2005) and Hill (2005) note the interactive nature of client, therapist, and technique variables in psychotherapy. Hill concludes that it is premature to attempt to quantify the relative significance of each class of variable as a determinant of outcome. However, in the cognitive therapy of depression, Trepka, Rees, Shapiro, Hardy, and Barkham (2004) found that a therapist's competence and the quality of the alliance were largely independent of each other (see also Paivio, Holowaty, & Hall, 2004).

In most of the studies reviewed by Martin et al. (2000), outcome was assessed in terms of a reduction in psychiatric symptoms. If clients value their therapy for reasons other than symptom change, it is possible that the actual correlation with outcome, measured differently, would be higher than this. These authors could not identify any characteristic of client, therapy, or scale that moderated the size of the correlation. Clients rate the alliance more consistently across sessions than do therapists or observers.

Martin et al. maintain that the therapeutic alliance can be decomposed into three main themes: the collaborative nature of the relationship, the affective bond between client and therapist, and their ability to agree on treatment goals and tasks. They also refer to evidence that the subscales of certain measures of the therapeutic alliance, presumably tapping into different aspects of it, are uncorrelated. However, their meta-analysis did not reveal a more subtle breakdown of the correlation between alliance and outcome. On the face of it, a global measure of the alliance does not make much sense, especially for longer term psychodynamic therapies that view working through transference and counter-transference relationships as the principal mechanism of change. Furthermore, in so far as therapists are able to analyze the source of reciprocal affective responses and foster insight, the working alliance cannot be viewed as independent of the skills of formulation.

There is unlikely to be a single explanation for the correlation between measures of the therapeutic alliance and outcome. This is made very clear in the conceptual analysis of Gelso and Carter (1994). In their view, therapist and client might genuinely like or dislike each other, independently of transference responses that distort what they call the "real relationship." Moreover, whether or not the therapist or client experiences strong emotional reactions, both recognize that they are working on a task that they have contracted to undertake together. Therefore, the positive and negative feelings that the client and therapist hold toward each other are both unavoidable, necessary (especially in psychoanalysis), and, at the same time, potentially destructive of a productive use of the "working alliance." Gelso and Carter speculate that the three components of the client/therapist relationship that they identify interact with each other, and that the nature of their interaction may depend on the type of therapy and its length. Drawing on research evidence and clinical examples, they offer 19 propositions to explain how the three components might interact. It seems unlikely that without greater sophistication of research designs, very much more can be discovered.

One of the limitations of group correlational studies is the difficulty of drawing any causal inference from them. In order to test a causal hypothesis it would be necessary to manipulate the independent variable in some way, assuming, of course, that the researcher was in possession of a sufficiently fine-grained classification of problem types, adequate measurement of goals, and some means of assessing the quality of a formulation. It is doubtful whether these requirements could be met in nomothetic research without doing an injustice to the unique features of each client's circumstances. Clients' problems in this type of research have mostly been described as a set of symptoms, and success has been measured in terms of their reduction, rather than the resolution of a problem. For example, the results of research on predictors of psychotherapy outcome reviewed by Castonguay and Beutler (2006) are organized into sections that represent categories of disorder (dysphoria, anxiety, personality disorder, and substance abuse disorder). While different predictors do show up for different disorders, a grouping of results in this way has no obvious theoretical basis, making it difficult to interpret the similarities and differences.

The aim of Castonguay and Beutler's (2006) book is to identify critical principles of change from empirical studies of predictors of a successful therapy outcome. The research points to common factors in certain groups of client. However, across all clients, there are modest correlations between some rather obviously important features of the therapeutic relationship and therapeutic success. In individual therapy these are: evidence of a strong working alliance being established and maintained throughout therapy, facilitation of a high degree of collaboration, empathy with a client, an attitude of caring, warmth, and acceptance, a therapist's self-awareness and her or his willingness to share it in the moment, being flexible and empathic when resolving ruptures in the alliance, and making sure that interpretations are not "overdone" and are accurate. Although it is good to have the importance of these features established empirically, they might be considered favorable in any collaborative venture between a professional and a client, whatever the joint endeavor. It is also unclear what creates these ideal conditions. They may be a consequence of successful interaction as much as their cause.

With regard to techniques that are conducive to success, two common principles are identified by Castonguay and Beutler as important. These are, first, a therapist being structured and focused on an intervention and, second, being skillful when acting in a non-directive way. There are also some general skills in engaging and motivating clients that apply to some disorders more than others. With regard to more specific interventions, the conclusions that can be drawn are extremely general in nature (e.g. address intrapersonal functioning, address interpersonal issues that relate to problems, facilitate change in cognitions, modify maladaptive responses, facilitate self-exploration, help clients either to accept or, at times, to control their emotions). With regard to particular client groups, the research also points to specific recommendations. For example, Castonguay and Beutler (2006, p. 51) identify six principles for matching dysphoric clients to therapeutic interventions. However, these findings from empirical research, important though they are, are not sufficient to guide a novice therapist. The conclusion seems unavoidable that when applying them, the devil lies in the detail. Essentially, each client is a new throw of the die. In fact, in some cases, a therapist might be better off admitting defeat from the start. Some problems, given their parameters, might be insoluble, just as an engineer would have to give up the idea of bridging a gorge without the necessary resources. In yet other problems, the concept of "treating a disorder" is inappropriate; therapy would be better described as accepting reality, forgiving others, or reconciling oneself to unbending circumstances. From a non-medical perspective, success cannot be measured only by a reduction in symptoms, and so correlational research predicated on this assumption has limited implications.

It is noteworthy that the index of Castonguay and Beutler's book contains no entry for formulation. Client characteristics are largely reduced to demographic variables, personality types, and coping styles. This underlines the absence of (or perhaps difficulty of developing) a suitable alternative to diagnostic classification of problems. Despite the importance generally assigned to formulation, there is almost a conspiracy of silence about its relevance in this literature. This is not so in Germany where a case formulation is mandatory if a therapist wishes to receive payment from a health insurance company (Muller, 2011). From an idiographic perspective, the frequent absence of any reference to formulation is not surprising, assuming that problems typically arise from a complex interaction of personal characteristics and unique life circumstances, and these are difficult to capture succinctly. Expertise grounded in nomothetic principles presumably has to be complemented by an intuitive appreciation of another's predicament, in other words, by empathizing with them and conceptualizing their problem. Empathy draws indirectly upon nomothetic knowledge (of values, norms, general expectations) and it perhaps entails a kind of summative opinion of all the different forces acting upon a person. It is not easy to formally represent these subtleties in a manner that allows for quantitative measurement.

In non-clinical situations, empathizing with another, if articulated at all, may be expressed in the form of a story recounting dilemmas, betrayals, conflicts, disappointments, etc. Everyday empathy tends to be more concerned with shared moral judgments than the attribution of causality, although feedback of the "cruel but kind" sort is also valued. An individual case formulation (ICF), at its broadest macro level, is also a storied account (see Chapter 6). It is not helpful, nor required by theory, to oppose narrative and causal accounts of human behavior (Hallam, 2009). A narrative account at a broad level is compatible with a formulation of problems at the micro level that relates events in a functional and causal manner. Of course, it may not be possible to achieve change at the micro level simply by means of a narrative reframing of a client's understanding of what is necessary to bring about that change. This is true of many human situations where change is desired. The end result can only be achieved by doing something, not contemplating what to do about it.

If the message delivered by an accurate formulation of a client's problems is to think or act differently, it may not be welcomed if the message is of the "cruel but kind" variety. A formulation diagram can benefit a client by helping him or her to make connections between past events and other circumstances in his or her life (Moore, 2007), but a formulation can also be received negatively and therefore impact on the therapeutic relationship (Leeming, Boyle, & MacDonald, 2009). The relationship between the skills of formulation and relationship-building is therefore a complex one.

WHAT ACCOUNTS FOR DIFFERENCES IN THERAPIST EFFECTIVENESS?

A large body of research conducted by Lambert and colleagues (Lambert, 2007) has produced results that have implications for understanding the relative importance of the therapeutic relationship and the skills of case formulation, even though this was not the aim of the original research.

If the process of formulation is rated as important, it must incorporate checks on its validity. One such check is feedback on improvement or deterioration as therapy progresses. When an intervention does not appear to be helping, this may signal that a formulation needs to be changed. An example of a failure to make a lasting impact on a problem is given in the Guidelines. Ideally, a measure of progress should be one tailored to a client's specific problem, such as the frequency of a particular intrusive thought. However, in large-scale research this is impractical. Lambert and colleagues employed a standardized measure of a client's mental health status, the OQ-45, a

45-item questionnaire covering emotional distress, interpersonal problems, social role functioning, and quality of life. It has been administered weekly, or before each session, by thousands of therapists employed chiefly in university clinics. These therapists were working in a routine practice setting and they adopted a variety of theoretical models. It has been shown in a number of studies that an increase in OQ-45 scores (or a less than expected decrease) successfully predicts final outcome status as early as the second session. Clearly, it would be an advantage for a therapist to know this in order to take corrective action or to switch his or her approach.

One important finding in this research has been the identification of a group of early responders to therapy, around 25% of the total, who also continue to do well at end of therapy and follow-up. Lambert argues that if improvement occurs before the introduction of interventions that are assumed to be theoretically important "it is difficult to attribute central importance to these techniques in the healing process" (Lambert, 2007, p. 6). While Lambert is open-minded about the mechanism of early response, one possibility is the benefit derived from a good formulation before any "techniques" are applied. It is not unusual for a client to undergo a radical change in self-understanding within a few sessions of assessment and formulation. There was no attempt in Lambert's studies to assess the adequacy of case formulation, although this is typical of correlational research on outcome. It would, in any case, be difficult to assess the quality of formulation, given that therapists followed different models (cognitive behavioral, psychodynamic, eclectic, and humanistic).

The desirability of giving feedback to therapists on their performance is indicated by the wide differences that can be demonstrated in their effectiveness (Okiishi, Lambert, Nielson, & Ogles, 2003). Although this variation is unlikely to have a single explanation, it would be valuable to know whether it relates to the adequacy of formulation or quality of the relationship. To indicate the size of variation, the top 10% of therapists had an improvement or recovery rate of 44% and a deterioration rate of 5%, while for the bottom 10% the corresponding rates were 28% and 11% (Lambert, 2007). In a review of the literature on differences in therapist effectiveness, Elkin, Falconnier, Martinovitch, and Mahoney (2006) conclude that these differences have been exaggerated, especially in studies like their own in which therapists were highly trained and worked to a manual. In such studies, they argue that any differences observed can be attributed to a few "outliers" in the data. However, it is in routine practice that the issue of differential effectiveness is most important from the perspective of maintaining professional competence.

In studies cited by Lambert (2007), in which therapists were asked to predict which clients would ultimately deteriorate (i.e. show no benefit at all), they performed very poorly when compared to the actuarial method of making predictions from OQ-45 test scores. In fact, in one study, only 3 of 550 clients were predicted to deteriorate (of which one eventually did) whereas 42 ultimately did deteriorate. In contrast, by using a carefully designed "warning" system based on the OQ-45, 77% of clients who failed to benefit were detected at an early stage. However, this warning system also generated a large number of false-positive signals. This may matter if therapists are deflected from continuing to use a successful intervention. However, it would matter less if they were merely alerted to the possibility of failure and did not change what they were doing without good reason.

Further research demonstrated that, in practice, the warning signals provided valuable feedback to therapists, as they were then able to reduce the deterioration rate in one study from 20% to between 8 and 15%. Lambert argues that therapists rely too heavily (and unjustifiably) on their clinical judgment and generally do not see the value of frequent assessments based on standardized scales. Although this criticism is well taken, the important point is that a form of feedback is required for a therapist to keep on track. This aim could be achieved by requesting feedback from clients in sessions or by using a problem-specific measure that makes more sense to a client than a global measure of well-being. It is not difficult to imagine a situation in which the administration of a standardized measure that is not quite on target could affect the quality of a therapeutic relationship, especially for clients who are sensitive to being evaluated. Some clients consider it an affront when merely asked to read some helpful literature. Therefore, the practice of requiring therapists to administer a standardized measure (of this length) at every session could have an adverse effect on the relationship. Feedback can presumably be obtained in ways that have greater face validity. There is, in fact, every reason to suggest that feedback should be sought routinely.

The inability of therapists in these studies to identify clients who would ultimately fail can be interpreted in another way. First, if one important therapist skill is to engender hope, this is inconsistent with an attitude of expecting a client to fail, and of oneself being too incompetent to prevent it. A bias toward optimism counteracts a possibly self-fulfilling prophecy of failure. Second, completion of a test of mental health status is an opportunity for a client to give concealed negative feedback, signaling, for instance, a dislike of the therapist, a lack of belief in the formulation, or some other kind of resistance to being helped. These concerns may be difficult for a client to admit to or discuss directly. It is possible that in Lambert's samples, therapists did not adopt a sufficiently collaborative style and therefore failed to be sensitive to feedback that was potentially available. The fact that they did produce better results when supplied with warning signals is at least consistent with the hypothesis that they re-examined their formulation, either of the problem or of a client's reservations and non-compliance.

In a subsequent analysis of the data supplied by 25 therapists, an attempt was made to account for their differential rates of success. A measure of "facilitative interpersonal skills" that assessed a therapist's ability "to perceive, understand, and communicate a wide range of interpersonal messages" did account for these differences (Anderson, Ogles, Patterson, Lambert, & Vermeersch, 2009). The skills were assessed by asking therapists to audio-record their responses to eight brief video scenarios of problematic client communications (e.g. confrontational, passive, confused, and controlling styles). Their responses were then rated on several scales by two independent observers. The results of this study provide some support for the importance of clinical experience, because facilitative interpersonal skills were correlated +0.45 with the age of the therapist. It seems likely that "facilitative interpersonal skills" involve skills of formulation as well, although this possibility was not addressed in the research.

SUMMARY

There is an intricate and so far relatively unexplored overlap between the skills of building a relationship and the skills of formulating a client's problems. Moreover, some clients are quite capable of doing without a therapeutic relationship when using a self-help book or interacting with a program delivered by a computer. The model of a therapist as healer or shaman is criticized, as it seems to underplay the role of helping a client to solve real-world problems. Correlational research into the predictors of a good therapy outcome has revealed the importance of certain therapist and client characteristics but empirical research of this kind has not yet led to greater conceptual understanding. However, it has identified a group of early responders to therapy who may well benefit from assessment and formulation, without the need for an intervention. It is noted that a client may not receive a case formulation favorably, even though it is able to identify correctly some key causes of a problem.

CHAPTER 8

A Functional/Systemic Framework for Case Formulation

The foundations for a functional approach to formulation were set out by Frederick Kanfer and George Saslow in 1965, and the soundness of their proposals means that they have not greatly changed since then. Kanfer and Saslow understood formulation to mean the identification of behavior patterns that constituted a problem, to discover the best practical means of bringing about change through altering the environment, a client's behavior, or a client's "self–attitudes." A formulation also speculated about how a problem behavior was acquired and was currently maintained. In marked contrast to the prevailing psychodynamic view, a client's history was regarded as being of mainly academic interest unless it contributed to the interventions designed to be helpful. A client's "symptoms" (e.g. complaints about moods and feelings) were viewed as consequences of "other important aspects of the patient's life," such as "life conditions, interpersonal reactions, and environmental factors" (Kanfer & Saslow, 1965, p. 532).

These authors stressed that a client should be continually assessed until information about "the circumstances of the patient's life pattern, relationships among his behaviors, and controlling stimuli in his social milieu and his private experience" was sufficiently well understood to suggest an intervention that resolved the problem. Perhaps significant in the light of the later development of cognitive therapy, Kanfer and Saslow (1965, p. 534) stressed that their view did *not* assume that "changes in thoughts or ideas inevitably lead to ultimate changes in actions."

The approach they adopted for organizing information was aimed at producing a "behavioral analysis" at a "relatively low level of abstraction." To summarize very briefly, this consisted of (1) classifying problems as "excesses" or "deficits," each defined along dimensions of frequency, intensity, duration, appropriateness of form, and stimulus elicitors, (2) clarifying how people and circumstances maintain the problem behaviors, and the consequences of the latter for the client and for others, (3) identifying which persons, events, and objects serve as reinforcing stimuli for both adaptive and maladaptive behavior, (4) a historical analysis in the sense of habitual behavior at different stages of development and how any variation is related to

Individual Case Formulation
http://dx.doi.org/10.1016/B978-0-12-398269-8.00008-9

changed circumstances, biological factors, or sociocultural events, (5) an analysis of the ways a client copes with his or her problem in his or her daily life, in other words, his or her ability to self-regulate his or her own behavior (this is relevant to the choice of therapeutic targets in the sense of strengthening weak control or replacing maladaptive methods with adaptive ones), (6) an analysis of a client's social network, particularly with regard to people who have influence over problem behavior, and (7) establishing the local norms of the environment in which a client lives, so that these can be considered when formulating the goals for therapy.

Kanfer and Saslow emphasized the importance of documenting a client's repertoire of effective behaviors with a view to developing her or his autonomy, and the importance of making use of strengths when planning an intervention. In their opinion, the proposed system for formulation was "rooted in contemporary learning theory" but, as can be seen, it was also a comprehensive and pragmatic approach. It was idiographic in the sense that the seven areas of assessment always produced results that depended on the unique circumstances of the individual. Practical guidance was offered on how to collect evidence by different methods and how data should be interpreted.

Functional frameworks for formulation have remained extremely influential. At their core is the provision of a causal account of relationships between situations and behaviors in context. One of the best-known examples is the Functional Analytic Clinical Case Model (FACCM) of Haynes and O'Brien (2000). In a functional approach, an "act in context" is defined by what it achieves; in other words, acts are related to their consequences (Hayes & Brownstein, 1986). The context for an act could be very narrow (e.g. picking up a pen), somewhat broader (e.g. buying goods in a shop), or very wide, such as a client's concern about the overall direction his or her life is taking. Most clients are fairly clear about the ultimate ends they find desirable although some may seek help to clarify their goals.

In contrast to a topographical (or structural) analysis, a functional description of behavior therefore relates to the ends that it serves. An example of different responses that serve the same end would be paying an invoice by check, cash, or electronic bank transfer. Although not topographically similar, each act has the same outcome—a debt is paid. "Paying a debt" is the functional unit in this kind of analysis. Similarly, events that are quite different from a physical point of view can be regarded as functionally equivalent when they trigger the same response. For a driver who is waiting at traffic lights, either the appearance of the color green or the spoken words, "It's now green" are likely to trigger moving off. A person's total behavioral repertoire can be conceptualized as consisting of a set of functional units, representing potentials to respond differently in different situations. Some behaviors will hinder and some will facilitate an adaptive solution to life's problems. Interventions are typically designed to encourage "constructive" solutions, that is, to develop behavior that leads to desired outcomes that might otherwise have been sought out in a maladaptive way. For instance, encouraging self-assertion in place of unassertiveness might be achieved by shifting an assertive response from one context (where it is expressed naturally) to another where a person would normally become aggressive or submissive.

It follows that in a functional case formulation it is not enough to make a list of problem behaviors. The functional unit includes that which contextually sets it up (or elicits it) and how the behavior changes the environment that follows afterward (e.g. in producing its outcome or pay-off). In the controlled conditions of a laboratory, it is possible to specify precisely the relationship between events but in the real lives of clients the investigation of functional units is inevitably much more indirect. At best, the most that can be achieved at the outset is to discern dependencies between events. A simple illustration would be insomnia occurring after drinking coffee late at night but not at other times. This kind of information is typically obtained by interview or from a client's self-observation (e.g. a diary) or by direct observation. The content of behavior is described (drinking coffee, not sleeping) but the analysis is directed toward identifying how events are related and linked to context. The description of actual behavior in this example requires only a low level of inference—in fact, it could be called non-theoretical. For this reason, it lends itself to a range of possible theoretical interpretations—from a behavioral analysis that draws upon learning paradigms (e.g. positive reinforcement, avoidance), through to interpretations of what is going on in the mind of the person, and to what is going on in the body (e.g. caffeine producing states of arousal in the central nervous system).

The "systemic functionalism" I am putting forward builds on the concept of functional units and a client's behavioral repertoire but is otherwise theoretically eclectic. A variety of interpretations are permissible at a higher level of inference. However, any inference should be backed up by evidence. In this way, different hypotheses (which are essentially interpretations of dependencies between events) can be ranked in terms of their credibility. The approach is similar to the one taken by Haynes and O'Brien

(2000) but with some important differences. Their basic analysis refers to "differential conditional probabilities of behavior across situations (and states)" (Haynes & O'Brien, 2000, p. 155). They stress the many facets and dimensions of a problem that might, in some cases, vary independently of one another. Haynes and OBrien's aim is to estimate the strength of causal relationships between the elements in the analysis, and these estimates are derived partly from assessment information and partly from what has been found in relevant nomothetic research. After subjectively quantifying the strength of all causal relationships and representing them in vector-graphic form, a mathematical method known as structural equation modeling is used to select an intervention that will impact optimally on those problems and also make the most difference to a client in terms of his or her goals. In the view of Haynes and O'Brien, a causal analysis should ideally be grounded in accurate measurement and empirical observation of relationships. Consequently, for these authors one important criterion for the validity of a formulation is an accurate functional analysis of behavior (Haynes & O'Brien, 2000, p. 280).

In place of this mathematical approach, I suggest that the credibility of competing causal hypotheses is assessed informally by careful interviewing (and sometimes observation) to clarify the situational determinants of behavior. The credibility of a hypothesis can draw upon other forms of reasoning, such as logical coherence, consistency, "best fit," and counterfactual reasoning, more typical of qualitative analysis.

The term "systemic" in "systemic functionalism" points to the fact that contexts are limited by a boundary, that is, behavior is viewed within a dynamic system of interacting elements. For instance, a person in their environment is a system in the sense that one act may compete with another act within a person's overall repertoire of potential acts. In the case of a person who cannot decide between advancing toward and retreating from a feared situation, she or he is in conflict because she or he possesses a finite set of possible responses of different strengths. The context for behavior is not fixed and care has to be taken when choosing an appropriate boundary. For instance, the dynamic interaction between the elements in the example provided will change if the context is changed to include one in which the person drinks alcohol or is offered a positive incentive for approach.

Functional dependencies between events are frequently mediated by language. Stories usually follow a characteristic plot structure that terminates in a certain outcome. For this reason, and partly because to do otherwise would entail an impossibly high level of complexity, hypotheses to account for "acts in context" may refer back to cultural norms, common myths, conventions, rules, and stories that specify typical event dependencies. People obviously do things deliberately to achieve the goals they imagine in advance of acting, and they can explain this in words. Interpretation at this level need not pre-empt hypotheses that refer to dependencies explained in terms of simpler learning processes. Most acts can be viewed as jointly determined by a language-mediated system (and therefore understood as "meaningful") and by more mechanistic processes. Radical behaviorists have attempted to account for verbal behavior in terms of its history of reinforcement in earlier contexts, and for certain problems, this type of analysis may be preferable to an interpretation based on the communication of shared meaning (Ahearn, MacDonald, Graff, & Dube, 2007).

A functional systemic analysis is compatible with a wide range of models in psychotherapy. The case illustrations in the Guidelines demonstrate the potential for an eclectic mix of hypotheses. Learning paradigms are certainly central to systemic functionalism but their application to the real world is often imprecise. A consulting room is not a laboratory, and a therapist may draw upon a variety of explanations that have little to do with psychological theory. For instance, a therapist might empathize by imaginatively placing her- or himself in the position of her or his client and speculate on this basis about a likely cause of behavior. Human life is simply too complex to be grasped within one conceptual model or method of interpretation. The main check on unrestrained speculation is the requirement to verify an interpretation or evaluate a hypothesis by seeking further evidence for or against it. To be open to different hypotheses does not imply sailing away with the first idea that comes to mind. One means of restraining a subjective "anything goes" approach is to set out observations and hypotheses in the form of an explicit formulation diagram (see Guidelines, Sections C and D).

The conventions I have chosen for the construction of a diagram have been influenced by trial and error, experience of supervising novices, and by the functional and systemic concepts outlined in this chapter. The first requirement in case formulation is to observe as precisely as possible how events are related. The formulation diagram distinguishes clearly between observations that involve few inferences and hypotheses that involve a higher level of inference. It is necessary to be confident that any behavioral and phenomenological description is an accurate representation of a client's reality. Thereafter, a therapist is free to draw upon whatever model of understanding seems appropriate.

BASIC COMPONENTS OF A BEHAVIORAL DESCRIPTION

The reader is referred to a large literature on behavioral and functional analysis in case formulation (e.g. Epling & Cheney, 2008; Follette, Naugle, & Linnerooth, 1999; Haynes & O'Brien, 2000; Haynes, Leisen, & Blaine, 1997; Hersen, 2004; Sturmey, 2007, 2008). My aim in this chapter is to summarize some foundational concepts and to provide a rationale for how the elements of a case formulation diagram should be represented.

In the familiar ABC (antecedent–behavior–consequences) model, an event or stimulus has the function of eliciting a response that, in turn, might have the function of producing a certain outcome. The apparent simplicity of this formula obscures the need for an extensive gathering of information in a variety of relevant contexts. Observation of behavior does not always provide clues as to which events are critical in maintaining it. It is necessary to explore (in reality or in imagination) whether adding elements to the situation or taking them away would affect the form of the behavior or its frequency of occurrence. A behavioral analysis of functional dependencies between events does not require knowledge of the causal mechanisms that lie behind an ABC sequence. However, a therapist is more likely to be successful in influencing a behavior when a correct causal interpretation can be placed upon it. In addition, it is necessary to ascertain any influences that "moderate" an ABC sequence in the sense of changing it in some way. The presence of a causal moderating influence could be fairly obvious, as in the case of a client whose problem changes as his or her mood cycles predictably between high and low. A therapist might also want to speculate about "mediating mechanisms" that act as links in an ABC sequence (see below).

An analysis usually begins with a client's immediate complaints, life circumstances, and social environment. Haynes and O'Brien (2000) suggest that a contextual analysis should be oriented around "target behaviors," meaning "the response class selected for measurement or modification" (Haynes & O'Brien, 2000, p. 312). However, it may not be immediately obvious what the relevant targets are. A certain amount of circling around the presenting issues is the rule before a crucial component of a problem can be identified. One complaint of client B (see Guidelines, Section D) was that she "no longer trusted her judgment." This was one of a number of complaints and it was not clear initially how they were related. In fact, in a subsequent review of the formulation, the therapist realized that he had missed the importance of the break-up of a recent relationship (a fact that she had played down initially). In other words, it is simply not known for sure what events are significant or how different functional units might be related. O'Brien (2010, p. 300) argues that "after data collection, effective evaluation procedures must be used to measure the magnitude of relationships between target behaviors and contextual factors." Again, the assumption here is that the target is known at an initial stage. According to O'Brien (2010, p. 310), data collection amounts to a "topographical analysis of target behaviors." However, assessment is more likely to involve a wide-ranging exploration that is not merely topographical; it will almost certainly be oriented to functional dependencies. The "evaluation" that O'Brien refers to is a refinement or further confirmation of an assumed causal relationship that has already been hinted at. If the target behavior is fairly obvious, such as a "panic attack" or "insomnia," precise measurement may make sense from the beginning. O'Brien and Carhart (2011) advise that any target selected for measurement should first be defined unambiguously and operationally. For instance, for a problem such as panic attacks, it is important to define exactly what is to count as an "attack" before instructions are given to a client to collect information about it in a diary.

An operational definition of a target behavior is necessarily a description abstracted from its context. The bar press of a rat in a Skinner box provides a good operational definition of a response but it does not exclude the rat accidentally sitting on the lever or variations in pressure applied to the lever that may go unrecorded. Although it is certainly desirable to have measures by which to assess change reliably, the formulation of a problem may change over time. What once seemed important may no longer come to seem so, either to the client or to the therapist.

Haynes and O'Brien (2000) advise partitioning target behaviors into three interrelated modes of responding: cognitive/verbal, physiological/affective, and overt motor. This partitioning is widely adopted in cognitive behavioral therapy (CBT) formulation and it is a form of topographical, not functional, analysis. Evans (1986) notes that the tripartite distinction began innocently with a reminder by Lang (1968) that the construct of fear embraces changes in three modes of responding—verbal, overt motor, and physiological. Lang saw these response modes as interacting with each other, although they could also vary independently. Evans points out that the boundaries between the response modes are arbitrary, often unclear, and that they do not correspond to anatomical or functional systems. For example, speaking involves verbal/cognitive, overt motor, and physiological activity all at the same time. Evans places more emphasis on an analysis of a behavioral repertoire into functional units and how these are interrelated (e.g. how changing one unit affects others) (Evans, 1993). Any single functional unit is likely to involve an integrated coordination of different response modes.

An analysis of functional dependencies is most closely associated, theoretically, with theories of learning. Contemporary models in CBT still rely heavily on concepts of contingency and types of reinforcement that define the common learning paradigms, about which a great deal has been discovered from laboratory research. The concept of a learning contingency has been widely misinterpreted as reducible to the "reward and punishment" of simple responses of animals in cages. As I hope to show, a functional framework for formulation has considerable depth and complexity. Despite its origins, chiefly in the behavior of animals, the findings of laboratory research have wide applicability, as B. F. Skinner himself tried to demonstrate (Skinner, 1953). When a client sets out to learn something new, this learning is always superimposed on past learning—the past contexts of responding in comparable circumstances—and also upon the contingencies that exist naturally in a person's world, such as the rules, social customs, and economic realities that determine the consequences of a person's acts (DeGrandpre, 2000). The likely success of new learning therefore depends on the possibilities that the social environment affords and on the repertoire of skills a person can already bring to bear on a task. Since the early phase of animal research (i.e. on classical and operant learning), the field has now developed to deal with the complexities of learning rules and the role of symbols, which research on animals could only partly address (Dougher, 1998; Hayes, Barnes-Holmes, & Roche, 2001).

CONVENTIONS FOR PRODUCING A FUNCTIONAL CASE FORMULATION DIAGRAM

The formulation diagram is a flow chart of interacting elements. It incorporates many factors simultaneously that would otherwise be difficult to express in a verbal summary. I will review some existing conventions for visually representing relationships between the elements, and make some simplifying suggestions. It seems best to aim for simplicity and clarity in practice settings because assessment yields information of variable quality. The process of assessing the significance of information borrows from the logic of single-case research but the latter requires much more rigor in its attention to measurement. The purpose of individual case formulation (ICF) is to apply knowledge rather than advance it.

With respect to the diagram itself, there are features of formulation that call for choices to be made about what to represent and in what manner. Symbols are needed to represent the elements of an analysis, the relationships between them, and their theoretical interpretation. This is usually done with different shapes (circles, squares, etc.) and with arrows or lines to indicate links, both causal and non-causal. Muller (2011) reserves a place in his diagram for treatments and for symptoms/disorders. Although the aim of formulation is to suggest interventions, I will not consider these as part of an ICF diagram. Moreover, symptoms and disorders are considered here to be theoretical interpretations of behavior (i.e. inferences) and not components of a behavioral description. My main aim has been to employ the minimum number of conventions in the diagram.

Behavioral Description versus Hypothesis Generation (Low- versus High-Level Inference)

One way to mark out the distinction between observation and inference is to place the description of situations, behavior, and its consequences (i.e. further stimulus events and behavior) in circles or ovals, and any interpretation of the links between them (i.e. hypotheses) in squares or rectangles. Quite clearly, hypotheses are not causes and so they simply point to descriptive elements (or the links between them) in order to show what they are attempting to explain. This pointing function can be represented by a dotted line to distinguish it from causal or other connecting links that are represented by a solid line. For example, some situations will be associated with a higher likelihood of a behavior occurring. This is observed as a dependency between events at a descriptive level. A possible theoretical interpretation is that the situation has acquired the properties of a discriminative stimulus, that is, an S^D signaling that a response will lead to a certain outcome. Thus, the behavioral description (i.e. a stimulus, placed in a circle) could be distinguished from its theoretical interpretation as an S^D (a hypothesis, placed in a rectangle). Other stimulus events, such as thoughts or sensations, might be interpreted as specific antecedents of particular responses. It might be assumed that a stimulus has acquired its power to elicit an emotional response through its association with past positive or negative events (e.g. a drug high or a sexual assault)—a hypothesis to explain the function of a stimulus.

A "problem" (which can be recast as a behavior targeted for an intervention) need not be considered a special class of event but just one element in the stream of events. Therefore, there appears to be no need to mark it out

with a separate symbol. Other symbols that can be dispensed with are special ones for "unmodifiable causal variables" and for "client resources" (see,
for example, Muller, 2011). An example of the former might be a client's
partner who refuses to engage with his or her problem. Although the
partner's response might be unmodifiable, it could be an important situational determinant in the descriptive analysis and may influence what
intervention is chosen. The attitude a client takes to an unmodifiable
situation may become a target for change. With regard to a client's resources,
these can also be represented as behaviors and situations. In a constructional
approach to therapy, resources are an integral part of the formulation and
not a separate class of determinant. For instance, a resource, such as a person
offering social support, could act as a moderator variable in an ABC
sequence. Expressed more concretely, the presence of a companion might
diminish the probability of a client panicking in a supermarket.

Theoretical (high-inference) explanations (placed in rectangles) can be
labeled as hypotheses (Ho1, Ho2, Ho3, etc.). There may be competing
explanations for the same observation. As more information is gathered
from session to session, certain hypotheses will drop out of consideration
if they are unsupported. The distinction between low-inference observations and high-inference explanations is not always marked out clearly (if
at all) in case formulation diagrams. Nezu, Nezu, Peacock, and Girdwood
(2004) draw out an example of a "clinical pathogenesis map" that does not
use different conventions for indicating *observations* (e.g. social isolation,
absence of sexual intimacy) and *explanations* (e.g. coping deficits, mistrust
schema). One advantage of representing the two with different symbols is
the ease of making changes to an earlier formulation. There are clear
advantages in supervision as well; a trainee's behavioral description might
be adequate but the interpretation placed upon it at fault. This means that
the observation can remain the same while its theoretical interpretation is
revised.

Written case formulations interweave factual information and interpretation, and perhaps this is why diagrams tend to do the same. This is not true
of the FACCM of Haynes and O'Brien (2000), which has a different convention for representing causal/moderating variables and behavior problems.
Nevertheless, some of their causal variables are a mix of observation and
interpretation. For instance, in one of their formulation diagrams, "daily
stressors" could be understood to signify either actual events or the perception (by client or therapist) that such events are stressful (Haynes & O'Brien,
2000, p. 284). Similarly, "negative self-statements" could have been indicated

in the diagram in a descriptive way (e.g. client says or thinks, "I am incompetent,"), which leaves open their causal interpretation as referring to a concept of self or as being necessarily negative.

The FACCM employs the convention of a diamond to represent unmodifiable causal variables. One example provided is "death of husband," which is, of course, a past event. An alternative way of representing this event would be in terms of statements about the death as perceived by a client (e.g. "says she misses husband's support" or "distressing thoughts about husband's death" or "blames self for not looking after husband's health better"). The concrete description, mirroring what a client says, is easier to link in a causal fashion to other ongoing events and is more suggestive of a possible intervention. It emphasizes a client's present construal of a past unmodifiable event in a form that may well be modifiable.

Representing Causality

Functional units of behavior can be conceptualized as being arranged in space and time. Responses are spatially adjacent when they are potentially available at the same time, but with different probabilities of expression. A rich behavioral repertoire is one with a wide range of potential behaviors. Problems can arise if a client lacks a required behavior, if a behavior occurs too frequently or in the wrong form, or if the same situation elicits competing behaviors at the same time with approximately equal strength, in other words, a client is in conflict. The functional approach to changing behavior involves rearranging events in time and space. In one strategy, an attempt is made to strengthen an adaptive behavior, and in another, the strategy is to encourage a behavior that is incompatible with, and therefore displaces, an unwanted behavior. New learning is assumed to be the result of arranging new temporal contingencies between events. This may not be a very deliberate or transparent process. Learning to ride a bicycle involves a few wobbles, and maybe falling off, but the assumption is made that successful balancing and steering is strengthened by its immediate temporal consequences. Therapeutic change is ultimately brought about by a client's exposure to a new pattern of events, although there are only some arrangements that are effective in bringing about a beneficial result. A formulation diagram is an attempt to specify which sequences of events in a client's life are causal. Having identified what appears to be a causal relationship, there are still likely to be competing theoretical interpretations of the mechanism involved. Getting the hypothesis right is necessary because different types of cause require different remedies.

Learning Contingencies

The simplest description of an event dependency refers to event A followed by event B. However, not all contiguous events in a person's life are causally related in the sense of being contingencies that produce learning. A may be unconnected with B, such as reading a book and then having lunch. For sequential events to leave a lasting influence, it is assumed that a contingency must relate to significant outcomes (positive or negative consequences). So, if having lunch is preceded by reading a book, and the two behaviors are not specifically linked to a common outcome, there is no reason to expect this sequence to produce learning. Moreover, there would be no contingency between them if it were just as likely that having lunch was preceded by reading a book as *not* reading a book. The situation would be entirely different if, let us say, a parent created the following contingency for a child: "You won't get your lunch until you have read the book." It might also be different if reading a book happens to be regularly and promptly followed by lunch more often than reading a book is followed by other events (such as exercise, watching TV, or not having lunch). Reading might then be accompanied by salivation in anticipation of lunch.

Clients are not necessarily aware of the contingencies that influence their behavior. Of course, a client might be aware of the *effects* of a contingency, as in: "It's funny, I always seem to salivate when reading." Or in the case of the child who is only given lunch after having read a book, he or she, as an adult, might feel that food has to be earned rather than taken as a pleasure. A client may not know the reason for this quirk in his or her personality. (These are merely fanciful examples to illustrate a point.)

The usual convention is to depict a causal relationship by an arrow: A→B (where B is a significant consequence). This does not necessarily imply that A is always or often followed by B, only that a causally effective contingency exists to some degree. In other words, B is more likely after A than after the absence of A. A contingency is therefore also present when A predicts the *absence* of B. For instance, the arrival of the weekend usually predicts the *absence* of work; in contrast, Sunday evening predicts the *presence* of the requirement to work on Monday morning. These contingencies may be associated with different emotional responses, especially when a client is subjected to stress at work.

The causal effects of contingencies are revealed by changes in the relative frequency (and form) of different events or responses. In other words, in a causal functional relationship, there is no direct reference to material causation between events—Sunday evening does not cause Monday morning's workload. However, the pattern of external events does influence a person's response to them. The effect is much less discernible when a contingency exists between combinations of events. To elaborate the earlier example, Sunday evening might have a different psychological impact depending on what is expected on Monday morning (the boss absent on holiday, a difficult committee meeting, etc.). Most combinations of event are much more complex than this.

The causal arrow indicates two kinds of influence—excitatory or inhibitory. If A makes B more likely to happen or more intense, the effect is excitatory. If it makes it less likely or less intense, it is inhibitory. An example of an inhibitory effect is the presence of a so-called "safety signal" when combined with an excitatory signal. So, for instance, a client might avoid walking in the street when there are dogs about (street + sight of dog→run away) but can do so when accompanied by a trusted companion. That is, the presence of the companion constitutes an inhibitory "safety signal" which, when combined with "street" and "sight of dog," reduces the likelihood of running.

Clients vary in their awareness of the influence of excitatory or inhibitory signals on their behavior. People usually pay more attention to what happens in a positive sense. So, a person who experiences a "panic attack" will certainly know when this is happening and what triggers it but might not notice what it is that makes it less likely that a panic attack will occur. Put differently, they are less likely to notice the presence of something that causes the absence of an event. Similarly, they may not notice the significance of the absence of something that causes the presence of an event, such as the absence of a trusted companion who acts as a safety signal. A related example is a client who has only limited awareness of the absence of something that, if present, would alleviate their feeling of unhappiness. A therapist may have to draw a client's attention to the absence of, let us say, an opportunity to work, or the absence of a partner.

It should be clear from what I have said about contingencies that it is quite in order to enter the *absence* of something as an element in a formulation diagram. To use the example above, this "something" (e.g. the presence of a trusted companion) has exerted an influence on previous occasions (e.g. by reducing the intensity of panic) and then its absence is found to have the converse effect. Social life raises general expectations about the presence of something that might be conspicuously absent for a client. Its absence might be felt as loss, regret, or disappointment. The absence of a *behavior* is also a relevant element in a formulation. If a client lacks a behavior that is generally required for success in some endeavor, this could be described as a "deficit" when it is absent. However, a client might be entirely unaware of his or her "deficits" as they are formulated by a therapist.

The presence of a "deficit" can be given a variety of theoretical explanations. It could be a response that has never been learned, a response that has been punished in the past and therefore suppressed, or due to the absence of a situation in which a potentially available response could be expressed. These are quite subtle distinctions for a client to grasp as well as for a therapist to formulate.

When events or behaviors do not appear to influence each other, there is no need to indicate a relationship with a causal arrow. It may be the case that two responses are simply non-causally associated together in time. For instance, when a person runs away from a dog, his or her heart is probably beating faster and he or she is using up more oxygen. Both responses are functionally related to the presence of a dog and the attempt to reach safety. The two responses may be causally related at a physiological level but functionally, they are simply correlates of the same events at the psychological level.

Similarly, certain responses might tend to occur together because they are functionally equivalent, even though they look dissimilar. If for a thirsty person, water needs to be conveyed to the mouth, it does not really matter whether this is done with a cup, a mug, a straw, or cupped hands. The important functional relationship is between the presence of water and assuaging thirst. The simultaneous presence of some of these responses does not indicate that they cause each other. Where events are assumed to be merely correlated or functionally equivalent (rather than contingently related), a convenient convention for linking them is the equals sign (i.e. $A = B$).

Haynes and O'Brien (2000) represent the estimated strength of a relationship between causal elements by the width of a causal arrow or by a numerical figure denoting the size of a correlation. As noted earlier, in the interests of simplicity (and usually the impossibility of giving a precise estimate of strength), a causal relationship is simply identified as being of a certain type (e.g. response X is cued by Y and avoids consequence Z). There may be alternative theoretical interpretations of observed events (e.g. that X is either likely or unlikely to be an avoidance response), in which case the hypotheses are simply ranked in terms of their probability of being true, rather than being given a numerical estimate. Judgments of causality are therefore made in relation to different kinds of evidence, and decision making depends on the relative certainty of different hypotheses that could account for a causal relationship.

Haynes and O'Brien's recommendation to assess the strength of an assumed causal relationship has been taken to a high level of sophistication by Mumma and Mooney (2007), who analyzed time series data. They persuaded a client (with some cash incentives) to make ratings, for 81 days, of emotional distress, automatic thoughts, assumptions, and core beliefs. The content of the negative cognitions had been selected by two clinicians after watching a video of the client being carefully assessed during an interview. One clinician was an expert, the other a novice. The client had been diagnosed as depressed, dysphoric, and generally anxious. The purpose of the study was to compare the accuracy of the cognitive formulations of the two clinicians by analyzing the covariation between fluctuations in cognition and mood over time. It was shown that the expert's formulation accounted for twice as much of this covariation as the novice's. As the authors state, the expert's formulation was not considered to be superior on a priori grounds (simply because he or she was an expert) but because it more accurately mirrored daily covariation between negative cognition and distress. The method is proposed by Mumma and Mooney as a way of helping clinicians to improve their formulation skills and also, where necessary, to revise a formulation when it does not account for causal relationships that are empirically demonstrable.

The authors concede that the method is time-consuming, in this case needing a couple of months of data collection before feedback was obtained. The method is a novel way of assessing the validity of a formulation but is rather unwieldy for practical purposes. Moreover, the method depends upon the early identification of key causal variables. All of this presupposes a prior stage of reasoning that is not itself grounded in statistical estimates of the strength of causal relationships.

Inferred Events

In the study just described, certain negative ways of thinking were treated as *intervening variables*, that is, as hypothetical but assumed to exist as real causal determinants. As such, they could be placed in circles in the ICF diagram because, even though their existence is speculative, their reality is assumed. It is inevitable that chains of events will include some that are unobservable yet deemed highly significant. Therefore, one feature of a description of the dynamic interactions in an ICF diagram is the inclusion of elements that can only be inferred indirectly. Let is suppose that a client's behavior is functionally related to her or his fantasied success as a rock musician. This client practices an instrument every day, belongs to a band, and has made some trial recordings. These are all observations from which it is inferred that the client's fantasied success is a strong driver of behavior. It is speculated that the anticipation of this future outcome (as the client conceives it) is a mediating variable that maintains current behavior, perhaps along with the pleasure of playing and previous encouragement for, and evidence of, success. The fact that the hoped for outcome has not yet happened need not inhibit a therapist from speculating about present behavior being functionally related to an anticipated (and inferred) future event. However, this conjecture is open to investigation. A therapist might inquire as to the imagined consequences of failing to achieve success; some attempt could also be made to ascertain the client's level of skill, or what feedback she or he has already obtained from others. These inquiries might suggest alternative hypotheses such as a fear of not matching up to the expectations of a parent who also happens to be a rock musician. The strength of a hypothesis is based on a number of separate observations considered jointly. Although care has to be taken to ensure that observations are reliable, the process of relating them together is necessarily conjectural.

The principal source of evidence for showing how the elements in a formulation are causally related is to investigate how a problem behavior (or a functionally related class of responses) is expressed differently under different circumstance. For example, perhaps it is observed that a client smokes when she says she is bored but not when working at her computer. It could be inferred that something to do with the client's absorption in this activity is connected with frequency of smoking. Event B (smoking) seems to be associated with condition A (boredom) but further investigation may indicate that A is neither necessary nor sufficient for B to occur. In other words, smoking might occur on occasions when the client is not bored—for example, when enjoying socializing with others. Without proper investigation, there is a risk of jumping to a conclusion too quickly and, in this case, accepting a client's hunch that smoking is associated with boredom. Perhaps, the key element in the association between working on a computer and not smoking has something to do with the fact that the client's hands are occupied in an activity incompatible with handling a cigarette. This activity could either be boring (e.g. housework) or interesting (e.g. sending out emails to friends).

As mentioned earlier, A and B may appear to be causally related, when in fact they are not, because they are both correlated with a third event. Consider another hypothetical example. Perhaps a client watches violent films late at night and then has difficulty falling sleep. These two events could be correlated effects of a broader pattern of swings in a client's mood from low to high. In other words, insomnia and watching films could both be features of an overactive or agitated state of mind. They are functionally dependent on mood, not on each other.

Noting that events seem to be related is only the first step in a functional analysis. Let us suppose that a client's insomnia really is causally related to watching violent films. In other words, insomnia rarely occurs when the client does not watch these films, and watching these films is almost always followed by insomnia. The causal explanation of this dependency between events is still open to interpretation. Perhaps the two behaviors are part of a longer chain of responses. A client might decide to watch violent films as a form of distraction or relaxation only when he or she anticipates having a sleepless night. This is a counterintuitive hypothesis but cannot be ruled out entirely. The client is aware of cues that foretell a sleepless night and does something (ineffectively) to forestall insomnia. In fact, the coping response may indeed have the paradoxical effect of making the problem more likely to occur—a not uncommon scenario in the presentation of problems.

The formulation process within any conceptual model pays attention to associations between events. For example, a psychodynamic therapist might speculate that a client harbors unconscious hostility, and for this reason violent films provoke disturbing dreams in which it is acted out and this wakes him up. This interpretation combines two hypothetical mechanisms—a structural mechanism (unconscious hostility) and a functional one (that disturbing dreams have the function of expressing hostility, and they generally wake people up). The first stage in developing a formulation is to observe what happens. The psychodynamic interpretation could be strengthened or weakened by collecting evidence about the frequency of waking up from sleep, the content of disturbing dreams, and state of mind prior to going to bed. The functional framework proposed here is compatible with a variety of explanatory models. However, a requirement for all models is to show how events are connected under different conditions so that evidence can be produced to support or refute a chain of causal reasoning. As pointed out in Chapter 5, therapists are prone to biases in the processing of information that lead to the perception of illusory correlations.

Some functional relationships can be interpreted as representing key arrangements (or paradigms) that provide the conditions for learning. In the avoidance learning paradigm, an event signals that something aversive is about to happen and a response is produced (the avoidance response) that prevents it happening. This could be one of the central hypotheses in a formulation. It is likely to motivate a therapist to inquire about the circumstances that have cued similar avoidance responses in the past and about any factors in the current situation that affect their strength. A particular avoidance response will almost certainly vary in terms of its strength or frequency in different situations. This can be illustrated with the example of "carrying an umbrella" in order to avoid getting rained upon, a response that will vary according to circumstance. If traveling by car rather than walking, a person might take the risk of getting wet (when getting into and out of the car) and not bother with the umbrella. The prospect of rain is therefore a necessary but not sufficient cause of carrying an umbrella. Mode of transport therefore *moderates* this form of avoidance behavior. Carrying an umbrella might also be *mediated* by certain beliefs about the probability of fine weather turning to rain. The umbrella would be dispensed with during obviously sunny weather.

Moderating and Mediating Causal Influences

The concept of moderating and mediating factors can be illustrated in relation to the earlier example of insomnia. If the behavior of watching violent films were to be related to an endogenous physiological factor, then a cycling mood state would be classified as a *moderating* variable. However, despite the inevitability of mood changes, a client might still become aware of the beginnings of a mood swing very early on and note that certain actions or events influence the impact of the change of mood. In other words, a client's awareness of the onset of a change of mood might *mediate* a response that ameliorates the causal effects of the moderating variable.

Haynes and O'Brien (2000, chapter 10) discuss the role of causal mediating mechanisms at some length. They note that a number of different functional relationships could be mediated in the same way. Let us suppose again that the insomniac client believes (wrongly) that watching violent films is an effective coping strategy for insomnia and also for other problems. The functional analysis might suggest the advisability of trying to change this client's belief in the wisdom of adopting this manner of coping. Of course, not all mediating mechanisms are beliefs (i.e. cognitive in nature). There could be a mediating factor that a client has not noticed and therefore is unable to say anything about. The mediating variable might only be revealed by careful questioning or by close observation of a client in a problematic situation.

It is rare that a contingent relationship between a situation and an important outcome is all or none. Relationships between events are usually far less predictable, usually being moderated by different facets of the situation. For instance, when it snows, the train to work might be delayed 10% of the time. When it is not snowing, the train might be delayed 2% of the time. The presence of snow predicts the relative likelihood of delay, and the latter might also depend on the amount of snow that has fallen.

Any alteration in the relationship between a situation and its expected outcome is likely to elicit an emotional reaction. With or without snow, a commuter expects to get to work. If the railway line is closed for a week, the habit of waiting for a train is no longer reinforced (technically the person is placed on an "extinction schedule"). The closure elicits frustration and the person has to resort to alternative means of transport. Consequently, when formulating a problem, especially one involving emotional distress, the broad context in which recent upsetting events have occurred must be carefully and fully explored from a functional standpoint.

Reciprocal Causal Relationships

The causes and effects of a problem, and the problem itself, are elements in a wider system of causal interactions. Reciprocal influences may produce amplifying feedback or have a progressive damping effect, and this is frequently a central feature of a formulation diagram. A excites B which in turn might excite A further and the result is a form of amplifying feedback. Alternatively, A excites B and B reacts back on A to dampen its influence, sometimes to the extent of inhibiting all further responding. Within the limits set personally or socially, feedback effects are adaptive; otherwise, they are referred to as vicious circles or cycles. These cyclical interactions may occur over the short term (minutes or hours) or over months or years. The causal arrows between A and B (and perhaps, in addition, other elements C, D, etc.) chase each other in a circle. Reciprocal influences can be symbolized with a bi-directional arrow ($A \leftrightarrow B$). For extra clarity, amplifying feedback effects can be indicated with a plus sign, and dampening effects with a minus sign.

An example of feedback with an undesirable effect would be a client who fears choking when eating. The vicious cycle could be represented as follows: food in the mouth→fear of choking→sensation of a constricted throat as a component of the fear response→increased fear of choking→increased sensation of constriction→increased expectation of choking. Positive feedback can also produce virtuous cycles, a process implicit in the phrase, "success breeds success." The virtuous circle might extend into the family or community. Couples therapy might diminish the frequency of violent arguments, thereby reducing the negative impact on children who might otherwise have become distressed when observing their parents arguing.

Vicious cycles can occur over very long stretches of time. A client who gambles may lose the trust of a partner and also get into financial difficulty, which, in turn, might increase the urge to gamble more. A client with intrusive thoughts of danger might seek reassurance from others, which only strengthens the tendency to seek reassurance again. A client who has obsessive thoughts about harming a child might be inappropriately investigated by a social worker as a potential child abuser. A client who avoids a situation that evokes fear might end up leading a life that becomes increasingly restricted and isolated.

Representing the Causal Effects of Past Events

Past events inevitably enter the formulation diagram in some form. Current events are also linked to physical continuities in a person's life. The house in which a client lives contains reminders of the past (possessions, photographs) and family and friends maintain patterns of relationship that may go back to childhood.

The influence of the past is usually represented in terms of significant marker events. For instance, a client might report a distressing memory of a dog that bit her at the age of eight. The client dreams about this event or is especially afraid of dogs that resemble that particular dog. This is evidence that could be gathered at interview and it indicates an enduring influence of the past. But if the same client with a fear of dogs cannot provide any current evidence of distress that connects her fear with the memory, its causal relevance remains at a conjectural level. It is possible that the event predisposed the client to react more strongly, later in life, to any encounter with a threatening dog, or to fearful events in general. However, evidence for this hypothesis cannot be derived from the memory alone. This general point rings more true when the past event was inappropriate sexual behavior from an adult toward a child. A client might remember this but still wonder if it has any current significance. Evidence to link past and present is needed.

The significance of past events seems clear when there is a common theme underlying problems at different periods in a client's history. The presence of a theme might generate a search for actual past events to which it could be related. For instance, a client who has a history of being jealous when someone else pays attention to his or her partner might prompt a therapist to explore disruptions to earlier important relationships. However, this exploration should avoid the bias of seeking confirmatory evidence for a favored hypothesis. Evidence could be sought in current behavior, including the use of imagery techniques, that is both consistent and inconsistent with the hypothesis.

One general point to make about the causal effect of past events is that all causal influences are current. Of major importance is a client's construal of past events. This is her or his own autobiographical understanding of what happened in the past that she or he recounts to her- or himself and to others—which, again, is a current behavior. In the absence of evidence that current behavior is linked to past events, the latter might still be represented in the ICF diagram as a hypothesis that a certain past event has exerted a lasting influence. Evidence might subsequently come to light that supports this hypothesis.

Private Experience and the Life of the Mind

The growth in popularity of cognitive therapies from the 1970s onward can be attributed, in part, to a failure of functional learning theories to come up with a compelling approach to language and the reality of a person's private experience. Rational emotive therapy (Ellis, 1962) and cognitive therapy (Beck, 1970) rapidly gained ground because they were seen to have obvious relevance to the problems of most clients. Beliefs, fantasies, and feelings could be explored directly and could be successfully influenced by verbal methods without resorting to a systematic program of "relearning." Clients are perfectly well able to reflect on their problems, follow suggestions, and experiment with new behaviors. However, enthusiasm for verbal methods alone began to wane when it was attempted with clients who had a long history of problems in relationships, usually originating in childhood abuse, emotional deprivation, and other traumas. New cognitive behavioral therapies were developed that relied more on slow behavioral change and experiential methods, such as dialog and role-play (e.g. dialectical behavior therapy, Linehan, 1993, and schema-focused therapy, Young et al., 2003).

Functional analytic therapy and Acceptance and Commitment Therapy (ACT) (see Chapter 2) formulate verbal exchanges between client and therapist from a functional perspective. There are some advantages in viewing verbal behavior as *behavior* rather than as signs of hidden cognitive structures such as irrational beliefs or schemas. The formulation can refer to what is literally expressed verbally, noting cues or situations that occasion a thought or emotion. This description of surface behavior permits a variety of interpretations of the significance of a reported mental experience in the stream of behavior. For instance, a statement of feeling could be related to a social strategy—it has a purpose in a social context. "I'm angry" might be intended to warn others to proceed cautiously. "I'm scared" might signal that support or encouragement is being requested.

In a similar way, an expression of belief can be described as if it is referring to observed events. Sarbin (1998) conceptualizes a belief as a product of the imagination, that is, as a sequence of imagined events. This way of representing a belief means that its content can be translated into what is actually expected to happen in a given situation. Not all private experiences lend themselves to this kind of analysis because a private experience is sometimes expressed through an analogy. "Feeling stifled" is an example. A case formulation may have to begin with a rather vague statement with the hope that it will be clarified later on. The point of taking a functional approach is that a statement such as "feeling stifled" will probably be raised in relation to a particular context—say work or family. The difficulty might be easier for a client to state metaphorically because the anticipated consequence of following through on a belief that one is *really* "being stifled" (in a psychological sense) may be too threatening to be stated literally.

A client's imaginings may have a strong or a weak effect on behavior. In the case of post-traumatic stress, intrusive images have a powerful emotional impact and may constitute the main complaint. A car crash victim who replays a sequence of frightening images when later traveling at speed is in a very different position to the person who rationally reflects on the fact that driving at speed is dangerous. A phenomenological description of the two situations would make it obvious that they differ. The advantage of being rather literal in describing a client's self-reported experience helps to avoid the risk of premature over-interpretation. The context in which private experiences occur might also give clues to tracing historical connections or repeating behavioral patterns.

It is perhaps rather too easy to characterize a client's beliefs as if they define the whole person and apply at all times. Clients often recognize that what they claim to believe or feel is not justified by the "reality" of their situation. An obsessional idea about the possibility of harming a child might be viewed as "silly" despite an inability to resist imagining it. Nevertheless, a client might feel compelled to act on this belief, in the sense of taking great care to avoid causing potential harm. The belief may powerfully deter-mine behavior in one context but not in another.

Early learning theory had its origins, primarily, in animal research. This led to a neglect of rule-governed and symbolic behavior. However, the importance of learning by imitation was recognized early on. People can learn quickly by observing on film or videotape how an action or skill is to be performed. Modeling circumvents the long process that an animal with fewer cognitive abilities would have to go through. Nevertheless, the sim-pler learning processes studied in animals still apply to humans. It is for this reason that insight into the causes of a problem may not be sufficient to bring about change. This is not to underestimate the importance of educa-tion, persuasion, and the rational examination of beliefs, but the problems of many clients are resistant to these methods.

Representing Private Events in a Diagram

Self-reports of thoughts, feelings, and sensations can be represented in a case formulation diagram and speculatively included in causal chains. Private events can be causes in the sense of being the immediate trigger for a response. As noted above, images of events can be intrusive and emotionally disturbing. A client's self-talk (overt or covert) might play an important role in the mediation of behavior. Self-critical thoughts are a common problem. Self-reported experiences can be represented by specifying content and modality (e.g. "image of dog," "thought of suicide," "anticipation of rejec-tion," "sensation of pain"). Some self-reports are forms of self-analysis best represented by verbal statements, such as "believes he may have been abused," "believes that delving into the past is not useful," "believes that medication is helpful." A client's expressed beliefs are not hypotheses but are treated instead as descriptive elements in the total situation. A belief that medica-tion is helpful could be linked causally to other observations such as the attitudes expressed by a client's spouse or a family doctor.

Self-Regulation

Therapy that is offered in a client's natural environment (as opposed to a closed institution) is only effective because clients can self-regulate their behavior to a significant extent. In self-regulation, a person conceives of his or her own "self" as a distinct entity and acts "on behalf" of that entity. This ability is strongly encouraged in Western culture, and where this training has been lacking in childhood, a client may lack a sense of being any kind of self that he or she can feel comfortable with. For instance, some clients, despite knowing they are a person in their own right, might subordinate their own needs to those of others, or even constantly berate themselves for being unworthy, guilty, or incompetent. A case formulation normally includes a description of a client's self-regulation strategies.

Skinner (1953) reflected at length on the nature of self-regulation but did not write very much on self-conception. He noted that people are often aware that they "lose control" when they place themselves in certain situations which are either so attractive or aversive that they fall under the control of external events. A person might say "I cannot speak to my employer about the problem because I know I would blow up and lose my job." Another might say "I cannot afford to leave chocolates lying around because I know I would eat them all at once." In both situations there is an imagined chain of events with a certain outcome that the person regards as undesirable in the long view (losing a job, putting on weight). A person can often exert self-control early on in the chain and can implement a response that prevents the chain's otherwise inexorable progression. Self-regulation is therefore usually possible when the ultimate outcome is sufficiently remote. As such it exerts only weak control over present behavior (see Watson & Tharp, 1989, for techniques to foster self-regulation). Skinner commented on commonplace forms of self-regulation, such as posting reminders in order not to forget something, shopping after a meal rather than when hungry (so as to purchase less), taking an analgesic when in pain, or choosing to engage in a social activity on the grounds that it attracts a certain kind of person.

Talking to oneself, in essence treating oneself as the recipient of good advice, is another form of self-regulation. Advice that is normally directed toward others, such as "Don't do that" or "Stop and think," is sometimes addressed to oneself as a way of checking behavior that could be harmful. Counting to ten before responding to a perceived slight might soften an otherwise over-forceful and counterproductive reaction. Many clients carry around in their head a self-commentary that is overly critical and typically unhelpful as a form of self-correction. Others mentally rehearse all the things that could go wrong for them in life. Self-regulation strategies are also directed toward achieving positive outcomes. A person might rehearse what it is they want to do or say, or plan ahead all the stages in reaching an objective.

All of the aforementioned self-regulatory strategies should be familiar to readers as an internal monolog (or a dialog if there are several imagined protagonists). As suggested earlier, "self-talk" can be described in an ICF diagram as a chain of imagined events. The imagined consequences of acting, thinking, or behaving differently in any given situation can be explored in an assessment interview. This might reveal why a person *does not* do something. A style of formulation that identifies private experience with self-talk lends itself naturally to interventions that rely on fantasy or dialog (e.g. Gilbert, 2010; Hallam & O'Connor, 2002; Young et al., 2003). These methods involve making something that a client rehearses in his or her own mind into something that can be publicly displayed and therefore accessible to modification. One form of exploratory assessment is simply to put down on paper what hitherto has only existed in a client's thoughts. Another is a role-play in which a therapist takes the part of a protagonist in a client's own private dialog (see Guidelines).

SYSTEMIC RELATIONSHIPS

The basic idea of a network of causally related elements is certainly not a new one in formulation. For example, the concept of a vicious anxiety circle was drawn out as a diagram by James (1940, p. 564). It was developed in conditioning terms by Evans (1972), as a feedback system by Hallam (1976b), and in terms of cognitive concepts by Clark (1986). The vicious circle concept, which has played such an important role in case formulation, was helped along by the new science of cybernetics that introduced the concept of a "servomechanism," a device for continually monitoring the output of a machine. The mechanism makes adjustments to the machine to match output to a predetermined set value (Sluckin, 1954). Of particular relevance is the concept of "predictive teleology" (Sluckin, 1954, p. 104) in which the feedback mechanism responds to extrapolations to future positions (e.g. a person might extrapolate to imagined future states such as insanity or loss of control and make adjustments accordingly). Feedback is informative and adaptive when it specifies the size of a deviation from a desirable range of values and when a feedback mechanism can reduce the degree of deviation. In problematic examples of vicious circle behavior, a client might be unable to specify meaningful values or be unable to respond in an adaptive way to correct a deviation.

Apart from its long association with family therapy, systemic thinking exists chiefly at the level of theory (Schiepek, 2003; Tarrier & Calam, 2002). Functional and systemic concepts have a natural affinity. A client's problem usually has implications for others, for his or her employment, and for social agencies. The family, local community, and nation state have their own priorities that may conflict with the client's. The social context may have to be considered from the point of view of a client's gender, social class, ethnicity, or sexual orientation. How these influences enter into a formulation will be highly individual and in part dependent on a client's willingness to raise them as significant. However, it is not necessary to formulate everything that can affect a person. The aim is to take into account those factors that have a direct bearing on a particular problem.

In one-to-one therapy, the interests of the client are usually placed above those of others, and a therapist becomes a kind of personal advocate. A boundary can be drawn that can be described loosely as the client's world; by implication, an ICF is concerned with a system in which the client is placed at the center. However, viewed systemically, a person as a subsystem is only partially autonomous. A client usually sees her or his "problem" as something that upsets the stability of her or his own world. Before taking a wider view, I will consider the boundaries that define this "subsystem."

The Person as Subsystem

A person is a bounded system in the sense that he or she possesses a finite repertoire of different skills, talents, habits, coping strategies, and other behaviors. These are not necessarily available at all times in all situations. Whether a person says hi, hello, good morning, or merely grunts depends on circumstance. Some behaviors in the repertoire are likely to be mutually incompatible, but this need not matter if they are expressed in different situations. For example, a person might be ruthless at work but kind to their children. The functional units that relate behavior to outcomes are typically compartmentalized. In so far as a person's behavior is finely tuned to the needs of a specific situation, and these situations can be discriminated, the dynamics of the whole system can remain stable.

A behavioral repertoire is therefore a dynamic and systemic construct. The removal of a problem conceived as a symptom or as a disorder is far too narrow a perspective. The dynamics of a repertoire have been investigated in animals by creating several learning contingencies concurrently and studying their interaction in terms of the responses they generate. This has led to important innovations in practice, such as changing an unwanted behavior by rewarding an alternative response that produces the same outcome but in a more acceptable or less problematic form. For instance, in the case of a client who is consuming too much alcohol, a change in their social activities might lead to an increase in the amount of external social control over drinking or reduce his or her access to alcohol. Another strategy is to create conditions that raise the probability of a response that is incompatible with the consumption of alcohol, such as consuming a non-alcoholic drink, while still enjoying the company of friends who are drinking. People plan changes to their behavior expecting it to impact dynamically on future situations. In all these examples, behavior-in-context is conceptualized as a system of dynamically interacting components.

Although many people are proactive in promoting their own interests, some clients seem to set up situations, wittingly or unwittingly, that lead to recurring difficulties of a similar nature. It is as if a client is following rules but ones that are inflexible, leading to self-defeating consequences. A client may realize this and it may be his or her reason for seeking therapy. There is a failure to profit from experience. A case formulation diagram should help to capture these repeating maladaptive patterns as a system of interacting elements.

The Wider Systemic Perspective

The systemic viewpoint is amenable to conceptualizations of causal interaction between different levels of analysis—biological, psychological, and societal. The "context" can be understood as consisting of nested dynamic systems. This perspective has helped to clarify concepts of emergence, reductionism, and upward and downward causation between levels (Sawyer, 2003). A case formulation would not normally put much emphasis on events occurring at a somatic level. There are semi-autonomous subsystems that usually take care of the integrity of the body. However, when a biological system malfunctions, it can have an "upward" causal effect on a higher level. Maladaptive respiratory habits can cause hyperventilation that produces disturbing sensations of lightheadedness or depersonalization. A vestibular disorder affecting balance can seriously affect such basic functions as walking.

A client is normally only aware of events at a "psychological" level—in the example above, dizziness and an ability to walk. For this reason, a therapist should always be on the look-out for the existence of unrecognized disorders or physiological influences. Moreover, a client may be unaware of the undesirable (and unintended) consequences of some of their habits, such as drug-taking. A case formulation has to take account of interpenetrating causal domains.

A client's personal world consists of whatever it is that she or he considers to be personally relevant. Perhaps a client believes that phases of the moon affect her or his behavior, although I have never actually encountered a client who registers lunar cycles. If there is a firm belief that the phase of the moon is significant, it is potentially relevant to the formulation. The grounds for the belief could be explored and perhaps evaluated with reference to actual lunar phases. A therapist might form a hypothesis that a belief in the influence of the moon (rather than any actual influence of the moon) plays a functional role but one quite different to the one supposed by the client.

A client is usually seeking to sustain her- or himself as a stable constellation of satisfied needs and ongoing activities, projecting into a future that inspires hope. The relationship with the wider system is fluid—there are bound to be porous boundaries that afford the possibility of change. However, clients may impose limits on themselves, refusing, for instance, to change their diet, reduce demands at work, or form new relationships. Despite attempts to help a client to be proactive in making changes, this may not be possible in practice. Given that therapy is voluntary, a client has to be the best judge of what works for her or him and how far she or he is willing to change.

An awareness of the wider implications of a problem can give rise to ethical dilemmas for a therapist. Should a partner or parent be asked to join a session in an attempt to make a change in family relationships? Should advice be given about ending a harmful intimate relationship on which a client is dependent? How far should a therapist intervene in a dysfunctional healthcare system that is purportedly attempting to help a client? Should a client be discouraged from continuing with a medication prescribed by a doctor? Should a therapist agree to reduce a fear of public speaking in a client who wants to spread a repellant dogma? There are no easy answers to these questions. They often involve a conflict between promoting a client's welfare and respecting his or her autonomy (Knapp & Vandecreek, 2007). A therapist's formulation might lead to the view that a client's goals cannot be achieved by means acceptable to the client. If, as a consequence, a therapist declines to offer a service (or the client decides to discontinue) this should not be interpreted as a failure of the formulation process. Not all problems are soluble.

CHAPTER 9

Future Prospects for Individual Case Formulation

Previous chapters have argued for the merits of an individual approach to case formulation that conceptualizes a problem systemically at different levels, draws upon psychological principles, and takes heed of the therapy outcome literature. The mental health professions loudly proclaim the importance of the skills of case formulation, but recent models of service delivery seem to demote them. Of course, the perception that many practitioners are failing to use effective methods may be accurate. If so, it would be difficult for them to mount a defense of the value of their independent judgment when formulating problems. Clearly, anyone adopting individual case formulation (ICF) should not ignore evidence that indicates a best way to influence a problem—to do so would be negligent. However, there are many ways to formulate a problem, and therefore likely to be many ways to resolve it. The case has already been made that disorder-specific models and standard protocols cannot be expected to provide guidance on all of the individual circumstances of a problem in which judgment is required.

DO MENTAL HEALTH PROFESSIONALS REALLY TAKE CASE FORMULATION SERIOUSLY?

Given the high regard in which case formulation is held, it is puzzling to find the skills it involves so little discussed or researched. The most likely explanation is that practitioners would feel at a loss if they gave up the diagnostic model. Without this model, the situation would be more or less as Fowers (2005) describes it:

The truly remarkable thing is that there is virtually no explicit, systematic training about how to recognize and respond to what is most important in a client's presentation.

In a recent issue of the journal *Psychotherapy: Theory, Research, Practice, Training* (No. 4, 2007) devoted to training in psychotherapy, formulation is scarcely mentioned. For instance, in their skills-based approach to training novices, Hill, Stahl, and Roffman (2007) refer to skills needed for the "exploration

Individual Case Formulation
http://dx.doi.org/10.1016/B978-0-12-398269-8.00009-0

stage," such as open questions, but consider that applying a theoretical approach to inform a case conceptualization is a broader skill that may be hard for novices to grasp. Fauth, Gates, Vinca, Boles, and Hayes (2007) also regard formulation as a higher level "meta-cognitive" skill, and make a case for teaching trainees to detect "patterns" in segments of audio and video-taped sessions. Once detected, a "sustained empathic inquiry" can be devoted to those areas. However, it is not clear whether this inquiry reaches the threshold of formulation. Angus and Kagan (2007) focus almost entirely on trainees' ability to establish an accepting therapeutic relationship in which a client can reveal his or her story, allowing him or her to reflect, construct new meanings, and engage in problem solving. At an advanced level, trainees transcribe segments of their therapy sessions and are required to analyze them "in terms of four basic categories: client utterances, therapist responses, alternative responses and comments, and reflections on the interaction between client and therapist." Again, it is not clear from this description that trainees need to develop an explicit formulation. In their literature review, Kendjelic and Eells (2007) could not "identify any studies evaluating a train-ing manual designed specifically for case formulation."

This review may have prompted Kendjelic and Eells (2007) to conduct their study evaluating the effects of a 2-hour workshop that was offered to a large sample of mental health professionals. The majority of the workshop participants were still in training but they were routinely conducting assess-ments in a university-based psychiatry outpatient clinic. The study is reveal-ing because it points once more to an underlying neglect of formulation in training. The workshop explained why formulation is important and described it in terms of the identification of symptoms and problems, pre-cipitating stressors, and predisposing factors, all of which should ideally be related together by an inferred explanatory mechanism. The participants had to submit single-paragraph written formulations based on actual clients they had assessed, which were then independently coded on various scales for quality of content. The participants had already had an average of nearly 3 years' interviewing experience. Half of them were randomly assigned to the workshop training and half (as a control group) were not. The average score for the latter group on the scale measuring overall quality of the formulation was between 1, defined as no presentation of a mechanism, and 2, defined as rudimentary presentation of a mechanism which is *not* linked to symptoms/problems, precipitating stressors, and/or more distant predis-posing events. The group who attended the workshop obtained an average score of less than 3 on the 5-point scale, where 4 was labeled as adequate.

Although the workshop resulted in significant improvement in the quality of case formulation, it seems that it may have done little more than explain what a case formulation should look like to clinicians who were not accustomed to think in this way.

Eells and colleagues had used their carefully developed coding scheme in an earlier piece of research in which they studied a group of experts whose credentials could not be questioned (Eells, 2010; Eells, Lombart, Kendjelic, Turner, & Lucas, 2005; Eells et al., 2011). The experts on case formulation were recognized nationally to have reached a level of pre-eminence, having published on the subject or led workshops. One half of the 22 experts were cognitive behavioral in orientation and half were psychodynamic. They were asked to respond to six vignettes of clients who demonstrated commonly encountered psychiatric problems. Each vignette took around 2 minutes to read out. They were then asked to spend around 5 minutes thinking aloud about how they would conceptualize the problem and construct a formulation. A little later, 2 minutes was allotted for thinking aloud about a treatment strategy. The responses were transcribed and coded, and the experts' formulations were compared with those provided by therapists who had a similar number of years experience (20–30 years) and with a group of novices who had approximately 2 years' experience. It is somewhat reassuring that the experts' formulations were more comprehensive, elaborated, complex, and systematic than those in the other two groups. It is less reassuring that the novices' formulations were superior to those of the experienced practitioners.

This research has grown out of a model of formulation (Eells, 2010) that bears little resemblance to ICF. Information gathering is seen as a stage prior to formulation rather than as a process that entails the ongoing testing of hypotheses. Eells (2010, p. 240) states that a measure of case formulation competence should show how "inferences are supported by case material" and that attention should be given to "potential judgment biases," but how is a practitioner to demonstrate these skills in the experimental tasks described above? An off-the-cuff response to vignettes is insufficient. We simply have to take on trust that the transcripts of the most outstanding expert commentary provided by Eells (2010) actually demonstrates these qualities. In fact, it is clear that the experts were throwing up speculative possibilities that they knew they had no opportunity of verifying in the absence of further information. The processes of "forward and backward reasoning" that Eells identifies are likely to be found in real practice situations, but evidence on the ground is needed to show that any strategy results in effective therapy (as, in fact, Eells and colleagues acknowledge).

Eells' concept of a case formulation is a staged process "beginning with generating a problem list, then developing a diagnosis, proposing an explanatory hypothesis of the problems and diagnosis, and finally planning treatment" (Eells, 2010, p. 238). From this description it is not clear how decisions made during this process actually play out in client/therapist interactions. Formulation seems to be presented as a summary evaluation, an "expert opinion," rather too closely matching the medical model of symptoms, diagnosis, and prescription. The terminology of diagnosis and problems underlines the problem of mixed conceptual models.

IS "GOOD-ENOUGH" THERAPY GOOD ENOUGH?

Most people imagine (realistically or not) that there is someone who has an answer to their problems. In the case of medical services, it is often possible to search for an individual who is highly recommended. Judging excellence in psychotherapy is a far more difficult task and a potential client may not know what to look for. From a health provider's point of view, a service will be shaped by a number of factors, including a concept of evidence-based practice. However, the actual service that is provided will depend also on whether it is affordable and sustainable, given a variety of pragmatic constraints. A typical organization of services is based on a hierarchy in the workforce determined chiefly by length of training. Those at the top of the pyramid of expertise research theorize and devise optimal interventions, while those at the bottom are advisers or facilitators of self-help. Therapists at a middle level may depend on a professional with greater expertise to screen new referrals, select suitable clients, and provide back-up in case of difficulty.

Clearly, not everyone will have access to the "top specialist" for his or her particular problem. As Crits-Christoff, Wilson, and Hollon (2005) put it, "the ideal of a doctoral level clinical psychologist who combines clinical skill and sensitivity, and who is informed by the relevant scientific research, is not a practical solution to the provision of mental health services." Typically, a service will be a form of manualized evidence-based practice (MEBP) that on average produces reliable results at a reasonable cost. It may or may not bear any resemblance to the service provided by the ideal practitioner (not necessarily assuming that this person would be a highly trained clinical psychologist).

In the body of research that constitutes an evidence base, outcome has been evaluated in so many ways that it is difficult to decide the meaning of "good-enough therapy." "High end-state functioning" seems to be closest to a lay concept of recovery. In physical medicine, one either "recovers" or is "cured," or one remains chronically ill and partially incapacitated. These concepts are much more fuzzy in the case of psychological well-being. For instance, a self-report measure of "dysfunction" might move to within normal limits but still lie close to a cut-off point for "caseness." From a problem-solving perspective, a high end-state means problem resolution, a concept not easily captured by normative measures of dysfunction. Moreover, clients often want to discuss their state of discontent, perplexity, or emptiness that does not directly affect everyday functions or show up on conventional measures of symptoms. The language of therapy and cure is not well suited to problem resolution or a sense of positive well-being.

Recent attempts to disseminate evidence-based practice illustrate the distance that exists between results that are "good enough" and outcomes that might be considered satisfactory by an impartial observer. An argument can be made that even a return to a normal range of functioning could be setting one's sights too low. This would certainly be true in the case of body weight or managing without regular psychotropic medication, since so many "normal" people fall short of a healthy ideal in these respects. It is typical in outcome studies to allow participants to continue with their regular medication while earnest attempts are made to change all other maladaptive coping habits. In fact, helping a client to manage his or her medication, or assessing the need for a new medication, is a stated treatment goal in some studies of the dissemination of MEBP (see below). In research on computer-assisted cognitive behavioral therapy (CBT) in primary care, Craske et al. (2009) reported that 69% of participants were already taking one or more psychotropic drugs. A passive tolerance of medication is an implicit acknowledgment that psychological methods alone are not "good enough."

The task of realistically assessing outcome is sometimes hampered by a fog of statistical data and effect sizes. The research itself may have conflicting aims, making the interpretation of results more difficult. One aim is to show that a principle, process, or method of change shows signs of being theoretically or practically important. In this case, even relatively small statistical effects may be worth noting if there is a possibility of building upon them with a redesigned study or a different sample. A rather different aim is to show that an intervention is effective in the real world—it produces substantial benefits, perhaps at lower cost than alternative methods. In this case, the benefits should be obvious in terms of clearly achieved criteria that could be readily understood by a non-specialist. The effects should be large in statistical terms or evident without a need to perform statistical tests. Unfortunately, outcome is often "benchmarked" with the change achieved on self-report scales in "gold standard" efficacy studies, which only defers the problem of interpretation. Marchand, Stice, Rohde, and Becker (2011) regard the results of randomized control trial (RCT) efficacy trials as indicating "optimal therapy," whereas, for all sorts of justifiable methodological reasons, an RCT optimizes internal validity rather than therapeutic impact. For this reason, it may compromise optimal effectiveness.

A recent claim from a community clinic that a policy of switching to empirically supported treatments (ESTs) significantly improved the outcome for clients highlights the issue of what is to count as "good enough" (Cukrowicz et al., 2011). The new policy amounted to a "culture change" in which therapists were required to adopt ESTs (usually in accordance with a protocol) and new supervisors were employed who were adequately trained in the new methods. Adherence to EST protocols was not monitored and so, at best, therapists were guided by the empirical evidence (a form of EBP). Prior to the switch of policy in 1998, therapists were *not* required to be influenced by evidence, and it comes as no surprise that an audit of outcomes found that "ratings indicated no change or even slight worsening of symptoms" (Cukrowicz et al., 2011). Presumably, any form of therapy guided by evidence would have improved this state of affairs. With regard to the improvements achieved, it is very difficult to judge whether the new regime is "good enough." The therapists were inexperienced (still in training), 60% of clients unilaterally terminated their therapy, and outcome was assessed by clinical ratings of improvement that were sometimes made by the therapist rather than by a blind assessor. It is not clear whether clients' problems were individually formulated, and choice of therapy was dictated chiefly by psychiatric diagnosis. The new regime in the community clinic led to improved outcomes, but were these "good enough"? The arguments presented in this book concern *how* therapy should be guided by empirical evidence, not *whether* it should be so guided. Nothing can be concluded about manualized therapy from the results of this study apart from the fact that a systematic approach seems to have been better than none at all.

The issue just outlined can also be illustrated with respect to the results of MEBP when it is delivered by means of the internet, email, text messaging, and/or telephone communication, described by Mohr (2009) as "tele-mental" delivery. This is a promising development, in part because it lowers costs and expertise can be accessed at a distance. Across four anxiety diagnostic groups, Craske et al. (2009) reported an effect size of 0.46 for anxiety measures and 0.34 for depression. These results are consistent with the findings of a meta-analysis of 12 RCTs of internet-based CBT for depression and anxiety (Spek et al., 2007). A consistent finding in self-help and telemental methods is that the availability of advice and support from someone with expertise augments the benefits; computerized therapy offered with the assistance of a therapist produces better results than the same program without support (Andersson, 2009; Andrews & Titov, 2009).

The effect sizes in these studies of telemental CBT are therefore small to medium. What they really mean in terms of real-world gains is far from obvious. Kiropoulos et al. (2008) compared internet-based CBT for panic disorder/agoraphobia with 12 weeks of face-to-face therapy. Bearing in mind that these were self-selected participants (who also met inclusion criteria), and most of them were in professional occupations, it is somewhat surprising that only around 30% in each group achieved panic-free status one month after therapy. It is certainly less than the 70–80% panic-free status achieved in a number of previous studies (e.g. Barlow, Craske, Cerny, & Klosko, 1989; Clark et al., 1994; Williams & Falbo, 1996). It seems it is possible to obtain statistically significant results while leaving a majority of participants only somewhat improved or unchanged.

In another therapist-guided internet-based intervention, Carlbring et al. (2011) achieved large effect sizes in clients given any anxiety diagnosis, and benefits were maintained for 2 years. Therapy was tailored according to client characteristics in the sense that a choice could be made from up to 16 different modules. The control group participants were invited to join a confidential online support group, which turned out to have little therapeutic effect. They were switched to internet therapy after ten weeks. On closer inspection, the results are less impressive. Mean scores on the Beck Anxiety Inventory were still at the mid-point of the "mild anxiety" range and, given the size of the standard deviation, some of the participants must have produced moderate and severe scores. Only 4% were rated as "very much improved" on a clinical global improvement scale. Forty-one per cent showed small improvement or no change. The clinical rating cannot be regarded as a measure of "end-state" because improvement was judged in relation to a client's baseline functioning. The authors present the study as showing the feasibility of broadening internet delivery to a wider spectrum of clients and introducing more flexibility in tailoring modules to client characteristics (in the absence, they admit, of a full case formulation). However, the participants were not typical of routine practice because they were recruited via news media outlets and information on webpages. Of 137 people assessed, 54 were included in the trial. After completing each module, they had to answer 3–8 essay-style questions and submit worksheets before being allowed to proceed to the next module. This level of compliance seems exceptional, and certainly not typical of the average client, even one who is well motivated.

While this RCT achieved strong effect sizes, they are not very meaningful when considered out of context. The suspicion is generated that in many RCTs, a minority of participants do well, leading to statistically significant results. What is not so clear is how participants would fare given a longer course of therapy by more experienced CBT therapists (the therapists in the study by Carlbring et al. were just completing their training). If the aim of the authors is to demonstrate the feasibility of a somewhat tailored modularized approach, the study has proved its point. The next stage would be to investigate why a large number of participants did not benefit and why internet-based therapy in this form was insufficient for their needs.

The detailed session-by-session monitoring of therapeutic change in natural settings casts serious doubt on the conclusions that can be drawn from time-limited RCT outcome studies (Lambert, 2007). Lambert argues that counseling centers that limit therapy to, say, 10 sessions, are unlikely to meet the needs of more than half their clients. The most important determinant of outcome seems to be the initial severity and complexity of a problem. Clients in this category can be helped—but they need more sessions.

Another threat to the external validity of efficacy trials is the existence of a group of clients who have come to be known as "rapid responders," estimated by Lambert to be around 25% of a sample. Clients may respond before they have been adequately exposed to the therapeutic technique that is under investigation. An early dramatic response is associated with better intermediate and long-term outcomes. In data collected by Lambert (2007), only 16% of rapid responders made no reliable change by the end of therapy. The processes underlying rapid response are unknown, although the phenomenon of "sudden gains" in psychotherapy has been reported for some time. Change may occur between the end of one session and the beginning of the next, rather than gradually, and it tends to occur early in therapy and to be stable (Hardy et al., 2005). Clients who make sudden gains in cognitive therapy for depression are less likely to relapse in the next 2 years (Tang, DeRubeis, Hollon, & Amsterdam, 2007).

The existence of a group that is particularly receptive to credible interventions could account for a statistically "good enough" result in RCT studies. It suggests that research should set its sights higher, formulate therapy failures, and aim to be effective in all clients.

TRAINING IN CASE FORMULATION

It would be easier to make recommendations for training if more was known about the skills of formulation. As Westen and Weinberger (2005) note: "As a field, we have paid surprisingly little empirical attention to identifying the kinds of information clinicians might find useful in guiding interventions and in ways to optimize reliability and validity of those judgments." One of their interesting suggestions is to find practitioners whose inferences show the strongest correlation with external criteria. An expert systems approach would then be followed, attempting to identify the procedures the experts are using, whether or not they have explicit cognitive access to those procedures. Assuming that there is a discoverable basis for expertise, the relevant principles could be taught to others. The studies of Eells and colleagues, cited earlier, are an attempt in this direction.

In the view of a Task Force set up by the American Psychological Association to produce recommendations for the assessment of professional competence, the core competencies have not yet been defined and widely agreed (Kaslow et al., 2007). One of the proposed competencies is an ability to reflect critically on the knowledge that a psychologist is applying, though the authors note that little effort has been devoted to measuring this ability. Nevertheless, there is a strong assumption that competence in all areas can be placed on a scale ranging from novice, intermediate, advanced, proficient, expert, through to master. In the absence of agreement about the nature of case formulation (and the role of psychiatric diagnosis within it), it would seem that we are a very long way from defining levels of competence with this exactitude.

It might have been expected that in an eagerness to disseminate manual-based EBP, an attempt would have been made to research the effectiveness of different training strategies for practitioners working in the field. However, a study by Sholomskas et al. (2005) claims to be the first. It highlights the importance of continuing supervised casework. Fairburn and Cooper (2011) review issues in training CBT skills and make a strong case for a web-based resource of training materials. Caspar, Berger, and Hautle (2004) have described an innovative text-based and computerized "expert" system to assist in psychotherapy training.

In the absence of much relevant evidence, I will consider one model of CBT training because of its authors' longstanding experience of teaching novices (Kuyken, Padesky, & Dudley, 2009).

These authors make it clear that their recommendations may be limited to their own theoretical approach when they state that "highly experienced therapists who are relatively new to CBT may need to start at the novice level of learning case conceptualization despite years of clinical practice" (Kuyken et al., p. 296). It is somewhat concerning that formulation skills are not generalizable but the same opinion would probably be expressed by psychodynamically oriented trainers attempting to teach their skills to seasoned CBT practitioners. Nevertheless, some of Kuyken and colleagues' observations would probably be widely accepted: (1) that formulation skills need to be smoothly integrated with a range of other skills such as establishing a collaborative relationship, empathic listening, observational skills, self-awareness, etc.; (2) that novice, intermediate, and expert levels of skill can be distinguished; (3) that a method is needed for summarizing a client's case formulation (e.g. diagram or written statement); (4) that as expertise is acquired, therapists begin to operate on automatic pilot within sessions and may need a period of reflection to explain their decisions; (5) that a distinction can be drawn between declarative knowledge and procedural skills (Bennett-Levy, 2006) and therapists at all levels need to update the former on a regular basis; and (6) that therapists should ensure they have an opportunity to reflect on their formulations and discuss them with others in supervision.

It therefore seems desirable to include the following in training: reading, workshop attendance, role-play, therapeutic practice graded in terms of complexity of client problems, re-reading of session notes, regular supervision, recording of at least a sample of sessions so that they can be reviewed in supervision, and provision of feedback on performance using standardized measures (see also McHugh & Barlow, 2010). It is not easy to assess formulation skills specifically because they have to be integrated with other skills. Moreover, experts may agree about the description of clients' problems but they frequently disagree about their higher level inferences and the implications they may have for choice of an intervention. In the case of cognitive therapy skills, which are specified in greater detail than in most other forms of therapy, inter-rater agreement of therapy competence on the Cognitive Therapy Scale (revised version, Blackburn, James, & Reichelt, 2000) is only moderate (Gordon, 2007). This scale is a relatively undifferentiated assessment (Vallis, Shaw, & Dobson, 1986) and therefore cannot be used as a measure of formulation skill as such (see also Fairburn & Cooper,

2011). Kuyken et al. (2004) review research on the reliability of cognitive case formulations and conclude that it is low at the more inferential level.

Case formulation is clearly a skill that deserves greater study. As already noted, investigation of responses to short case vignettes seems a poor substitute for the real thing. It would be interesting to pursue the suggestion of Westen and Weinberger (2005) to compare and contrast the reasoning processes of experts who follow different conceptual models (see above).

THE DISSEMINATION OF EVIDENCE-BASED PRACTICE

Few commentators would dissent from the opinion that there should be wider public access to effective forms of psychological therapy. The cause of dissemination has been taken up at national, state, and local service delivery levels (McHugh & Barlow, 2010). A larger workforce has to be trained if this goal is to be achieved. Kazdin (2011) is concerned that the traditional one-to-one model of therapy fails to reach the large majority of individuals in need of psychological services. This is partly because trained professionals tend to be concentrated in cities, and partly because one-to-one therapy, and traveling to obtain services, is costly. Kazdin welcomes innovative modes of delivery, such as computerized methods, as long as they yield benefits. Kazdin sums up the challenge as "designing ways of delivering or packaging them so that they can be extended without degradation."

The skills of ICF do not apply only to traditional one-to-one, face-to-face psychotherapy. The word "individual" in ICF signifies "uniqueness" rather than the "individual" person. A "client" could indeed be a person in direct contact with a therapist but a client could also mean a couple, family, group, or organization, each with its own unique problems. A formulation is undertaken from the point of view of a client in this wider sense but it need not be conducted face-to-face. The problem presented is a practical one in which different players have competing interests; a therapist is therefore drawn into the position of an advocate. Problem resolution for one client might disadvantage others.

As an alternative to EBP based on adherence to a manual, a case has been made in earlier chapters for a *principles-based* form of practice in which there is peer and public scrutiny of the reasoning processes a therapist employs. All major developments in therapeutic practice over the past 50 years have grown out of close contact with clients. It has been entirely understandable that attempts have been made to systematize, research, teach, and *improve* on what had already been discovered through practice. Manualized therapy has been a part of these efforts. However, adherence to a protocol only makes sense if it produces superior results, and this question is still largely untested. Chorpita and Regan (2009) point out that uptake of EBP might be higher if it were seen less as an either/or adoption of a manual but instead as "enhanced usual care," incorporating principles and procedures generally associated with positive outcomes.

In the dissemination debate, it is practitioners who seem to be placed on the back foot. For instance, in their discussion of one example of MEBP, McHugh and Barlow (2010, p. 79) state that, "A drawback, however, is that clinicians must make a number of individual decisions on which modules are indicated, and the reliability of these decisions is not yet clear." Decisions must of course be made in a consistent fashion but the validity of the whole treatment package has to be established first. In any case, therapists may not make identical decisions in identical circumstances because they (together with their clients) may vary in the priority they give to different goals. Barlow and Carl (2011) emphasize that it is important to work toward outcomes that are not merely symptom based but also increase quality of life. However, quality of life is always judged from the perspective of an interested party.

One aspect of practice over which there may be disagreement is the desirability of psychotropic medication. Underlying the drive to offer psychotherapy rather than medication lies the value judgment that the former produces longer lasting benefit, has fewer (or no) side-effects, and is quite possibly cheaper in the long run. These considerations are bound to be of concern to health providers, although a client's preference to take medication is normally respected. One of the false impressions conveyed by advocates of manualized therapy is that it is quite obvious what a client's therapeutic goals should be. However, any reading of how therapy is actually conducted (e.g. the cognitive therapy described by Kuyken et al., 2009) shows that it involves complex collaborative decision making. Some clients may even prefer to "hang onto their symptoms" rather than change, and it cannot be assumed that this is necessarily a bad decision for them.

The planning of services on a large scale naturally includes a consideration of cost-effectiveness. One temptation is to lower costs by reducing the length of therapists' training and by opening up the field to a wider range of entrants. For instance, in the UK's Increasing Access to Psychological Therapy (IAPT) service, a new cadre of workers has been created called "personal well-being practitioners." IAPT was initially designed for people presenting with complaints of anxiety and depression, although it has now broadened out. It provides a first-stage "low-intensity" intervention but clients can be stepped up to (or may start with) "high-intensity" therapy. It is intended that IAPT be delivered universally and equitably across the country. It aimed to have treated 900,000 people by 2011 (Department of Health, 2010b) although it is currently falling a little short of its targets. Low-intensity interventions consist, in the main, of guided self-help, and high-intensity therapy is chiefly CBT, although other modes of therapy are available as well.

Two evaluations of IAPT have been made available online and summaries have been published (Clark et al., 2009; Glover, Webb, & Evison, 2010). Clients who use IAPT are assessed in terms of psychiatric symptoms rather than a problem list and so it is impossible to judge whether clients felt that their "problems" (apart from dysphoria) were being solved (client satisfaction data were not collected). The evaluations rely primarily on change scores on two self-report symptom scales of depression and anxiety. A client is designated a success when his or her score on both of these scales drops below a cut-off for "caseness." In theory, a change of a couple of points could convert a client from someone who is "ill" or "sick" (in the language of the reports) to someone who is "well." Clients are also offered employment advice (if needed) and changes in welfare benefits are recorded. A large proportion of referred clients were already taking psychotropic medication, mainly selective serotonin reuptake inhibitors (SSRI). Although reduced reliance on medication is an intended outcome for IAPT, the data do not appear to have been collected sufficiently well so far to assess whether this goal has been achieved.

Given the restricted focus on psychiatric outcome criteria, the process of formulation at assessment is unclear. According to the published reports, most referrals come from general physicians who also supply a psychiatric diagnosis. Assessment, including an appraisal of risk, is carried out by IAPT caseworkers. At one of the two pilot sites, 8.5% of referrals were considered unsuitable, 28% of potentially suitable clients failed to engage with the service, and a further 25% came for only one session, half of whom refused further therapy or discontinued unexpectedly (Clark et al., 2009). This is a high rate of attrition. Those who completed therapy (i.e. came for two or more sessions) received an average of 2.6 hours of contact time spread out over a mean of 4.9 sessions. Only 2.7% were referred on for "high-intensity" CBT, although this might have been due to the unavailability of local therapists (Richards & Suckling, 2008). The mean post-therapy score of clients who completed two or more sessions was 7.4 (on a 27-point depression scale with a cut-off of 10) and 6.8 (on a 21-point general anxiety scale, cut-off 7). Only one-half of clients provided follow-up data, on average 10 months later, by which time mean anxiety scores were above the cut-off, and mean depression scores had slipped back to 8.7. There was some indication that clients who were not followed up did less well than those for whom data were collected.

The results are presented as a 50% recovery rate at follow-up for this pilot IAPT site (Clark et al., 2009). However, the number "recovered" represents only 27% of the referrals deemed suitable for the program and many of them still score close to the threshold for "disorder." They are probably still taking medication. On present showing, the evidence is not convincing that the program produces results comparable to those achieved in RCT studies of the kind that regularly get reported in academic journals. Moreover, as this was an evaluation without a control group, it is not known how many of the "recovered" clients would have improved without help.

The results for the first year of IAPT (2008–2009) that followed the initial pilot stage were reported in 2010 (Glover, Webb, & Evison, 2010). Perhaps most surprising is the brevity of interventions—a median of two sessions for low-intensity and three for high-intensity treatment, including assessment. This might account for the fact that the median change-score (post-therapy minus pre-therapy on scales of depression and anxiety) was zero. However, as in the pilot sites, there were gains for the subgroup who completed two or more therapy sessions. Of these, 56% achieved scores that placed them below the cut-off for caseness, although mean scores were again close to the cut-off point. Those who did not complete therapy improved slightly but their scores remained above the cut-off. Clients had a better outcome when they were stepped up to high-intensity therapy or received more sessions (Clark, 2011). Of some concern is the wide variation in "recovery rates" between the 42 different treatment sites. The 95% confidence intervals for recovery rates for the best and worst third of IAPT sites showed almost no overlap (Glover, Webb, & Evison, 2010). The completers represented only 38% of the 41,724 people for whom data were analyzed and it should be noted that a large number of people were assessed but were not considered suitable for the program. It would be misleading if effectiveness were to be assessed in terms of treatment effect sizes for completers only. The general impression is gained that the program is setting its sights too low (see commentaries on Richards & Suckling, 2008, and their defense).

The reason for presenting these results in so much detail is to make the point that enthusiasm for dissemination of MEBP (at least on some models) might be misplaced. There is still disagreement over what is to count as sound EBP. For instance, Gambrill and Littell (2010) express reservations about disseminating "multisystemic therapy" on the basis of a lack of evidence for its effectiveness. With respect to IAPT, it is not yet clear whether caseworkers are trained to a sufficient depth or whether other aspects of the model of service delivery need to be changed. A program in the early 1970s that trained a small number of psychiatric nurses in CBT provided a much longer, full-time training period, with close supervision of casework (Marks, Hallam, Philpott, & Connolly, 1976). Client benefits matched the published outcome data available at that time.

A different model for low-cost dissemination is an internet-based service in which therapy can be continued on an "as-needed" basis, with relative ease of client contact using telephone calls, videolink, text messaging, or regular emails. The contribution made by expertise in formulation skills could be investigated by monitoring decisions and analyzing the reasons for making them. Alternatively, the results obtained by caseworkers with different levels of training could be compared.

THE FUTURE OF DIAGNOSTIC-LED FORMULATION

The combined pursuit of two incompatible paradigms (the diagnostic and problem-centered) has led the field of psychotherapy into contorted descriptions of its own practices. It is common to refer to clients' symptoms and problems, an even-handed recognition of the diagnostic and non–diagnostic positions. All of the major traditions within psychotherapy, with perhaps the exception of some radical behavioral approaches, have been required to accommodate to evidence-based outcome research that relates to diagnostic categories. This is evident in Persons' adherence to an individualized approach in her earlier writings (Persons, 1989) and a hybrid, top-down, approach in her recent book (Persons, 2008). The concept of therapy as problem solving, an essentially non-medical approach, also sits very uneasily with evidence-based treatment of disorders (Nezu, Nezu, & Lombardo, 2004).

If the concept of psychiatric disorder were to be no longer seen as relevant, this would have very serious implications for "mental health" professions that have allied themselves to medicine and psychiatry. Barlow and Carl (2011) make a rather provocative suggestion to redefine the terms "psychological treatment" and "psychotherapy." The former would be restricted to EBP addressing psychopathology and pathophysiology within a healthcare context, while the latter would be a term reserved for procedures designed to enhance personal adjustment and growth outside of healthcare systems. Barlow and Carl are concerned that helping clients to work out problems to do with the meaning of life, with failed relationships, or personal growth will "never be reimbursed by health-care dollars" (Barlow & Carl, 2011, p. 908). They argue that psychotherapy should have its own evidence base in the burgeoning field of positive psychology (see below). This is a rather neat solution to the dilemma but not one that seems likely to catch on. It is also inconsistent with a constructional approach to therapy, which is just as applicable to "pathology" as it is to personal growth (Evans, 1993; Goldiamond, 1974).

Looking to the future, the whole issue may be decided out of the hands of healthcare professionals. Apart from "severe mental illness," chiefly reserved for the diagnosis of the psychoses, so-called minor forms of mental illness have largely been de-stigmatized. For instance, the term "neurosis" is hardly ever used. Self-help books have been published on every conceivable problem and seem to be widely consulted and read. Self-help is now a multi-billion dollar industry (Wilson, 2003). Techniques such as "assertiveness training," originally introduced by Salter (1949) as conditioned reflex therapy within a clinical context, have now transferred to an educational one. The main obstacle to de-medicalizing the field of personal problems is the widespread and still growing prescription of psychotropic drugs, supported by heavy marketing and lobbying from very powerful commercial interests. While there is still a place for medication, psychological therapies have clearly proved themselves to be an effective alternative. Barlow and Carl (2011) have perceptively observed the dilemma in which psychological therapy finds itself. The links with medicine and health services cannot be severed without a potential loss of influence. This is despite growing evidence that the most commonly prescribed medications, antidepressants, act through a placebo effect (Kirsch, 2009).

THE TREND TOWARD POSITIVE PSYCHOLOGY

The growth of the positive psychology movement within academic psychology has had spin-offs in the area of psychotherapy (e.g. Seligman, 2002). A focus on a client's strengths and resources is not new in psychotherapy, and in a constructional approach to CBT it is integrated into the formulation. In principle, a positive psychology framework for formulation could replace a diagnostic one. In practice, only a few positive psychologists have embraced a radical position by rejecting the medical model (e.g. Maddux, 2005). Many therapists influenced by positive psychology have simply

soft-pedaled on this issue. Wong (2006, p. 137) describes a social constructionist, virtues-based psychotherapy, and states that, "diagnostic labels are
merely one of several ways to discuss clients' concerns." He also suggests that
his virtues-based approach might have to be modified "when clients present
with severe psychopathology" (Wong, 2006, p. 143). Wong's position is
therefore consistent with Barlow and Carl (2011); "real psychopathology" is
different from run-of-the-mill complaints. Keyes and Lopez (2005) and
Magyar-Moe's (2009) conceptual framework for "positive therapy" is even
more accommodating to a diagnostic approach. To complement a dimension
of high to low symptoms of mental illness, they propose a dimension of high
to low symptoms of well-being. In other words, the aim is to "broaden Axis
V [of the DSM] to include two global functioning scales" (Magyar-Moe,
p. 16). The idea of symptoms of positive mental health making up a syndrome of well-being is a very ingenious application of classificatory thinking.

McNulty and Fincham (2012) point out that psychology as a science is
neither positive nor negative in its effects. They also cite many studies showing that psychological traits regarded as positive, such as forgiveness, kind-
ness, and optimism, can produce harmful effects in certain contexts. In other
words, none of these traits or values is inherently good. One lesson to draw
from this is that a judgment of benefit for an individual should be formulated within the unique context of that individual's life.

In the version of ICF presented in this book, both the positive and negative aspects of a client's life are considered to be indissolubly connected. By
focusing on "problems," the terminology I have used may seem too negative
but, on the whole, clients do not seek therapy when they are content with
their lot. Problem resolution normally has two connotations—of overcom-
ing an obstacle and moving on to a better place. Therapy that resolves problems typically pays attention to a client's positive goals.

Some forms of therapy have shifted their sights beyond problems as a
client defines them, and on to general advice (or a philosophy of living) to
which a client can aspire. This may account for the assertion that Acceptance
and Commitment Therapy (ACT) "goes beyond CBT." It aims to develop
broad, flexible, behavioral repertoires rather than solutions to specific individual problems (Hayes et al., 2006). For example, ACT assumes that some
clients are too "fused" with certain of their own beliefs and values, and this
seems to be a formulation that makes an implicit claim about a better way
to live. Given that current beliefs and values reflect the frames of thinking of
an endless number of previous generations in their now lost contexts, a
formulation of this type is a kind of socio-historical explanation of typical

problems of the present generation. Discontent with current cultural values may explain the popularity of oriental philosophy and its meditational practices. In other words, it may be an antidote to the overly rational, intellectual, and self-oriented attitudes typical of Western thinking. The aim of some techniques within ACT, and also in mindfulness-based cognitive therapy (Segal, Williams, & Teasdale, 2002), dialectical behavior therapy (Koerner, 2007), and meta-cognitive therapy (Wells, 2008), is to achieve an attitude toward one's thoughts that diminishes their literal, believable, and rational character. Instead of "living in" one's thoughts and beliefs, they are accepted simply as thoughts and examined as interesting phenomena.

Any waning of the influence of psychiatric diagnosis within the field of psychotherapy and its replacement by promotion of positive philosophy is likely to have far-reaching consequences. The attribution of unhappiness or disease to internal disorders of the body has been with us at least since the time of the ancient Egyptians. From around 2000 BC, phenomena that have since come to be known as "hysteria" (derived from a Sanskrit word for stomach or belly) were thought to be due to wandering movements of the uterus. This style of thinking is unlikely to disappear soon because it probably serves the purpose of explaining, to ourselves and to others, one form of adjustment to life's difficulties. Consequently, case formulation goes to the heart of people's beliefs about threats to the "good life" and how to account for them. In this book's presentation of ICF, an attempt has been made to view it as a reflective process rather than the prescription of any definite type of solution. Nevertheless, it does advocate rationality rather than spirituality or a particular credo. It cannot be assumed that clients will necessarily like the formulations that their therapists produce, even when they are collaboratively constructed and perhaps could be judged as valid causal explanations. People are often more at ease with medical diagnoses than with psychosocial explanations when accounting for their distress (Leeming, Boyle, & Macdonald, 2009). A psychosocial explanation could be interpreted as implying that a client is weak, shameful, or antisocial. In addition, clients may be reluctant to blame others for their distress, especially when they happen to be close family members. A medical diagnosis can also be useful to explain troubling bodily experiences in the absence of a likely biomedical cause. It may simplify the process of accounting for oneself to others (e.g. "I was just suffering from depression at the time"). Therapists and their clients are both collaborators and adversaries. As Leeming et al. remark, "We need to be more active in placing more sophisticated explanations of psychological problems within the public domain."

Guidelines for Assessment and Constructing an Individual Case Formulation (ICF)

SECTION A. GATHERING INFORMATION FOR THE INITIAL FORMULATION

The phrase "initial formulation" carries the implication that formulating continues throughout therapy as new information is received and changes are made to hypotheses. A complete revision of the formulation is sometimes required.

The initial phase is usually completed within 1 and 4 hours. It ends when:

1. Agreement has been reached about the therapeutic approach to be taken, including its estimated length, and the frequency and timing of sessions. Depending on a client's level of knowledge, information is supplied about the nature of problems (e.g. post-traumatic stress) and techniques (e.g. re-living). This can be explained directly but it is usual to offer supplementary reading matter such as a leaflet or self-help book.

2. All of a client's background details have been documented and all potentially relevant problem areas have been explored (see below). This may be done by interview (structured or unstructured), life-history questionnaire, fantasy exploration, behavioral observation, diary recording, role-play, behavioral tests, and self-report psychometric scales.

3. The general aims and specific goals of therapy, in order of importance, have been provisionally agreed.

4. A provisional formulation of the main problems has been developed and there are sufficient grounds for deciding upon an initial intervention, the rationale of which has been explained.

5. There is agreement as to what will count as problem resolution in terms of a change in behavior (e.g. reduced frequency of worrying, increased levels of a specified activity, etc.). A means of charting change is agreed,

even if this is done only informally, such as meeting performance targets or a diary recording of relevant changes. An idiographic measure tailored to a certain problem might be devised (see below). Where baseline recording is desirable, this is implemented for an agreed period before intervening. Standardized assessments are carried out where these are required for normative comparisons, quality control, or legal purposes.

Variations in relation to the above

The interview strategy favored by the author involves the generation and testing of hypotheses (see Section B). This strategy is combined with the aim of obtaining an accurate description of behavior. Background information (e.g. living arrangements, employment) is normally discovered "in passing" and then supplemented by direct questions to fill in any gaps. Some therapists prefer more structured approaches. For instance, a questionnaire can be sent out in advance of the first appointment to gather background information, details of presenting problems, and a life history (e.g. see Appendix in Kuyken et al., 2009). A semi-structured format for the interview is sometimes preferred. Mumma (1998) has devised a structure that is designed to yield a cognitive conceptualization.

General considerations:

1. Assessment should be relevant to a client's problem, otherwise it is perceived as unnecessary and a waste of time. Very long questionnaires sent out in advance may be offputting if they ask for personal information that a client does not want to divulge (or considers irrelevant).

2. Assessment should not take an unreasonably long period of time. The initial phase is not expected to yield everything a therapist needs to know.

3. Assessment should aim to be comprehensive in the sense of not omitting anything of importance.

4. The information gathered should be useful in decision making, that is, it is not simply collected out of interest or to follow up a hypothesis that has no immediate significance.

5. The description of the problem and the circumstances surrounding it should be reliable in the sense that if the information were to be sought again using the same methods (or obtained by another person), it would not give a substantially different view of the facts.

6. The information obtained should be valid in the sense that it truly reflects or means what it purports to mean. This does not imply that there is only one true account of a client's life. Information is rarely

provided from an impartial point of view. Clients interpret themselves, other people, present and past events, from their own perspective. It is only to be expected that others will give a different account and that there will be inconsistencies in a client's account.

7. A great deal is often left ambiguous or unsaid in normal conversation. For this reason, a therapist may have to be persistent when rooting out the significance of what a client is attempting to communicate.

8. The assessment should aim to seek out information from multiple sources in different modalities (verbal questioning, behavioral observation, fantasy, self-report scales, etc.) because each has the potential to throw a somewhat different slant on a client's problem. It is advisable to cross-check information gained from different sources.

9. The employment of standardized measures has the advantage of enabling comparison of a client's scores with those of a well-defined sample of participants. For instance, it might be useful to know how a client's post-traumatic complaints compare with the scores of a population of war veterans. The reliability and validity of formal tests are carefully assessed before they are published and distributed for professional use. However, it is important to bear in mind that a client may not match the characteristics of a standardization sample, in which case comparison with published norms may not be appropriate.

General considerations in assessment by interview

The reliability and validity of informal interview assessments can always be questioned. In other words, it may not be possible to repeat them and reach the same conclusions. This weakness is offset by the strengths of face-to-face communication. In the first place, given that therapy will continue in this manner, an interview assessment is the means by which a trusting relationship is established. In the second place, an interview yields information in several modalities, verbal and non-verbal. Third, as a method of inquiry, it is highly flexible and responsive to questions that arise moment to moment. Inconsistencies can be resolved, omissions rectified, and information cross-checked with that obtained from other sources. A therapist needs to have mastered the skills of interviewing, especially in respect to asking open-ended rather than leading questions. An interviewer should be able to clarify and explore a client's meaning in a sensitive manner, and structure an interview so that it flows coherently.

However experienced an interviewer happens to be, the interview situation is one of information overload. It is necessary to attend to the content of what is said while at the same time the interviewer is bombarded with signals from a client's non-verbal behavior, as well the distraction of personal emotional reactions and thoughts. Not only is it necessary to respond without too much hesitation, but information also has to be remembered, organized and recorded. Ideally, an audio or video recording is made of an interview but this cannot always be done routinely. Moreover, reviewing these records is extremely time-consuming. A novice will probably become too distracted if he or she attempts to write everything down, although it is advisable to make written notes at the time or immediately afterwards. Note-taking while interviewing becomes easier with practice. The written notes might contain words or phrases that are recorded verbatim and intended as prompts for questions to be asked later on. The phrase can be repeated, just as it was spoken, in the same or a later session ("You said just now," "Last week you said," etc.). An interviewer cannot respond to everything that is said but must selectively attend to one thing at a time. As an aid to organizing and structuring an assessment session, an interviewer should have a mental or written list of the topics the interview is intended to cover.

Given that the situation is one of information overload and multitasking, a therapist is likely to resort to the thinking shortcuts that were discussed in Chapter 5, and should therefore be aware of them. Fortunately, an interview can be self-correcting if the interviewer is careful to review what can be inferred safely from the information obtained. In relation to overload, there is usually an opportunity to take more than one bite at the cherry. When doubt creeps in, a question can be repeated or a client assessed again. A picture is gradually built up over time, and inconsistencies or contradictions usually begin to stand out. A client can be asked to validate a particular inference that may have been drawn from the evidence. Inconsistencies can be clarified. For instance, a client may claim to be severely dyslexic but nevertheless supplies an email address for communication. It is necessary to inquire whether written messages are sufficiently well understood or whether a client calls upon others to help. Perhaps the strongest safeguards against inadequate assessment are the tendencies for clients to repeat themselves and to correct a therapist if they are getting things badly wrong. For this reason, a therapist should provide opportunities for a client to make corrections (e.g. "If I understand you correctly, you are saying that …" or "Have I left anything out?").

Information about a client is collected for different purposes at different times. I have therefore organized this chapter as follows: (1) Knowledge about a client prior to first interview. (2) Issues and tasks in the first assessment interview. (3) Ongoing assessment and monitoring of a problem during therapy. The style of interviewing that is driven by hypotheses is described in Section B where interview transcripts are given with accompanying commentary. The conventions for a case formulation diagram are introduced in Section C.

Knowledge of a client prior to the first interview

The information available prior to the first interview can vary from words exchanged in a brief telephone call to voluminous written reports. It is clearly important to read official records and to list issues that need to be checked out or investigated further. It is best not to make too many assumptions about a client at this point except to be sensitive to the small cues that can often be found within the wording of a report, such as what it has left out or any implied recommendation that is not actually stated explicitly.

The nature of a contract with a client might need to be clarified in advance, such as the limits of confidentiality. A therapist may be playing a role within a wider professional network, in which case mutual expectations and obligations may have to be spelled out to a client such as requirements in terms of future communication and reports. Contact numbers and addresses need to be recorded. It is important to know whether a client is receiving other forms of therapy (medical or psychological), and whether these are compatible with the approach on offer. This includes medication, and it is essential that a client's daily prescriptions are recorded (this information is usually obtained at the first interview). A therapist should also be aware of past or present use of illicit drugs and excessive consumption of alcohol. However, information of this nature may not emerge until a client feels trusting enough to reveal it.

Issues and tasks in the first assessment interview

The primary purpose of the first interview is to assess and formulate a problem(s). However, these are not the only tasks that need to be performed. In addition:

1. The therapist introduces her- or himself and explains the purpose and need for assessment. It is usual to request permission to make notes or record a session. Reassurance is given about the confidentiality of personal information and, if needed, the rare conditions in which it may be broken. A client is asked about setting limits on communication with, for instance, a partner, an employer, or a personal physician.

2. A therapist acts in such a way as to inspire a client's trust and confidence that what is on offer is acceptable and desirable.

3. It is established that a client has the kind of problem that a therapist feels competent to deal with and that she or he wants to work with a client.

4. A provisional agreement is reached on the goals of therapy and the therapist makes a best estimate as to how they might be tackled and in which order. Success and probable length of therapy is indicated. Reservations might be expressed if there are potential difficulties, and back-up arrangements might be put in place.

5. A therapist asks about knowledge of, or prior experience with, therapy. He or she shapes a client's expectations of the therapy on offer and may have to correct misconceptions or dissociate her- or himself from a client's previous experience of therapy. Therapy should be explained in terms that a client readily understands, depending on level of education and prior knowledge. As noted earlier, reading matter might be supplied (or this is left until later when a client is more likely to be receptive to it).

6. It is established that there are no medical, psychiatric, legal, housing, or other issues needing urgent attention.

Given that a relationship between therapist and client is just developing, there need be no fixed format for the structure of the first interview. An approach that is too formal might have the disadvantage of not allowing an inhibited client from opening up freely. On the other hand, a client who is too verbose may have to be reined in and directed to the task in hand.

A typical structure for the first interview is as follows (not necessarily in this order):

1. A brief account of the main problems, ensuring coverage rather than depth (5–10 minutes).

2. Elicitation of recent events that prompted seeking help.

3. A description and history of the main problems and associated life events.

4. Collection of key background information, such as marital status, living conditions, employment.

5. A brief medical and psychiatric history, noting medications, psychiatric admissions, and current or past episodes of depression. It may be necessary to judge whether a more detailed assessment of suicidal thinking is needed.

6. Assessment of response to previous psychological therapies (if relevant) and apparent motivation for present help. If a client seems to have reservations, the reasons should be sought and met. The first phase of therapy may consist of "motivational interviewing" (Miller & Rollnick, 2002).

It is rarely possible to complete all these tasks in one session. In a loosely structured style of interviewing, background and history data can be gathered incidentally, the therapist stopping briefly to clarify factual matters without disturbing the overall flow of the interview. Gaps can be filled in later and, in any case, most clients do not mind repeating information that they may have already supplied. While it is clearly necessary to give a client full attention, this has to be balanced by the time needed for writing things down.

Having completed these preliminary tasks, the therapist goes on to explore and define problems and goals in greater depth. Clients may know broadly what they want to achieve—such as expanding their social activities or feeling less anxious in the presence of others—but not know how to achieve it. The steps towards the main goal involve setting subgoals. This process is in turn dependent on an adequate formulation of the existing difficulties. In other words, problem definition, formulation, and goal-setting go hand-in-hand rather than representing clearly demarcated stages. In some cases, the problem and its potential solution are fairly obvious. However, when a client's problems are multifaceted, he or she may only be able to register a sense of being stuck, "empty," or beset by negative emotions. The first three tasks of the assessment process listed above are therefore more complex and continue for much longer.

In the course of exploring a problem, the following kind of information is likely to be collected:

1. The first instance, a typical instance, or the worst instance, of a problem.
2. Life events that may have preceded instances of a problem in the past.
3. Any pattern in the occurrence of a problem over the life span (e.g. a series of episodes of depressed mood).
4. Current cues that seem to be occasions for the expression of a problem. Events associated with fluctuations in the frequency or severity of a problem. Situations in which the problem does not arise when it might have been expected.
5. Possible cyclical effects (e.g. related to endogenous physiological factors).
6. Repeating themes in a client's life. Problems in work, relationships, family life, etc., that seem to recur.
7. An overall sense of the narrative of a client's life. What were his or her past aspirations, and were they fulfilled or unfulfilled? Where is the

client's life going now? Is the client at a choice point? What life events are upcoming (marriage, starting a family, change of job, retirement, etc.)? Questions tend to move from the general to the concrete but they also return to a more thematic level when patterns are identified. A client's recall of events is facilitated by requesting concrete details, which then lead on naturally to further questions, guided by hypotheses. It is necessary for both client and therapist to distinguish a description of the circumstances of a problem at the level of "reality" (i.e. what actually seems to have happened or be happening) from how those circumstances are interpreted by the client or others. For instance, why has an employer referred an employee for counseling? What is the "real" situation concerning the employee's performance at work, the employer's reason for making the referral, and the employee's wishes with respect to work? There may be a number of competing interpretations of "the facts of the situation" and their significance and role in relation to the purposes of therapy has to be ascertained. For most interviews, the best attitude to adopt in relation to the information obtained (rather than in relation to the client her- or himself) is tolerance of uncertainty and skepticism. It should not be assumed that a client's agreement with the way a therapist represents the facts of a situation signifies that his or her interpretations are valid.

Examples of questions to elicit the concrete details of a problem are as follows:

1. Tell me about a recent example of feeling distressed in this way.
2. What is the first thing you notice when this problem arises?
3. What's going through your mind when you experience … ?
4. Tell me about a typical day from the time you get up.
5. How does the problem affect you?
6. What will happen if this problem continues?
7. Does this problem prevent you from doing anything?
8. What has been the effect on your life since … ?
9. How would your life change if you were able to overcome this problem?

In addition to taking care when appraising information, a therapist should be alert to any limitation on a client's ability or motivation to give a reliable account. The following questions should be considered:

1. Does a client know what information is being requested? This might not be so if questioning does not follow a logical sequence or is confusing in other ways (e.g. if a question is badly worded or double barreled). A therapist should avoid being side-tracked by "interesting" information

that is essentially irrelevant. It is usually helpful to prime a client about the general nature of the information requested (e.g. Now, I would like to discuss X …). If a reply is insufficient or vague, a client should be asked to expand upon it until its meaning is clear. Unresolved ambiguity is likely to trip up a therapist later on in the interview.

2. Does a client understand the therapist's frame of reference? A client might start to talk about recent and emotionally significant events before the purpose of an interview has been established. A client's own frame of reference, such as a belief about the cause of a problem, might determine what he or she chooses to talk about. It helps to explain why information about a particular topic is important. Some investigative cognitive techniques, such as the "downward arrow," need to be explained to a client in order for the interviewing style to make sense. Otherwise, a client might feel that she or he is being interrogated.

3. Is a client being truthful, being economical with the truth, or simply lying? For many reasons, a client might not wish to divulge information.

4. Does a client have access to past events or are these so painful that memory of them has been suppressed?

5. Has a client been misinformed about the relevance of information provided in the past? A therapist might need to correct a client's understanding of, say, the significance of a medical disorder or their understanding of the nature of therapy.

6. Is a client ignorant of the significance of facts about him- or herself and therefore unlikely to mention them?

7. Is a client sufficiently articulate to provide useful information in an interview? A therapist might have to rely more on behavioral observation or other indirect methods.

8. Is a client wishing to make a certain impression and therefore distorting information accordingly? Perhaps a client wishes to exaggerate or minimize a problem. Is a client over-compliant and likely to agree too hastily with any suggestion the therapist makes?

Additional methods and sources of information
Non-verbal behavior during the interview

By non-verbal behavior is meant hesitancy, gestures, posture, manner of speech delivery, patterns of breathing, eye contact, and many more. In the second interview transcript presented in Section B, the client was fairly forthright and articulate. He held a strong view of his previous counseling. He did not seem to be nervous or hesitant. At times, he could reflect, analyze, and sum up the content of what he was saying. This feature of his speech delivery did not support his conception of himself as someone who was highly anxious and lacking in assertiveness. From this it might be concluded that his anxieties were rather specific and, as he explained, related to the opinions of others, especially those of his peers at work. The interviewer also noted his rather disjointed style and tendency to pile up one complaint on top of another, with no clear-cut theme to his concerns. This conversational style was interpreted as supporting a hypothesis about his interpersonal coping strategies.

Feelings in the therapist induced by a client

In the interview just mentioned, the therapist felt slightly out of control of the flow of information as if, in the assessment, he was trying to scoop up a globule of mercury. This led the interviewer to speculate whether others felt the same way when interacting with him. He began to wonder what sort of social role the client was (probably unwittingly) trying to place him in. Perhaps this was an interaction in which advice is sought and then undermined. Might this tactic relate to the client's childhood response to a mother, who, according to his description, appears to have been anxious, indulgent, and perhaps over-controlling. Was the client encouraged to communicate directly or did he use a confusion strategy as a method of counter-control? Does the client understand that others might find his style frustrating (if they do)? These were all hypotheses suggested by the interviewer's attention to the feelings induced in him.

Direct observation of behavior

Another important source of information comes from direct observation in situations in which a problem is expressed. These could be situations in a client's natural environment, in simulated situations, in fantasy, or in role-play. A client's behavior might also be observed with a partner or family member who is invited to take part in a joint interview.

A real-life situation is an opportunity to observe a client's spontaneous thoughts and feelings. This situation would be easy to set up for a client who has a fear of a small animal. In the case of an obsessional problem, a client could be visited at home where rituals and associated thoughts could be observed directly. It is also very instructive to witness intense feelings of anxiety at first hand, such as a panic attack. A therapist might suggest going to a situation in which a client is normally very anxious (e.g. shopping mall or bar). Although the presence of the therapist is likely to change a client's usual behavior, a client can always be instructed to carry out a task alone and return to report what happened. In the case of clients traumatized by road traffic accidents, it may be possible to return to the site of the accident in order to investigate triggers for flashbacks or to prompt memories of it. Stimuli that play a significant role in provoking a problem can often be created in an office situation (e.g. for a client who experiences panic attacks, giving instructions to over-breathe or spinning a client in an office chair to produce dizziness).

The purpose of observation is rather different when the problem itself consists of a behavior that needs to be regularly monitored as part of an intervention, such as the number of cigarettes smoked or documentation of prescribed tasks. In this case, a therapist has to pay more attention to operationalizing the way in which a behavior is described, is sampled, and is measured. The ongoing monitoring of a problem is a means of showing that a formulation has generated an intervention that is effective (or ineffective). The assessment and ongoing monitoring of behavior are too large topics to be covered here (see Barlow, Nock, & Hersen, 2008; Haynes & O'Brien, 2000).

Fantasy simulations

When clients recount their difficulties, they are often simulating a situation in their imagination. A therapist can push this process much further by prompting for concrete details of the situation. A therapist can ask: "What sort of room are you in?" "What time of day is it?" "Is anyone else present?" or might suggest a hypothetical scenario, as follows: "What would have happened if … ?" "Suppose that you had done/said X … ?" A client's involvement in a simulation, and consequently its vividness, can be increased by setting up, with his or her permission, a re-enactment in fantasy. It is important to explain why a simulation would be useful. The therapist asks the client to close her or his eyes, relax back in the chair, and speak in the first person, present tense. These instructions are given to enhance the vividness of the simulation. (A client might refuse to close his or her eyes, which is an observation of interest in its own right.)

Brief instructions can be given to set the scene, allowing it to unfold with no more than a little prompting. Alternatively, a therapist can ask questions during the fantasy re-enactment to evoke specific information. A client might be asked to respond to changes in the situation as suggested by the therapist. A simulation can be very short (a minute or two) or much longer. It should be followed up, when the client opens his or her eyes, with a request for immediate reflections, asking "How did that feel?" "What did you notice about yourself?" Debriefing is essential, not only to reassure a client, but also to allow time for an extended discussion of a client's reflections. Debriefing is likely to take much longer than the fantasy enactment.

Fantasy simulation sometimes produces a spontaneous and less censored expression of a difficulty than direct questioning. The following illustration is a simulation of a childhood memory that always brought tears to the client's eyes, although she could not really say why. The memory concerned her as a young child discovering a nest containing a fledging bird, picking up the bird, and dropping it. The client is asked to imagine the situation and speak to the bird:

> T. What are you saying to it?
>
> I want to say sorry.
>
> T. What is the bird saying?
>
> There's nothing it could say! Not, it's all right, you shouldn't have done that. (Said with strong emotion).

In the debriefing following this extremely short scene, the client expressed the opinion that what had happened had been total abuse and that the bird was entitled to be unforgiving. The therapist asked if her feelings during the image reminded her of any other feelings in her childhood. The client immediately identified with the bird and saw a parallel with her relationship with her own mother.

It is possible that the significance of her relationship with her mother as a child would have been revealed during assessment but the simulation was a rapid (and emotionally convincing) demonstration that this aspect of her history was a key to some of her, seemingly unrelated, presenting problems.

The following example is taken from an investigation, through a fantasy retelling in the first person present tense, of events during a road traffic accident in which the client was traumatized.

> Sandra (wife) is shouting. She gets out of the car and shouts at the guys in the van. It is a blue van. Cara (daughter) is saying my neck is sore, my head hurts. She was thrown forward onto the back of the seat in front. Sandra is telling them "we have kids in the car"—she is angry as well as upset. … I stay very quiet in the car—just sitting there for five minutes. … The van driver just says: "I was talking to my friend." He does not try to cover up. The van driver is apologetic. I didn't get angry. I said everyone's OK. Nobody has been seriously hurt.

In the debriefing, the client revealed disappointment with his own response—staying silent and smoothing out the situation with the offending driver who was clearly at fault. He could not understand his silence. He was shocked that his wife was the angry one, in some way taking charge of the situation. This amounted to a role reversal in their marriage in which he normally took the initiative and his wife was the quiet one. As in the example above, the re-enactment of a scene (plus reflection upon it) allowed the therapist to assess very rapidly an aspect of a client's response to the accident that may not have emerged at all if assessment had been limited to direct questioning.

Role-play simulations

Role-play is especially useful for problems that relate to social interaction, whether past or present. Having established certain key features of a social scenario, such as the key players, a therapist may take on the role of one of the protagonists. The initial role-play may have to be tried out repeatedly until the therapist, with a client's guidance, strikes the right manner and can simulate another person sufficiently well for the role-play to be realistic. In fact, the client might act out typical statements and mannerism of the person concerned so that a therapist can imitate them. Playing this role, a therapist can increase or decrease the provocative nature of the difficulty and/or allow a client to experiment with different ways of handling a situation.

As with a fantasy simulation, time must be allowed for a subsequent review and analysis when out of role. The analysis might reveal why a client feels blocked and unable to act differently, perhaps through lack of skill or fear of the consequences. The role-play can be varied and repeated in the light of critical cues revealed in the discussion.

Role-play can be used to explore historical situations. One client who had problems managing his anger reported that he sometimes walked down the street "looking up at the sky at his dead father," shaking his fist and shouting abuse at him. The client had been badly treated by his father and, in order to explore his thoughts and feelings about this, the therapist elicited the kinds of things his father would say to him as a child. The therapist then simulated the father's comments and requested that he respond to them in any way he wished. By this means, underlying beliefs, resentments, and helplessness as a child were revealed.

Consensual opinions

It is helpful to have a second observer record his or her impressions when information is gathered by informal means, such as by interview or role-play. This person could be in the room or observing from behind a one-way screen. When evaluating information obtained in this way, several heads are often better than one. However, it is often simpler, with a client's consent, to audio or video record an assessment so that it can be reviewed later or brought to supervision. Another method is to require that trainee therapists carry out their interviews in pairs, in which one takes the interviewer role and the other contributes by invitation. The "observer" can act as a note-taker, leaving the interviewer to focus on establishing rapport and asking questions. The two trainees can then learn a great deal from a post-interview discussion between themselves, and when a problem is brought for supervision, the supervisor has two perspectives to compare. A supervisor could, of course, sit in on a session but this may feel threatening to a novice, and a client might be somewhat confused by the presence of another person who seems to be of higher status. This method is also very time-consuming.

Corroborating evidence for an observation or hypothesis can also be sought from someone who knows the client well, such as a family member, a teacher, or a general physician.

A client's written description of a problem

Creative self-expression can take many forms, including a poem or artwork. However, it is often sufficient to ask clients to write about key events in their life as a story. Another valuable source of information is a time-line in the form of a list of dates and associated events. If a client's problem concerns making plans, a list of possible courses of action could be requested. If an important decision has to be made, a client could be asked to write down arguments for and against the alternatives.

A client might not want to reveal everything that has been written down if there is some shame or embarrassment attaching to the events in question. An account of a rape was handed to the author on a piece of paper that had been folded down to minute proportions. He was instructed to read it in private. However, it later freed up the client to talk more openly about what had happened. In another client, a "free expression" diary revealed self-cutting that she said she had given up many years earlier.

Questionnaires

Once it is clear what areas need to be assessed, a questionnaire that covers the area is often a rapid means of surveying it. The purpose is not so much to obtain a score that indicates severity (although that could be valuable as well) but to explore checked items in greater depth by direct questioning. Questionnaires are readily available to cover signs of depression, fears, worry, post-traumatic stress, obsessions and compulsions, and fluctuations in mood. Progress in therapy can be assessed by changes observed in scores on a standardized questionnaire. The score might be interpreted in relation to norms that indicate the range of normal and high scores. A score can also be meaningful when compared with an earlier score. A so-called "pathological" score might represent an improvement from an even higher score obtained earlier. Questionnaires can be extremely economical in terms of time, and help to ensure that an assessment is comprehensive (i.e. they are used as a checklist, and checked items are followed up in an interview). There are self-report measures covering almost all areas of potential relevance to assessment (see Hersen, 2004).

Physiological measures

These measures are normally obtained from outside sources unless a therapist is equipped to make them. They are more typical of research studies because they require technical skill and specialized knowledge. For clients with health anxieties, the results of physiological and medico-diagnostic tests might have to be obtained from records or by request. However, when a client holds a faulty belief about an aspect of bodily functioning that can be assessed easily (e.g. pulse rate) there may be good reasons to include a physiological measure in the assessment.

Ongoing assessment and self-monitoring of a problem during therapy

Both client and therapist need to know whether progress is being made in dealing with a problem. Sometimes there are obvious and concrete milestones to indicate progress. For example, if a client, for the first time, has attended an evening class, is managing to sleep normally, has stopped taking antidepressant medication, has given a public speech, or has had successful interpersonal encounters, it is obvious that significant progress has been made. Verbal feedback from a client is often sufficient to verify this. When progress is slow and occurs by small increments, a daily or weekly record is valuable in providing reassurance that an intervention is working and that there is no need to reformulate. Clients sometimes rapidly forget what progress has been made. A record is therefore a reminder and a spur to motivation. Examples of slow change are a decrease in obsessional checking, an alteration in mood, or a change in the frequency of certain thoughts. Identical measurements should not be repeated too often because, if boredom or fatigue sets in, a client may begin to respond in a stereotypical way or no longer take the measure seriously.

Problems can be investigated by asking a client to complete a daily or weekly diary in a standard format. Diaries form an integral part of cognitive therapy techniques and the information they reveal not only helps to specify what the problem is but can also be used to prompt a client to adopt a more realistic interpretation of events or employ better coping techniques.

Some procedural considerations in self-monitoring

Self-monitoring may be undertaken chiefly as a source of information for the case formulation rather than as a measure of progress. One purpose in requesting completion of a diary is to provide feedback about a hypothesis. The reasons for self-monitoring should be explained carefully because, for many people, keeping a diary is an onerous task. There could be a problem of where to keep a diary so that it remains private. Some clients find it easier to keep a record on a computer, the results of which can be emailed to the therapist.

Given that keeping a diary can feel like a burden, it is often best to shape up successive approximations to the kind of diary that would provide optimal information. When the entries are discussed, it may become obvious to a client that certain refinements, though adding complexity, are necessary and worthwhile. Ideally, examples of "successes" as well as behaviors or distress that count as examples of a problem should be recorded. To begin with, therefore, a client might simply be asked to note down brief details of significant events. The sort of events that occur, and similarities across events, gradually become more apparent. At this point, the familiar ABC columnar structure of the diary can be introduced to separate events that elicit a problem (its Antecedents, A) from the Behavior/thoughts/feelings (B) that are provoked. The C column refers to the Consequences, either immediate or medium short-term, in other words, to what happens subsequently (the consequences, C). These are events/responses of positive or negative significance to the client. Information about positive consequences, such as examples of successful coping, should be requested as well as instances that represent persistence of a problem or failure to cope.

Therapist and client are often looking for common themes in events, and a diary is a good method for raising awareness. When a pattern becomes obvious, it can be helpful to label it with a name of the client's choosing.

Gradually a common language for talking about problems emerges that facilitates the formulation process.

Self-monitoring of a problem should be geared towards measures that have strong face validity for a client. A standard measure might not be available, in which case a scale can be devised that is tailored to a client's unique problem. The items that are monitored should not be based on subjective impressions or defined vaguely. It is usually not too difficult to define a behavior in clear operational terms. In the case of self-reported experiences, the set of points on a scale should indicate clearly to a client exactly what is meant. The following scale, based on a client's own words, illustrates the daily measurement of mood as he cycled between different states. It was not clear how his mood related to daily events and so the client also recorded significant happenings in his daily life. He was happily married and satisfied with his work, and so there were no obviously critical triggers, except a few daily hassles, to record. The aim of self-monitoring was to reveal patterns in coping and to raise awareness of the onset of a change of mood.

Individually tailored mood rating, 0–4, definitions negotiated with the client:

0   = Fitting too much into the time available, switching from thing to thing, no time to relax or reflect
1   Intermediate point
2   = Mid-point. Not too stressed. Fairly positive. Normal socializing.
3   Intermediate point
4   = No motivation to start or continue things. Being a difficult person to associate with.

Column headings for the daily record:

Day of the week	Situation/ event that brought about a change in your mood	What did you do, feel, or think that indicated to you that you felt better or worse?	What happened afterwards? (immediately or a bit later, i.e. how you coped, what your thoughts were, etc.)	What could have been done better? (how could the situation have been improved, avoided, etc.)	Overall mood for the day (0–4)

This survey of modes of assessment is not intended as a prescribed set of requirements. Tools may be selected to fit the needs for feedback about a hypothesis that a therapist wants to test. This should become apparent in later sections.

SECTION B. HYPOTHESIS-DRIVEN INTERVIEWING

This section explains a style of interviewing that focuses on specific lines of inquiry, motivated by the testing of hypotheses. The term hypothesis is not used in the sense of a single explanation that is arrived at after several sessions of assessment. This is a "macro" concept of a hypothesis, which is often a summary opinion that identifies a key concept, sometimes called a lynch-pin that ties everything together. The aim of formulation is, of course, to produce a causal conceptual model that accommodates as many facts as possible, but in this section, the term hypothesis is used in a "micro" sense. A hypothesis (Ho) refers to any kind of theoretical interpretation placed on the facts, whether this is no more than a hunch or speculation. However, it should be connected with observations that have been made, and can continue to be made, in order to test whether the hypothesis has any validity. Typically, there are a number of competing hypotheses to explain the same observations. The general aim is to entertain several hypotheses at the same time until one or more of them is well-supported. An investigation of a problem therefore continues until it has produced a result, even if it turns out to be a dead end. At this point, new information may be sought or the inquiry proceeds down a different route.

This style of assessment interviewing is therefore in strong contrast to one that amasses a pile of facts and leaves it until later to analyze their significance. The style is illustrated below with annotated transcripts of actual interviews, and also in Section D.

It was Joseph Wolpe, a leading figure in the development of cognitive behavioral therapy (CBT), who illustrated how an interview guided by hypotheses could be carried out (e.g. Wolpe & Turkat, 1985). Wolpe and Turkat gave the example (1985, p. 13) of someone who reported a "fear of passing out," after which Wolpe, the interviewer, formed the hypothesis that this was a variant of a fear of losing control. This would have led naturally to questions about situations that fell under this general category but Wolpe chose the route of asking about any prior experience of passing out (of which there were none) and then asked if the client could remember how the fear began. This elicited a description of an incident of being dizzy during a church service at the age of 17. Due to the client reporting inner ear problems at the time, Wolpe kept in reserve a hypothesis about a fear of passing out being related to dizziness or imbalance. Further questions about current episodes of the fear were directed towards finding evidence for this hypothesis or generating alternatives. The client was then asked about precise stimulus antecedents for passing out, methodically narrowing them down to ones that were critical. The client was asked for a precise description of how "passing out" would happen (if it did). This prompted a vivid memory of an "out-of-control" experience at the age of five when the client was in hospital by herself and about to be given an anesthetic before surgery. This example illustrates the way several hypotheses are entertained at the same time and the interview is driven forward by a client's answers to questions.

General features of the hypothesis-testing interview

In general, there are no wasted questions in this style of interviewing. Each question has a purpose and evidence is gathered until it eventually favors some hypotheses over others.

Open and closed questions

There is a mix of open and closed questions as hypotheses are tested. Occasionally, a question can be completely open-ended, "How can I be of help?" or "What's your problem?" When working on a specific line of inquiry, this should not be so obvious to a client that questions are answered as expected or a client attempts to provide counter-examples. In other words, questions should retain their open-ended quality. A question may be attempting to answer a specific hypothesis but it should not make assumptions about expected answers (e.g. "Tell me about your typical diet" rather than "How often do you eat fruit and vegetables?"). Closed questions are used to obtain factual information (e.g. "How old are you?" "Do you live alone or with others?") or when a previous response is unclear in its meaning (e.g. "Do you mean X or Y?").

Hypothesis testing

Although there is an attempt to follow up on one line of inquiry at a time, it is more typical to keep several lines open simultaneously. Moreover, a client often drops in a new "lead," thereby opening up new areas to explore. While this lead is still "hot," the interviewer might allow a brief diversion to explore it, perhaps saying to a client that he or she wishes to come back to the topic later on. This serves the purpose of acknowledging that the remark is significant and has not been ignored.

A therapist persists when a client has difficulty describing something, and may offer a choice of examples with which to compare the experience, based on predictions from current hypotheses. A therapist also notes any discrepancies in the account provided, bearing in mind differing implications for the hypotheses that she or he is entertaining. A therapist might frankly admit to not knowing how to make sense of a discrepancy and asks a client to explain it.

A hypothesis is only abandoned when disconfirming evidence builds up to a critical point. When a therapist is reasonably sure that a hypothesis is being confirmed, it may be presented as an interpretation and the client is invited to respond. Alternatively, a different tactic at this stage is to test out a prediction by asking, say, "How do you feel in situation X, or with person Y?" having in mind a certain answer if a hypothesis is true (or false). It should be clear that the style of interaction is collaborative. It is inevitable that a client's own understanding of a problem begins to be shaped up by the interview itself. This greatly facilitates the introduction of an intervention based upon a formulation derived from the assessment.

The interviewing style is now illustrated with transcripts based on two assessment interviews. The personal circumstances of each client have been heavily altered and anonymized. The interviewer's hypotheses and general strategy are explained. The aim is to illustrate the hypothesis-testing style of investigation, not to demonstrate how successful it was in the case of these clients (which it was not). As these are first interviews, no attempt is made to draw out a formulation diagram. This is done for a different client in Section D, using the conventions outlined in Section C.

In the following transcripts, the text in *italics* describes the therapist's reasoning process in terms of the hypothesis being tested and the strategy being followed. Neither interview provided sufficient information to reach a satisfactory formulation, but this is not unusual after one session of assessment.

Assessment interview: Client one

The client (P) is a married woman in her early 30s. She reports on the telephone a worry that her son might be autistic. She cannot get this idea out of her mind and she says that anxiety is disrupting her life.

The brief details of the problem obtained over the telephone may not represent the full extent of her concerns, and so T asks an open-ended question as an invitation for her to elaborate.

T: You gave me some idea about the difficulty you are having but where do you want to start today?

P: Well, I'm not sure.

For whatever reason, P does not want to elaborate and so T asks a closed question.

T: How long has this anxiety been bothering you?

P: For around six months.

Again, P answers the question without elaborating. T makes a comment to elicit a response.

T: Right, so not for so very long.

P: Well, it doesn't seem like that to me.

P seems to want to impress on T the severity of the problem. T acknowledges the response and decides to obtain background details.

T: Right, so to you it seems like a long time. How old is your son?

P: Three years.

T: And what is his name?

P: Gerald.

T asks for his name to personalize the discussion (and wants to know how to refer to her son). T tries another open-ended question.

T: And have you had any problems like this before?

P: Well, I have been prone to depression, but since he was born it's been a very happy time. Since the age of five I have always wanted a baby to look after, not necessarily my own, even an adopted one. I had lots of siblings and I have always done a lot of baby–sitting. I have always been crazy about babies. After he was born I was thrilled. I have always thought about having a child and how I would bring the child up. Over the years I have thought about strategies for child-rearing—maybe because my parents divorced.

P has revealed many facts about herself in this one answer: that she has many siblings, that she is prone to depression but not currently depressed, that her desire to care for a baby began at a very young age, that she thinks deeply about how best to raise a child, and that she thinks that the latter stems from her own parents' divorce. Her response, in sharp contrast to earlier responses, illustrates the problem for an interviewer of information overload. There are many more background details for T to discover (e.g. is this her first child, at what age was she when her parents divorced, etc.) but T's opening strategy is to test the hypothesis that her high expectations regarding Gerald's child-rearing have not been fulfilled (Ho1). This might account for her worry that he might be autistic.

T: And how has it turned out with Gerald?

P: OK. It's amazing. He doesn't have tantrums, he's advanced for his age. Everything was perfect.

This is not quite the expected answer and so T says nothing, noting the past tense "was," waiting for P to elaborate.

P: Then suddenly I got this suggestion that he was not so amazing. That he is advanced in being focused on things, like his airplanes, because he has Asperger's. That he's focused because he is withdrawn. He loves music, and I think, maybe, that's because he has Asperger's.

T has no reason to question P's beliefs about her son's development but entertains two hypotheses—that the concern relates to Ho1 (excessively high expectations) or that there is something abnormal about Gerald's development (Ho2). P had earlier mentioned autism in a telephone conversation but now she is referring to Asperger's [syndrome]. The features of Asperger's have been understood to lie on a continuum with autism but at the mild end, signifying a variant in personality rather than any language problems or cognitive difficulties. T wants to know where the sudden suggestion came from, as this might help to differentiate Ho1 and Ho2.

T: What happened to trigger this off?

P: I had an unsuccessful weekend with a friend. She has a child about the same age as mine. She can be a bit impersonal and put her foot in it. She was supposed to bring toys for her children but she didn't. So Gerald was there with his airplanes, which he loves, and he hates it if others mess them up. He wants to be in charge and gets irritable if others interfere. But he does love it if others join in and help. It was stressful, and my friend suggested that she had noticed a few things—signs of Asperger's—that I didn't need to do anything about it but she recommended a book to read. I was worried because I have a relative with a child who has autism. I got angry and asked why she had said that. I was devastated. I asked her if I should get an assessment. Now she says she doesn't think he has autism.

P reveals her close attention to Gerald's development and seems to weigh up evidence that he is both over-involved with his airplanes but also likes others to join in with him. She is aware of characteristics of children with Asperger's syndrome (which she equates with autism) and it is not clear whether this possibility had occurred to her prior to the weekend. P's high expectations (Ho1) are supported by her strong emotional response to the friend's remarks. Ho1 needs to be narrowed down in a number of ways: Is P's anxiety a general concern about any kind of mental or physical health problem affecting Gerald (Ho3) or is it an isolated new worry about Asperger's (Ho4)? The possibility that Gerald actually shows features of Asperger's (Ho2) still remains, or he might simply have some distinctive behavioral characteristics that would not raise any concerns in a child specialist. T is curious as to why P has taken her friend's remarks so seriously. As the friend has changed her mind, the question is phrased to follow on from P's last remark.

T: So did she say why she doesn't think he has Asperger's?

P: No—but she said she is sure, but just not to take her word for it.

P clearly takes her friend's opinion very seriously, but the friend's denial of any problem is equivocal. P may be offering a selective account of what the friend said and so it may not be an accurate memory. T asks what P did next in order to explore the seriousness of her concerns and to empathize with her story as it unfolds.

T: So what did you do?

P: I researched it on the internet and there are some similarities with children who have Asperger's. There is a list and I compared him on each one. I checked them off. Asperger's are like gifted children so perhaps he is just gifted, that's another possibility. He's not literal, in fact he's good at imaginative play. He's very reciprocal emotionally.

> *P's anxiety is beginning to sound as though it is an exaggerated specific concern (Ho4); she has been able to think rationally about it, weighing up the evidence that he does not match the features of a child with Asperger's syndrome. T decides to obtain more information about Gerald's age and general development in order to choose between Ho1 and Ho2.*

> *T: You said he was three—and how many months?*

P: He's just turned three. He started nursery three months ago.

> *T: How is he doing in the nursery?*

P: They don't really give any feedback. They like the children to be focused and calm. They don't really encourage the children to socialize. If they become disruptive, the teacher steers the children apart. I want him to socialize more and I told them so. They told me he is quite normal in his emotional development as far as they are concerned. They said they would get in touch if they saw a problem. In the email they wrote, they said it wasn't necessary yet and it was that "yet" that got to me. It seemed like they were confirming there was a problem. From their point of view he has settled well.

> *P's concern that the nursery should be socializing Gerald more adds support to Ho1 that P has very high expectations regarding his development. P has really received no evidence that Gerald is behaving abnormally in his nursery. The extent of her concern is indicated by her interpretation of an ambiguous use of the word "yet." T decides to explore the extent that P has sought further evidence, a sign that P is distressed by an exaggerated specific worry (Ho4).*

> *T: Have you done anything to check out your concerns?*

P: Well, there are some online tests for autism but he passed all those. I know that theory-of-mind is delayed in Asperger's and I read a book that said difficulty with theory-of-mind is universal in autism. But Gerald is actually advanced in that area. But I still can't relax about it! It's destroying my life. I can't even see my friend any more. I'm too angry and upset with her. She realizes that and even wrote me a letter saying why she didn't think he had autism. I felt better temporarily.

> *P's attention to Gerald's 'theory-of-mind' at the age of three (or less) supports Ho1. P has followed up all possible lines of inquiry but not yet, it seems, sought the opinion of an expert. Her concern that Gerald is abnormal seems to be exaggerated, and to some extent she seems to accept this. Nevertheless, she is still unsure about his*

normality. T seeks to confirm the hypothesis that the worry is excessive by asking about the opinion of other important people in her life.

T: And what about your husband, what does he think?

P: He knows that our son is different from other children but he loves him. He says we are very lucky to have a child like him. He doesn't think about it—he couldn't care less anyway. He says it's irrelevant and says I have been going on about it too much. So I have stopped talking to him about it.

Even though P has clearly sought reassurance from her husband, and gets it, she still seems to interpret his remark that Gerald is "different" in a negative light. It is not clear whether her husband actually used the word "different" or, if he did, what he meant by it. T would still like to be more sure that Ho2 (that Gerald is not normal in his development) is not supported.

T: What is it exactly that sets you off worrying about him?

P: When we can see him doing something differently from other children. I can feel myself tensing up inside right now. I can look at it in one way or another—it's silly or it's a real problem. He has this total obsession with airplanes. Well, not exclusively. He will pester me sometimes for attention when he is playing with airplanes. Sometimes, he wants to be shown other things instead, but he notices airplanes everywhere, say, when we are passing a shop window. Also he's not good at recognizing people—that's a sign of Asperger's. At a birthday party recently, I pointed out a child he knows well, but he couldn't pick her out by name. Not recognizing people is one of the symptoms of autism. I thought maybe his eyesight is poor and I got his eyes tested.

P seems to go to great lengths to check Gerald's normality, presumably to seek reassurance, and this adds support to Ho1 and Ho3. Although Gerald may be an unusual child, it seems unlikely that he is abnormal in any way. T explores other worries in order to be sure of this and to make a comprehensive assessment.

T: Is there anything else that worries you?

P: I'm not sure about his coordination. He spoke early, he's advanced. He can signal and gesture. But when he runs, he does it in a weird way. He always pointed well. His balance is good. There's nothing strange except the way he runs.

T: And you said he is advanced in his language development?

P: Well, pronoun reversal. I know that's a symptom of autism. He did that but I thought originally that was normal. I pointed it out to him when it happened and he got it right eventually. Sometimes, he still uses names instead of pronouns.

P is clearly very highly sensitive to Gerald's developmental milestones and is very well informed. T now regards Ho2 as very unlikely to be true and goes on to explore the extent to which P's anxiety is an isolated one (i.e. focused only on her son, on this particular developmental issue), or whether P's concerns about health are of a more general nature and concern other people or herself as well.

T: I can see you have a lot of worries so I have to ask you whether you have always had a tendency to worry about other things as well?

P: I was OK as a child. But as an adult I do worry. For instance, if one of my parents has to go to the doctor with something odd, I can hardly exist until I've got the results. I feel sure they are going to die. But my gut feelings are not trustworthy.

What P says is strong evidence for generalized concerns about others' health (Ho3). T continues to investigate them.

T: Do you worry over a long period?

P: With my father, we knew there was something not quite right for a long time. One day I realized that he really was ill. So my worry was proved right.

T: How old is your father?

P: 80 years.

T: Do you mean that your worry was proved right in this case and so that makes it more likely that your other worries will be confirmed?

This is a closed question designed to clarify the meaning of P's statement that she had been proved right. (The ambiguity could have been approached differently with an open-ended question, asking what it meant to her to be proved right.)

P: I thought my Dad had cancer and, in fact, the tests proved negative, so I was wrong about that. My mother had influenza, which worried me a lot, but she was fine.

P accepts that her worries are sometimes unfounded.

T: Are there any other worries that you have had as an adult?

P: There are times when I have been jealous. I pester people and drive them mental. This problem reminds me of that.

P's reply suggests to T that she cannot live easily with uncertainty (i.e. with respect to the possibility of any potentially negative event (Ho5)). T poses this as a hypothesis to P, knowing that she is quite capable of reflecting on the meaning of her own behavior.

T: So for you, certainty is very important?

P: Yes, I want to disprove something completely and finally. It's not safe to let go and think it's OK.

T takes this as support for Ho5. T needs to inquire later about the risks of "letting go." T decides to gently challenge P's belief in Gerald's abnormal development by suggesting that it is an example of her need for certainty. In this way, T is testing whether P is ready for a therapeutic intervention in which she deals with her problem as concerning something that is not based on a realistic assessment of probabilities. The question is phrased as an exploration of Ho5. It is possible that P would reject this hypothesis and stick to a firm belief that Gerald's development is abnormal.

T: So even if you went to an expert on autism and were reassured, that wouldn't help?

P: No, because he might have got it wrong and missed something. I would like to think of this as a phobia. I once had a friend with a fear of heights and I helped her with that in a gradual way. I'd like to use the same method with this but I don't know how. I did get hold of a book on cognitive therapy and followed the method. I wrote down my automatic thoughts and I challenged them, and wrote down how much I believed in them afterwards. But I had so many automatic thoughts, it would only help temporarily. The thoughts come back so fast.

P is one step ahead of T and has clearly considered the possibility that her thinking on the matter is irrational. However, she has not been able to use cognitive techniques to her own advantage. T explores further whether P is open to changing her beliefs.

T: So the question is really whether this worry about Gerald being Asperger's is like a phobia or whether you really believe it to be true?

P: I am genuinely convinced by the rational scenario but then I can't stop getting anxious about it.

P seems to be ready for tackling her problem as a "phobia" or irrational worry and so T begins the process of explaining the rationale for a way forward and ascertaining P's motivation and goals. T also begins to explore the meaning to her of Gerald developing abnormally, as she may be harboring a "disaster scenario" that is the source of her anxiety.

T: It seems to me that you are worrying about something bad that could happen in the future and it makes you very distressed anticipating this possibility, even though, as you say, you think it is unrealistic. The anticipation seems almost worse than the thing itself. You would like to have certainty, but the feeling that goes with uncertainty is unbearable. This is rather like someone who worries about germs and tries to make sure that their worries about, say, getting ill don't come true by washing their hands many times instead of just once. They are uncertain about getting ill and think that washing once might not be enough. Let me ask you, what would be the implications for you if your son was not developing normally?

P: There are different things—about having my child admired, about him being lovable, about being lucky with my child.

T notes that these concerns all refer to P rather than to any particular implications regarding Gerald's future development.

T: How would you put these in order of importance?

P: Well, first, that others didn't find him lovable or I did not find him lovable. I think, second, about admiration, I guess I want my child to be admired. And then, third, I always felt I was very lucky with my child—that would have to change.

P is very clear about the consequences, and these seem to provide evidence for Ho1, that she has always held very high expectations about how her children should turn out. This suggests that the origins of the problem are not simply anxiety about the health or normality of her child (and the consequences for him), but how his behavior (if he really were showing features of Asperger's syndrome) would affect her feelings for him (and others' views of him). This aspect of her problem will need to be explored in another interview, as it raises some completely new questions about P's concept of herself as someone needing this kind of confirmation from others.

T: If I understand what you said earlier, you do find him lovable now and have a close and warm relationship with Gerald.

P: I think I just worry about having weird children, and that I am not properly relating to them. But yes, I have a very close loving relationship with Gerald. I'm very responsive to his needs. Sometimes, I wonder if I reward him too much.

P's reply confirms that the assessment should be broadened out to include her expectations about the kind of child she wishes to raise, to her investment in them, and how her expectations relate to her self-image. There followed a discussion about the theme of her anxieties and some strategies for reducing their current intensity were outlined.

Reflections on the assessment

T was not completely confident that P accepted the message he was giving and P did not request a further appointment. It is possible that P was simply seeking a professional opinion (her first) and expected to be told that her worry about Asperger's had no basis. Had T done so, it is very unlikely that this reassurance would have had a lasting effect, given that a persistent search for certainty is one of the features of her anxiety problem. A second interpretation is that P wanted to deal with this problem by herself, as she had attempted to do in the past. The impression received of P's personality was that she greatly valued her independence of mind and preferred to rely on her own resources. For instance, she no longer expressed her worries to her husband because he had apparently dismissed them. Given P's quest for certainty and her independence of thought, T's opinion might not have counted for very much in her eyes.

The source of P's anxiety is not easy to discern. It did not seem to relate to her own health—at least, she did not mention any personal health worries when asked about other worries. Her anxiety seemed to be primarily about the health of others, and also about the normality of her child. The effect of her child being abnormal or "weird" seemed to be mainly of concern because this would have consequences for her own ability to love him as much as she would like. In fact, she admitted that she might be currently "rewarding" her son too much and therefore, presumably, she did not want to undermine any grounds for doing so. This might link to her own theory, briefly mentioned at the beginning of the interview, that her problems are related to the divorce of her own parents in her childhood. This points to the need for a broader conceptualization of the sources of her anxiety. At the same time, P seemed ready to acknowledge a general trait in her personality that relates to an intolerance of uncertainty, and this seems to be an additional contributing factor.

The last few minutes of the interview suggest that future assessment should focus on her ideas about child-rearing, its importance to her, how it relates to her childhood experiences, and the importance of producing a child that everyone can admire in maintaining her own view of herself. This is not to imply that there is just one correct formulation for P or that the way she copes with her specific anxiety about Gerald's development should not be an important goal for therapy. It seems likely that P has intersecting problems relating to health anxiety, insecurity about her image of herself, and personality traits that predispose her to generalized anxiety and worry. Furthermore, there was insufficient time to explore the possibility that P is subject to other life stresses that might be contributing to her current anxiety.

Hypotheses—State of conformation at the end of interview

Ho1. P has high expectations that her child-rearing practices will produce a lovable/admirable child. [Substantially confirmed, although precisely what her expectations are has yet to be determined.]

Ho2. Gerald actually expresses features of Asperger's syndrome. [Very little evidence to support this hypothesis.]

Ho3. P has general concerns about Gerald's mental and physical well-being. [Partially supported, but re-evaluated in light of Ho6.]

Ho4. P has an isolated worry and fear that Gerald is expressing features of Asperger's syndrome. [Although this is the main anxiety, it seems that P has other concerns about Gerald's developmental milestones and may be concerned about this for different reasons.]

Ho5. P has a generalized expectation of negative events and an intolerance of her own distress when in a state of uncertainty about them, motivating a search for certainty. [Strong suggestion of support but needing further confirmation. P may not worry about all types of negative outcome.]

Ho6. Having a normal child that can be admired and loved (and continues to meet her present expectations and concept of herself) is very important for P's happiness. [Hypothesis strongly suggested but needs to be explored further.]

Assessment interview: Client two

The results of an assessment interview with a second client were also tentative. As in the first case, a large number of hypotheses were generated and they did not point strongly to a unifying formulation. The therapist found it difficult to steer the interview and follow a consistent line of inquiry. The transcript illustrates the beginnings of a process that would have to be continued in later sessions. In fact, this client chose to take up an offer of a free service and so no further information was obtained subsequently.

J is a male in his 30s and he works in a residential facility for adolescents with behavioral problems. He complains of being in an emotionally distressed state and not coping well at work.

J: I saw a therapist a few months ago but it was "just talking" and it was a lot about my past, my parents. I want to deal more with my immediate problems.

J may have seen a therapist with a psychodynamic or non-directive orientation and now wants a problem-focused approach. Check this out later but for the time being obtain an idea of what the problems are.

T: Just tell me more about what they are.

J: I've been with my partner for 4 years, it's a major commitment, but I panic at the thought of marriage. I can't face it. I think I would be better off single, but I feel guilty. I always drift into relationships. I had one of 6 years—she was a real drama queen—but I couldn't break away—or cope on my own. My general problems are lack of assertiveness, low self-esteem, although I'm confident in some areas. My partner Carol is a great girl but there's not much sexual passion.

J has produced a wealth of information and his account suggests both longstanding and immediate problems. There is an immediate life dilemma (stemming from a pressure, as he sees it, to decide about getting married) as well as a suggestion of a pre-existing pattern of indecision in intimate relationships (Ho1). This may be related to a general lack of assertiveness (Ho2), as he states, or to more specific patterns of interaction, or deficits, in maintaining such relationships (Ho3). It is hoped that patterns in his relationships will eventually emerge and so, in the interests of maintaining a natural flow, the interviewer continues to explore the theme that has just been introduced and asks a concrete question to prompt further reflections.

T: Was there passion at the beginning?

J: A bit at first, more affection really. We get on great but I feel constrained. Carol has to work hard and she gets home late. I spend a lot of time playing the piano. I'm an obsessive personality but what I do doesn't come to fruition. When I was in my teens I had this thought, "I might get AIDS." When the going got tough, this thought would freak me out. I am a panicker. I have high blood pressure. I can't deal with responsibility—I bury my head in the sand. I know it's immature behavior. Now I'm in my 30s but there are things that are too worrying to tackle—like marriage or splitting up. I'm not in charge of my own life. I've always been in relationships with strong-willed women—but Carol is not overbearing.

The story of J's life expands by the minute but the presentation is disjointed, as if J seems to be living in a muddle and cannot begin to sort it out. This may represent a style of relating that he uses in other interpersonal situations—conveying his own confusion to another person and perhaps seeking to be rescued by a stronger personality (Ho4). J is able to analyze and label his problems but this may be his undoing—his analysis does not seem to lead to a systematic ordering of the issues that allows him to make firm decisions. At times, he seems to be quite capable of doing what he needs to do or wants to do (working, playing the piano) and so it is unclear what factors inhibit him from translating his wishes into action. There is a history of what appears to be an intrusive obsessional thought about getting AIDS (Ho5) and at some point it needs to be confirmed whether this is an example of a persisting pattern of obsessional phenomena. Given that discussion with J at a general level seems to lead to a rather confusing amount of information, T asks once more for concrete detail.

T: What happened at the end of the last 5-year relationship?

J: She had tantrums whenever I talked of splitting. I thought suicide was the only way out. I'd tell her I was moving back to my parents or I would just sulk and not say anything. I thought I had no right to leave. I'm overly empathetic when others get upset. Finally she accepted it. But she left a note saying she had been admitted to hospital and was seriously ill. When I got to the hospital, I found it was all untrue.

The question has yielded important information about J's inability to translate intentions into action. He is overly concerned about upsetting others—and seems to feel that he has no right to follow his own inclinations — supporting the hypothesis of a lack of assertiveness (Ho2). In this vignette, his ex-partner seems to have played on his weakness. The whole episode may have been so upsetting (or even traumatic) that he doesn't want to repeat it with Carol (Ho6). It is necessary to explore whether his lack of assertiveness affects him in all situations or just some. It is also unclear what he thinks would happen if he were to upset others. However, given that an essential objective in the first interview is to get a comprehensive overview of J's problems, T returns to some concerns he has already mentioned.

T: Let's come back to what you were saying about being panicky.

J: I'm disorganized—I can never get my act together. I can't focus because I'm too worried. I'm too aware of myself.

J continues to convey a confusing array of difficulties, now mentioning worry, self-consciousness, and general disorganization. T decides to check out whether J really is so disorganized or simply wants to present himself in this fashion (Ho4) for reasons yet to be determined. Once again, a concrete enquiry is made—about his experience at university, as he had been successful in obtaining a degree. If he is really so worried and disorganized, obtaining a degree could not have been easy. This tactic is employed in an attempt to resolve potential inconsistency in the facts.

T: Were you worried when studying at university?

J does not directly answer this question but elaborates instead on his ability to cope in general.

J: Well, my work now with the kids is tough but I force myself to be confident in that. I've been on antidepressants twice. At college I had the obsessive thought about AIDS but I've not had it in the last 8 years. Well it came back for a while after I split with my girlfriend. Then I went out with Jane who was very nice and nurturing. I became very dependent on her. I nearly failed my training as a youth worker. My tutor tried to get me thrown off the course. I thought I was useless. I had brain scans because I thought there was something wrong with me. I've always had headaches. I'm never living in the "here and now."

On the one hand, J's answer confirms that his problems are longstanding and there is evidence (medication and his tutor's actions) that he has functioned poorly in the past. On the other hand, he succeeded in getting qualified and also manages to cope with a group of adolescents with behavioral problems. While obsessional thoughts no longer seem to be an issue for him (Ho5 not supported), he has thrown in some new complaints—headaches, illness fears, and feeling unconnected with his immediate reality. This suggests some anxiety about his health (Ho7). He indicates that he gets into relationships in which he becomes dependent on a nurturing other (Ho8). Given that a therapeutic relationship can be perceived in this light, it may be that J is presenting himself in an unduly "pathological" manner in order to elicit T's support. T first wants to confirm that J no longer has obsessive thoughts.

T: Do you have any obsessive thoughts now, like the one about AIDS?

J: No, not now.

J clearly worries about many issues and obtaining a list of them might take forever. T therefore returns to the problem first mentioned, of having to decide about marriage, in an attempt to determine whether this is inducing a period of acute stress (Ho9). If so, some of his anxiety and concerns could be related to this immediate problem and might resolve if these issues were to be addressed.

T: You began by talking about your relationship with Carol. Can you say a bit more about that?

J: I'm totally dependent on Carol. I have a yearning to be free. I'm in a state of constant unease. I mess things up for myself. I wonder if an issue is real or not. Will I be better off single? I've never had many girls. When I did my high school exams, my worries really affected me. I am very self-conscious, I think everyone is looking at me. I am overly concerned about the opinions of others. I think, "You're an idiot"—it's crippling. I would like to be able to deal with something there and then. Actually, I think I'm a nice guy and considerate to others. With the kids at work, I don't value their opinions, so I don't take anything personally. But with my peer group, in staff meetings, I'm terrified. I can't say anything in front of my peers. I want to organize an outing for the kids but I don't want to speak in the staff room. Then I think, what if a kid gets lost, and I procrastinate. I don't face up to where I'm at.

J always produces far more information than is requested and it might be supposed that greater discipline should have been exerted on the interview, so that each issue could be explored more thoroughly. However, given his fulsome and sometimes disjointed style, it is not obvious that clarity could be achieved in this way. His answer suggests that his worries are quite generalized and that he procrastinates about many decisions. He has also been more specific about his concerns in social situations (e.g. that others will think he is "an idiot"). The hypothesis about unassertiveness seems too narrow and his problems in making his wants known and his social fears (Ho10) will have to be explored further. However, what he believes others think of him is not necessarily what he actually thinks of himself. He has indicated that he has a good opinion of himself—that he is a nice guy and considerate (Ho11). J produces evidence that some situations do not bother him—he is not concerned with what the boys he works with think of him, only adults. This is a small step towards a more precise description of his social anxieties and view of himself. He produces evidence that he is handicapped in carrying out his job in relation to members of staff. He avoids speaking up in the staff room—another piece of information relevant to his social fears. J's answer does not give much support to the hypothesis that stress arising from his relationship with Carol is the main problem (Ho9)—or, at least, it seems to be part of a repeating pattern in intimate relationships, probably with a variety of causes. T is not content that J has sufficiently displayed his positive assets and skills and so questions him along these lines. The purpose here is to test the hypothesis that J likes to present himself as rather hopeless and inadequate and in need of others on whom to depend (Ho4).

T: But you seem to have achieved quite a lot.

J: My work is difficult and I have stuck at it. When my tutor wanted to throw me off the course, I fought back. But I'm not consistent—I don't treat work as a pleasure. I don't have any disciplinary problems. But there's arguments with kids, noise, screaming, fighting, it grinds you down. I've always got my music. I would like to succeed more with my music. I play in a band at the weekends. I'm probably the best musician. We play and people come up and sing—at pubs, parties, weddings.

J's answer confirms T's suspicion that J has been over-concerned with demonstrating his inadequacies. The picture of a popular musician is not entirely consistent with what else he has had to say. T is now favoring the hypothesis that a display of helplessness may be the way he copes in difficult situations, justifying his procrastination, and serving as a means to solicit help from nurturing partners (Ho4). T wonders about the nature of his relationship with his previous therapist in an attempt to investigate the idea that he seeks to be dependent on others.

T: Do you feel you learned something from your previous counseling?

J: It was too much about my childhood. The therapist made wrong assumptions. My mother over-indulged me, my Dad was harder, but he was a great guy as well. My mother would always say I was wonderful, and spoilt me. She was a worrier as well. My Dad would never admit his flaws and would always try to make himself look big. … I want to write songs well. I like to be a performer and get the attention. People say I'm funny, and I can entertain people. I would like to do some stand-up comedy.

Once again J's depiction of himself changes with kaleidoscopic rapidity. Although it would be interesting to pursue in what way the previous therapist made wrong assumptions, J has produced an interesting summary of his family relationships that may support the hypothesis that J has left decision making to nurturing others (Ho4) and may explain why, given his mother's indulgent attitude, his image of himself as a person is generally positive (Ho11), while his perception of what others think of him is negative. It is noted that his image of himself as an entertainer and stand-up comedian seems to be inconsistent with a fear of being negatively evaluated by others, as in the staff room (inconsistent with Ho10). It seems likely that his social behavior is highly dependent on context. Future assessment would need to focus on why this is so. J continues to talk about his childhood.

J: My parents were Catholic and I think they used to panic about sex. When I was growing up, I thought I would go to hell when I fancied women. I got depressed at the age of 10 with images of naked women. I don't think you can ever find one perfect relationship. I feel guilty about wasting Carol's time. She's a career woman and earns a lot more than me. She doesn't talk about family but if she wants to start one, she has to think about it soon. I could just drift along or I could run away. I end up with a nervous stomach and full of regrets.

J reveals a longstanding tendency to become fearful when faced by new challenges. There are too many leads to be followed up in the time available with regard to the nature of his relationship with his current partner. J returns to the dilemma he faces about commitment and its role in his current distress (Ho9). He recognizes a need to make a decision but is unable to do so. However, he has not yet provided evidence that his partner wants to get married to him, and this may be an unwarranted assumption. He has nicely summed up the relationship between his procrastination, the implications of drifting, and the effect on his emotional and bodily state.

Reflections on the assessment
In this first assessment session, no clear account of J's problems has emerged, nor has a definite focus for intervention been identified. A good description of his behavior in specific situations has not yet been obtained. There are inconsistencies in his self-report and so it would be important to have it supplemented by direct observation and information from third parties. The therapist has not been able to explore hypotheses in a detailed sequential manner but instead has opted for broad coverage. The session has generated 11 hypotheses but they are still in an embryonic and largely untested form. Nevertheless, there are already signs that some are more credible than others. Given the complexity of his problems and their interwoven nature, several sessions of assessment are likely to be needed. J digresses repeatedly, which may be an example of his difficulty making decisions and his inability to stick to one line of action. The transcript contains 92 words spoken by the therapist and 969 by the client. He is likely to need considerable help in formulating his aims in life and adopting a problem-solving attitude. It might be helpful to gather information by standardized questionnaires of mood (anxiety, depression), obsessions, social anxiety, assertion, and health anxiety. However, it is possible that all these questionnaires would yield high scores, reflecting a response set rather than a veridical account of his difficulties. The session ended with a discussion of possible therapeutic methods, and the need to work out objectives.

Provisional hypotheses and associated level of confidence in their credibility:

Ho1. Indecisive in intimate relationships. [Strong support.]

Ho2. General lack of assertiveness skills. [J's ability to assert himself seems to be dependent on the situation. Low support.]

Ho3. Lacks interpersonal skills to maintain intimate relationships. [J does not seem to lack interpersonal skills necessary for beginning a relationship, but there seem to be specific difficulties in expressing his true feelings and in ending a relationship. Medium support.]

Ho4. J passes his own confusion and disorganization on to others and waits to be rescued. [Medium support.]

Ho5. J is prone to experience intrusive obsessional thoughts. [Strong support, but currently no evidence of obsessions.]

Ho6. Previous ending of relationship traumatic and J wants to avoid a repetition. [Not investigated but hypothesis is still a viable possibility.]

Ho7. Health anxieties, as yet unspecified. [Present in the past, unclear support in the present.]

Ho8. Life-long pattern in intimate relationships of becoming dependent on nurturing or strong-willed others. [Highly supported according to the account he gives of himself.]

Ho9. Acute stress due to impending life decision (i.e. as seen by J, whether to remain in his relationship and/or marry). [Medium support.]

Ho10. Social anxiety, as yet unspecified. [High level of support but anxiety seems to depend on the situation.]

Ho11. Client's self-concept is that in some respects he has a high opinion of himself. [Moderate support, but needs further exploration.]

SECTION C. CONVENTIONS FOR AN ICF DIAGRAM

The rationale for choosing the elements of an individual case formulation (ICF) diagram has already been given in Chapter 8. The diagram separates observations about a client (the more descriptive element, in circles) from interpretations that attempt to explain how the observations are linked together (the hypotheses, in squares). The value of the diagram lies in clarifying a therapist's thought processes because it makes explicit what inferences are being drawn from the observations. The diagram can also be independently evaluated and used in supervision. The main purpose of the diagram is to assist in the choice of an intervention.

The observations or "facts" of the case are expressed in simple, everyday language that avoids superfluous interpretation. This should ensure reasonable agreement between people who are discussing it. Hypotheses are not limited in this way, and therefore they are more likely to become a focus of disagreement.

Client and therapist will interpret the facts as they see them from their own perspective. In an ICF diagram, a client's interpretations are part of the description of her or his behavior (in circles), and identified in the diagram as statements of belief. They are distinguished from the therapist's hypotheses (in squares). Hypotheses are always provisional because new information is quite likely to lead to their revision. However, they are associated with different degrees of confidence, that is, credibility as causal explanations of behavior and its links. A therapist may have to proceed with an intervention having only modest confidence in its conceptual rationale. However, this can be discussed openly with a client, perhaps admitting that an intervention should be undertaken in the spirit of an experiment.

A hypothesis (Ho) is often based upon established principles and research evidence but, in the absence of a credible causal explanation, could consist of any form of speculation as to why behavior is expressed in a particular way. This openness to ideas is essential, given that a problem is a practical difficulty in the real world. It may be necessary to call upon many forms of knowledge and practical wisdom.

The process of drawing up an ICF diagram is collaborative, and the end result is intended to benefit both client and therapist. A client might be asked to check a diagram to ensure that it makes sense and does not contain inaccuracies. The diagram helps to explain the rationale of therapy, bearing in mind that the initial formulation is unlikely to get everything right. A client might be quite unaware of how a problem has arisen (e.g. why he or she feels depressed) and the ICF diagram should help to clarify the what, where, how, and why of these feelings.

An ICF diagram therefore serves one or more of the following functions:

*   To help a client make sense of her or his situation and create a basis for further exploration. (This assumes there is broad agreement about the goals of therapy and the general therapeutic approach.)
*   To place the problem in a social context, including family and friends, and other aspects of the social environment. When the social context includes circumstances that make a major contribution to a problem, and these realities cannot easily be changed, this should be acknowledged as a dilemma. In fact, if a problem is maintained by overpowering external circumstances that cannot be changed at all, therapy is unlikely to help. The aim may shift towards support rather than problem solving.

- To identify gaps in the assessment or contradictions in the available evidence.
- To clarify a therapist's thinking about a problem. Confusion can often be addressed by setting out a description of a problem, and inferences already made, in a visual form.
- To suggest potential interventions/solutions and how they might be implemented.

Intrinsic limitations on case formulation

- There are usually very many causal factors to consider, including some a therapist has not thought of.
- One of the richest sources of evidence comes from observing how a client's behavior varies in different contexts. However, most of this evidence is reported second-hand, there being few opportunities to observe it directly.
- The time available for gathering evidence is usually limited, and there is often pressure to intervene quickly before a case formulation has been well constructed. This pressure may come from a client or from a service that imposes time limits on contracts. This pressure is best resisted.
- Information about a client's life history is frequently incomplete because it may not be remembered or a client is unwilling to talk about it.
- The evidence used to test a hypothesis is often ambiguous and open to interpretation. It may be an indirect report of what happened on a particular occasion. Evidence from different sources is usually needed to test a hypothesis.
- A client might "manage" the information he or she divulges, even to the extent of deliberately creating a false impression.
- Observations are frequently difficult to distinguish from interpretations. Suppose that a client believes that other people dislike him and a number of examples are given. A therapist can attempt to elicit a concrete description in a variety of situations and in this way tease out descriptive observation from a client's own interpretation. Often enough, there is a theme that cuts across him or her, perhaps a feeling of being negatively evaluated in a certain way in a certain kind of situation. Generalizations of this kind are treated as hypotheses for the purposes of the diagram because these are inferences, and revisions are often necessary.

Clarification of hypotheses

In the example just given, a clarification of hypotheses might look something like this:

1. Although the client usually feels negatively evaluated in certain contexts,
it may or may not be true that the client is actually evaluated in this way—
one hypothesis is just that he feels/believes this to be the case.

2. Perhaps the client is actually negatively evaluated at times but not in an
unreasonable way (and so the hypothesis is that he is over-sensitive to these
remarks or cannot cope with them appropriately).

3. The hypothesis is that the client is, in fact, unreasonably negatively evaluated by others. The client believes correctly that he is undeserving of these
evaluations and that others are unfairly critical.

4. The hypothesis is that the client behaves in such a way as to elicit negative social evaluations (and may or may not be aware of doing so).

5. The hypothesis is that the client believes (incorrectly) that the negative
opinions of him are true and that he completely justify his negative
self-image.

Evidence is collected until a therapist is reasonably confident that it adequately explains the circumstances. Implicit in the five hypotheses listed
above are notions of situation, response, belief, feeling, and so on. A labeling
scheme for behavioral description suited to a functional approach is likely
to differ from the way the client might analyze his or her situation. The
proposed conventions were outlined in Chapter 8. The aim of an ICF diagram is to combine a causal analysis with an appreciation of the open-
ended nature of a client's potential behavior. On the one hand, the
immediate reality and determinants of a problem need to be conveyed; on
the other hand, space must be created for behavior that has a low probability of occurrence or is merely a potential to respond in a given situation.
These possibilities are normally explored by discussion or exercise of the
imagination.

Conventions for the formulation diagram
Circles or ovals

These are used for low-inference descriptive observations of behavior
and situational context. Observations can be divided into "triggers" or
"cues" for action (including thoughts and feelings, and events in the
body) and "responses" to those stimuli, including unheeded bodily
reactions. It is often sufficient to describe a "situation" that is not

broken down into its stimulus and response elements. The need to do so varies with the problem and the level of precision required for analysis. The descriptive element is expressed in text within the circle, indicating the nature of a situation/stimulus and the modality of the response, e.g.

- feels alienated
- driving on busy street
- tension in neck muscles
- urge to escape
- anticipates rejection
- receives request to work late
- thought of suicide
- worry about child's safety
- imagines a dog
- blames partner
- shows sympathy.

As shown above, a verbal description of a situation/response refers to its modality (as thought, feeling, behavior, etc.) but is not otherwise marked out symbolically. Of more importance is the need to show how situations and responses are connected in the diagram. For instance, an observation that a particular muscle group is tense could be related to situations that evoke emotional memories, to work stress, to certain kinds of personal interaction, etc. Thoughts, feelings, and sensations are included as descriptive elements whether or not they are conceptualized as stimulus, response, or both. As explained in Chapter 8, historical events are entered as hypotheses if they are judged to have causally influenced current events but there is no clear evidence for this in current behavior. However, some current descriptive elements might include situations/responses that closely resemble past events, implying an obvious causal link.

Squares or rectangles

These are used for for high-inference hypotheses, interpretations, and conjectures of all kinds.

Dotted lines

These link a hypothesis to the situation/behavior/causal connection it is intended to explain.

Solid double lines (without arrows)

These are used to show that elements are correlated but not causally related. This convention can be used to indicate that stimuli, responses, or "acts in context" are functionally equivalent. Apparently unrelated elements are not shown as linked at all, and an element can be included in the diagram without any links if is assumed that it will be relevant at a later stage.

Solid single lines (with arrows to indicated directionality)

These are used to represent a causal link (e.g. A→B). Reciprocal causal links are indicated by a double-headed arrow (A↔B).

Further considerations

Level of detail in the description

The aim is to characterize typical eliciting situations and typical responses. Precise description may not be needed. For example, for someone with an obsession that concerns cleaning his or her teeth, it may be sufficient to describe an eliciting situation as "standing in front of the bathroom mirror after getting up in the morning, and about to clean teeth." The time the person gets up, or what day of the week it is, may not be significant. (This can be established by checking the facts and omitting unnecessary refinements from a description). Similarly, the act of cleaning the teeth could be described with more or less precision depending on the need to do so (e.g. whether there is a ritual aspect to the cleaning action).

The timing of events

Accurate dating is necessary for tracing the causal development of a problem. A client can usually say what has happened in the previous 18 months but cannot always remember the precise order of events. However, it is often important to know what happened when because causes are understood to precede effects. Knowing the temporal order of events over very short sequences of behavior can also be crucial in understanding what it is that maintains a problem. This is particularly true when there is a vicious circle of mutually interacting elements.

The absence of "expected" elements

A client may be lacking certain skills or unable to avail him- or herself of opportunities that would normally be expected for that person in his or her social circumstances. These "deprivations" and "deficits" may need to be included in the ICF even though they represent the absence of something (see Chapter 8).

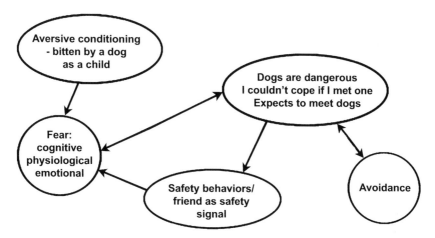

Figure C1 Trainee's first attempt to represent the individual case formulation (ICF) of a dog phobia.

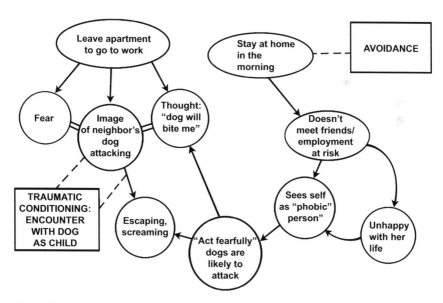

Figure C2 Trainee's second attempt to represent the ICF of a dog phobia.

The number of ICF diagrams

If a client has a number of unrelated problems, a diagram will be needed for each one. It might also prove helpful to "zero in" on a specific situation or "zoom out" to a macro level of description. It is not necessary to cram everything into one diagram as long as the relationship between separate ICF diagrams is understood.

Difficulties experienced by novices in producing an ICF diagram

The difficulties that may arise in utilizing these guidelines are best illustrated by giving examples of difficulties encountered by trainee therapists learning cognitive behavioral case formulation. The problems being formulated were fairly straightforward and, for this reason, illuminate the difficulties clearly. The ICF diagrams were discussed in a small supervision group. Subsequently, trainees saw their clients again, gathered further information, and produced revisions to their diagram and formulation. It should be said, in passing, that the reason for using these illustrations is to exemplify a teaching method, not to comment on the validity of the ICFs actually produced by trainees.

Example 1: Dog phobia (see Figures C1 and C2 for first and second attempts to formulate)
Difficulty 1: Leaving out the problem and its context

The first illustration is a client who complained of an excessive fear of dogs. The trainee formulated the problem as "Dogs are dangerous," "I couldn't cope if I met one" and "Expects to meet dogs." These observations could be classified as a statement of the client's beliefs. Typically, clients do not complain about their beliefs, but about what they feel or about what they do or about the consequences of their actions. Beliefs, as such, are merely one aspect of a problem, something that a client might think or say in certain situations. Without a context, we do not know whether all possible dogs are considered dangerous in all possible situations. Would a dog caged in a zoo be experienced as a dangerous animal (in general) or fear-provoking when observing it? Likewise, the belief about coping is non-specific. Would the client be able to cope when encountering a toy dog or an imaginary dog?

The lack of contextual detail can be remedied by analyzing concrete situations that a client regularly confronts. The actual problem for this client was that she had a fear of leaving her apartment in the morning before walking to the station to catch her train to work. It would have been helpful to know whether the dog she expected to meet was large or small, barking or jumping, and so forth. When the problem was explored in this way, it turned out that a resident of the apartment block in which she lived did in fact own a large and rather vicious-looking dog that other residents had already complained about. This was not the sole source of the client's problem but it was a relevant factor to consider when the formulation was constructed and an intervention was planned.

Difficulty 2: Failure to distinguish between an observation and its interpretation

With respect to the client's behavior, the client was described as showing "avoidance," although this was moderated by the presence of "safety signals." Both elements were placed within circles to indicate that they were observations, whereas, in fact, avoidance and safety are theoretical concepts (hypotheses) and should have been placed in rectangles. In terms of actual behavior, the client asked a friend to turn up at her front door in the morning and accompany her while walking to the station. Although it was probably correct to interpret her reluctance to walk alone to the station as an example of avoidance (i.e. of encountering a dog) this was not the only possible explanation. Perhaps she simply preferred the company of a friend when going to work. All possible interpretations should be considered in order to avoid the processing bias of selecting the one that is most available or fits a stereotype. Although the avoidance hypothesis was probably correct, in many formulations there is a range of credible hypotheses to choose from.

Labeling the friend as a safety signal seems sound but the concept of safety could have been explored further by asking the client to imagine seeing a dog in the street when accompanied by her friend. What would happen? In what sense does the friend ensure safety? The formulation diagram could then incorporate these observations as *potential* situations with certain consequences. The fact that they are based on imaginary scenarios is fairly typical of case formulation. If a therapist is confident that certain situations lead to certain consequences, they can be incorporated as observations in the diagram, even though their existence is based on inference. They are not hypotheses of a theoretical nature but a client's assumptions about the nature of their reality, in other words, what it is that would actually happen in certain circumstances. They could be labeled as a client's "beliefs" but in many cases they represent assumptions about a reality that is shared with the therapist (e.g. that there will actually be a train to catch at the station).

The trainee could have inquired about the contingencies that related to staying at home (i.e. acting as a phobic person) or going to work. When this was done, it revealed sources of the client's motivation to seek therapy (see Figure C2). She disliked seeing herself as someone who had a phobia and believed that acting in a fearful manner increased the likelihood of a dog attacking her. Identifying the adverse consequences of staying at home on her social life and availability for work also raised questions about the extent to which her friends or employer knew about her difficulties. Mitigating the adverse consequences of her avoidance could then become one of the goals of therapy.

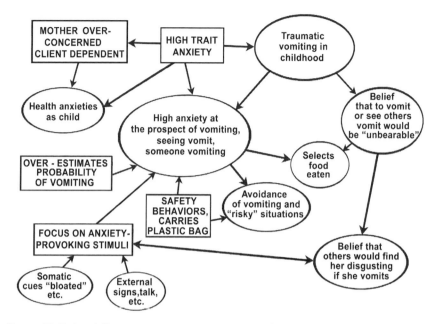

Figure C3 Trainee's first attempt to represent the ICF of a vomit phobia.

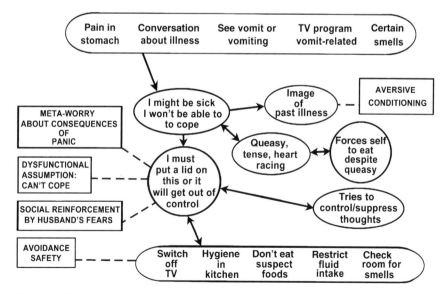

Figure C4 Trainee's second attempt to represent the ICF of a vomit phobia.

The client's response of fear was separately described as "cognitive," "physiological," and "behavioral" following a formula commonly adopted in diagrams (as discussed in Chapter 8). Without further specification, these are examples of conceptual labeling rather than literal statements grounded in what a client said or did. In any case, since some verbal expressions of fear had already been described, further reference to the cognitive element without further specification did not seem to serve any useful purpose.

Difficulty 3: Assumption of causality in past events

An observation that the client had been bitten by a dog as a child was labeled as "aversive conditioning" (and therefore placed in a circle). As noted in Chapter 8, her memory of being bitten might simply have been a reported fact or it could have been an active memory in the sense that it was re-lived in the present. In this instance, the trainee inferred that the dog bite was the basis of an aversive conditioning of fear to dogs. As such, it is a theoretical interpretation of the verbal report of the memory. The latter is an observation, and the former is a hypothesis. Further observation would be needed to add credibility to the conditioning hypothesis. For example, is it consistent with the client's behavior before and after the original bite?

Example 2: Vomit phobia (see Figures C3 and C4 for first and second attempts to formulate)

Difficulty 1: Inadequate specification at the descriptive level

As in the first example, observation and interpretation were not clearly distinguished. The target problem was described as "High anxiety at the prospect of vomiting" which is too vague and lacks any contextual detail. "Health anxieties as child" were included as observations but these were neither direct reports of what had been said nor clearly stated hypotheses about the significance of past events.

"Carrying a plastic bag" was described as a safety behavior but safety is a theoretical hypothesis (rightly placed in a rectangle) whereas carrying is a behavioral observation (rightly placed in a circle). The client's focus of attention on "anxiety-provoking stimuli" was labeled as a hypothesis, but no observable examples of this phenomenon were described. Hyper-vigilance for threat might have constituted the relevant theoretical hypothesis, in which case several observations supporting this inference could have been grouped together as functionally equivalent, simplifying the diagram.

Difficulty 2: Undue complexity

It is easy to be overwhelmed by a mass of observations and have difficult organizing them. One strategy is to deal with different aspects of a problem in separate diagrams, only later piecing them together. Alternatively, irrelevant or redundant elements can be removed or simplified.

The gain in this trainee's understanding was considerable after further assessment. The reformulated diagram was far better organized and theoretically more coherent (see Figure C4). A variety of situations that evoked expectations of vomiting were specified. The trainee elicited the client's images of past episodes of illness relevant to vomiting. Different physiological sensations were identified. Responses that could be interpreted as safety-seeking or avoidance were clearly labeled and grouped together. It was discovered that the client sometimes forced herself to eat despite feeling queasy, and the trainee drew out a vicious circle of interacting elements relating to the effects of this behavior.

The later assessment interview identified the client's reflections on her own thoughts about the consequences of vomiting. These included "I must keep a lid on this anxiety or it will get out of control." These self-reflections were interpreted theoretically as "meta-worries" (i.e. a further worry about what was worrying her) which was in part a consequence of (and maintained by) the "methods of thought-control" that she used. It was also discovered that the client's husband was concerned that she might end up in a psychiatric hospital. The hypothesis was formed that the client's secondary worries about the effects of her phobia were being additionally maintained by her husband's response to her problem.

It was largely through being forced to concentrate on observations and separate them from hypotheses that the formulation process improved. The first diagram was muddled but it was an important stage in the learning process. Drawing out diagrams enables trainees to become aware of their own confusion. This can be resolved in supervision and through further exploration with a client. Open-mindedness in formulation is helped by a supervisor's tolerance of inevitable inadequacies and a trainee's willingness to see this as learning process, not as a test of getting everything right at the first attempt.

SECTION D. EXTENDED ASSESSMENT AND ICF

This section analyzes the transcripts of three consecutive assessment interviews, providing an account of the interviewer's reasoning when developing hypotheses and strategies. Hypotheses are labeled sequentially as they are explored and evaluated. Some are dropped and new ones are introduced, culminating in a ICF diagram that summarizes what has been concluded. Provisional ICF diagrams are presented at different stages of the process.

In the following transcripts, the text in *italics* describes the therapist's reasoning process in terms of the hypothesis being tested and the strategy being followed.

Information obtained over the telephone

B, a single woman in her late 20s, inquired about private therapy over the telephone. The therapist obtained a brief account of her reasons for self-referral in order to ensure that her problem was of a kind he felt competent to deal with. B reveals that she is feeling depressed, is having panic attacks, but does not want to take medication. She has taken antidepressant medication on three previous occasions during episodes of depression. B says that she has never really been happy with herself, and that she wants a form of therapy that deals with fundamental issues rather than just her current mood. B admits to having cut herself periodically as a way of obtaining relief from her distress. She says she has rarely ever "felt fine" for longer than a few months at a time, although there had been a been a longer period in the previous year in which "she had felt really good." B says that "nothing happened" to trigger these changes of mood. She explains that previous therapy has not been particularly helpful and that she now wants a "good therapist." Both parents are alive.

It appears that B feels that there are longstanding "deep issues" to be dealt with and that her problems cannot be solved by medication or superficial therapy. A question that needs to be clarified is the type of therapy that she wants. B gives no reason for the causes of her depressed mood and panic attacks.

Assessment session 1 (see Figure D1)

B comes across as an attractive, well-dressed young woman who is articulate and polite. Before the interview gets underway, B produces a written list of current problems and proceeds to read them out:
1. Intrusive nightmares, two or three per night, don't sleep well.
2. Wasting my creative possibilities.
3. I hate my job in an office.
4. If I sell my home, I will have nothing.
5. Am I deluded about my creative talents?
6. People dislike me.
7. I'm wrong about everything (*at this point B dissolves into tears*).

8. I'll never be at peace.

9. I have self-harmed in the past—it's a bad thing but I don't see it that way.

It is unusual for a client to proceed in this way but perhaps B does not want to waste time in the session. The list shows that B is able to reflect on herself but she has not identified a theme to link all her problems. The fact that she admits to cutting herself suggests that she wants to be open with her therapist (T) and lay her cards on the table. T senses that B expects him to focus on the cutting (or disapprove of it) because she has already defended herself by claiming that, in her view, it is not a bad thing to do. T is therefore aware that this is likely to be a sensitive subject and he doesn't want to give the impression that he is overly concerned about safety issues or disapproves of her cutting. Therefore, he takes note of this information, reserving it for later exploration as and when appropriate. Based on knowledge of the frequency of this kind of phenomenon in relation to life-history events, her cutting might suggest a history of emotional deprivation or abuse in childhood (Ho1) and T will bear this in mind. T would initially like to know the severity of her current low mood and how often she has been depressed in the past. It is not clear why she should worry about losing her home. T is curious about situations or events that may be stressing her and whether there are any current precipitants for her present state of mind. The fact that B feels people dislike her and that she is wrong about everything suggests that B is uncomfortable with how she comes across or presents herself to others, or cannot understand others' opinions of her (Ho2). Before exploring hypotheses, T decides that some background details would help to start off the interview and therefore he asks about her current circumstances.

B reveals that she works in an advertising agency but the company has gone into liquidation and she is currently unemployed. She has a large mortgage to keep up on her house.

T infers that having lost her job, which she says she did not enjoy, B is at a choice point with respect to her future (Ho3). This may account for the way she questions whether she has any creative talents. The loss of her income, and potentially her home, could account for her distressed state and nightmares. A possible interpretation is therefore "acute situational stress" (Ho4). T decides to leave these lines of inquiry until later and asks about the nature of the depressed moods she has experienced at various times in her life, as this is her leading complaint and likely to be more significant, in the larger picture, than acute stress.

B says that she has had periods of depression around four or five times in her life. However, she says that between these episodes, she has never really been "at ease" or "in the right place." With regard to her current distress, B says that her nightmares are a form of persecution in which she experiences guilt and has to be deceitful, and "won't get away with it." She adds that she doesn't know "where or who I am." Her current distressed state has been going on for about two months. B says that there are moments that she thinks are "panic attacks" but she is "less scared of them now than before."

It seems that B has been unhappy more or less continuously for a long time. An onset to this state of affairs, if there is one, needs to be established. However, the first 10 minutes of an interview is not the right time to examine historical events in great detail. As T is keen to establish a working relationship, he adopts a relaxed conversational style. He decides to obtain more information about her current low mood and panic-like episodes.

B says that the triggers for panic are "not being able to cope" and "something I can't do well," that is, events that place demands on her that she feels she can't handle. On further exploration of what this means to her, B says she fears that "If I get worse, what will happen?" When asked about typical situations that elicit panic, she says that she felt less panicky when she was at work and feels more anxious now that she is alone by herself.

B's reply indicates that her panic-like episodes may involve a vicious circle of thoughts of a catastrophic nature, in which the outcome is some kind of mental breakdown. The nature of the triggers (not meeting demands) suggests the possibility of B having high standards when judging her own level of competence (Ho5). However, it seems that in the absence of work, and having time to reflect on her circumstances, her increased anxiety while alone may be related to her status as unemployed. Clearly, the nature of her anxious feelings and what triggers them is deserving of greater exploration but T's initial aim is to obtain a thumbnail sketch of all of B's current problems. He moves on to clarify the general nature of her distress.

B states that her distress is "Not an outside thing." "It depends on me and how I feel." The depression "is getting worse every day," and even affects getting dressed in the morning and an inability to decide what to wear.

B emphasizes the internal nature of her distress and seems to be arguing that her mood is primary and external events are secondary. Given her history of repeated episodes of depression, B may be right that there are influences unrelated to immediate external circumstances that affect her mood, or perhaps she is simply prone to significant levels of depressed mood whenever life gets tough for her (Ho6). It is possible that her panic-like episodes are an aspect of her depressed mood because research shows that panic attacks are commonly associated with depressed mood. T attempts to determine what has triggered earlier episodes of low mood in order to find out if there were external factors. In this way, T searches for themes in the triggers (perhaps related to being overwhelmed by demands) or if there are no obvious triggers, T wants to know whether her mood has changed without apparent reason (as she reported in the past year). In this way, T is investigating whether the triggers for her changes of mood are primarily internal or external. An answer to this question would help to determine the causes of her episodes of depressed mood.

B says that in the past there was always a trigger for depressed mood. As a teenager, "I wanted to kill myself." However, while talking about this, B expresses the idea that she is frustrated with her troubled personal history and needs "to pull herself together."

Her answer suggests that external triggers are usually prominent and that there are significant events in her history to uncover. B, for the second time, gives hints about her way of coping with difficulty—that she needs to be strong and put the past behind her (Ho5). However, rather than being drawn in to explore these leads at this stage, T continues to ask about her current depressed mood in order to assess typical signs and their severity, beginning with sleep. In other words, T is trying to be systematic about gathering information, while realizing that B is leaving many signposts to further inquiry.

B says she is currently getting a lot of sleep and would like to sleep all the time. She usually sleeps from 12.00 p.m. to 9.00 a.m. She talks in her sleep and is often woken up by nightmares. After waking, she usually gets back to sleep again. She says she does not want to go to bed in the evening. "If I just shut my eyes, it is a nightmare."

Sleep disturbance is common in a depressed mood but in the more endogenous forms of depression (i.e. related mainly to internal factors), a person usually wants to sleep in the evening and wakes early in the morning. B's pattern is the reverse of this. She dreads sleeping and again mentions nightmares; her disturbed sleep seems to relate to an over-aroused mental state and to her nightmares. This type of insomnia seems more typical of anxiety, stress, or worry, supporting the hypothesis that her disturbed sleep is part of a reaction to current circumstances (work/finance, Ho4). However, her nightmares might also relate to past traumatic events (Ho1). Loss of appetite is another typical sign of depressed mood and so T asks about this.

B confirms she has little appetite but says she normally loves food and is in the habit of cooking. However, she adds that she was recently diagnosed with a spasm in the colon caused by excessive consumption of alcohol. She has not had a drink for two weeks now, and no longer feels sick. B says she used to drink three to four glasses of wine in the evening in order to relieve her distress.

Her loss of appetite seems to be partly related to digestive problems caused by alcohol. The quantity of alcohol consumed does not seem too excessive but it may be an underestimate. T bears in mind that present and past use of alcohol is something that requires further investigation. However, if B is currently using alcohol to relieve stress, this would be consistent with an attempt to cope with her emotional reaction to acute problems such as loss of her job (Ho4) or her nightmares. B's ability to stop drinking on medical advice suggests that she is not dependent on alcohol and has a rational approach to coping. Although T has not yet fully assessed B's mood, he notes from her behavior that she is not lethargic, nor mentally slowed up and, in fact, gives a rather lively impression. She is likely to be pessimistic about the future at present and the risk of suicide needs to be explored. Her present cutting does not appear to be suicidal in intent and T accepts her explanation that it is a way of coping with emotional distress. T decides returns to the task of obtaining background information about her current circumstances (job, family, relationships, etc.).

B says she is close to her family and speaks frequently on the telephone to her mother. She visits her parents regularly. She spends leisure time with her current boyfriend, and with other friends. She says she is "always doing something" but also likes to have evenings at home by herself. Her previous work was generally "tedious and depressing," mainly because it was for business corporations.

T notes that this level of activity does not seem to be consistent with a severely depressed mood (Ho6). B seems to have adequate forms of social support, which also lessens any risk of suicide. T returns to the theme of her career in light of her complaint that work has been tedious and that she might be wasting her creative talents.

B studied arts subjects at university and then went on to a music college. She has always enjoyed literature and the arts. B gave up her career as a musician because there was little work available. She is uncertain how she could now develop her interests from a career point of view.

T infers that B is capable of a creative career and keeps this in mind for further discussion. B seems genuinely blocked in her career (Ho3). T asks about the consequences of her current lack of employment in order to evaluate the hypothesis of acute stress (Ho4).

B says, "Finances are a massive worry. I am bad with money. I have a big tax bill. I procrastinate and don't act. Sometimes I have no food in the house and no money." B says that she was unexpectedly left without an income when her company went into liquidation, and that she cannot keep up her mortgage repayments. She says that she has always worked in the past.

T infers that B is someone who has generally been successful in her work but now has severe financial problems and risk of losing her home. These problems could be sufficient to explain her current low mood, nightmares and panic attacks — the "acute stress hypothesis." It may be necessary to help B deal with this high priority problem before tackling others. In other words, she is unlikely to be able to think about her long-term problems while there is a threat of losing her home. In order to make a comprehensive assessment, T now inquires about intimate relationships in order to check recent events in this sphere of her life.

B says that she used to be passionate about things, like finding the right partner. Now, she thinks she is settling for second best. There was a boy-friend that she liked a lot but he messed her about and she felt hurt and left him. B regards him as young and unreliable, although he is still trying to contact her. Many years earlier, she had had a satisfactory long-term

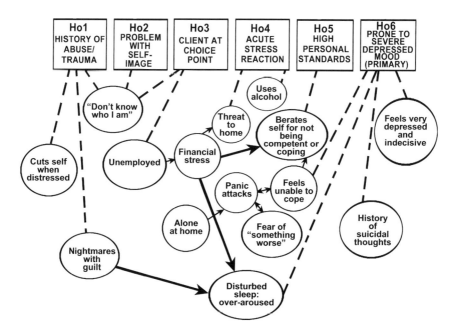

Figure D1 Individual case formulation (ICF) diagram after assessment session 1. Principal observations together with hypotheses (Ho1, Ho2, etc.).

relationship for 6 years but eventually they had drifted apart. B now has a new boyfriend who earns "lots of money and could support her" but he is "second best."

> *T infers that although B has been unsettled in her recent relationships, her present emotional state is unlikely to be directly related to their ups and downs. The session is coming to an end and T informs B that more time will be needed to reach an understanding of her difficulties. T expresses the opinion that B will find it difficult to work on longer term issues while she is acutely stressed over her finances. T explains that some of her emotional distress could be attributed to realistic causes, and temporary solutions are discussed, such as obtaining a new job even if it is boring. It is suggested that in the future she might be able to combine a well-paying part-time job with a more creative job as well. The point of saying this is to suggest a pragmatic solution to her need for creativity and to instill hope. B says she will plan to look for work and apply for a range of jobs. In giving the advice to look for work, T judges that B's depressed mood is not as severe as she first intimated. It is also an expression of his confidence in her abilities and an attempt to normalize her situation and give her control. A further session is arranged for a week's time. B appears to be much relieved by having someone listen to her difficulties.*

B telephones a few days later to cancel her next appointment the following week. She says she is still feeling very low. However, she has been invited by friends to spend a few days on holiday abroad and has decided to go with them.

> *T is somewhat surprised by this decision as B says she has no money and is feeling very depressed. It perhaps indicates that she feels secure that she can rely on her parents or new partner to support her financially. Alternatively, B might think it will help to improve her state of mind. T reasons that a severely depressed person is unlikely to take the initiative to arrange a holiday. T begins to favor the hypothesis that her low mood is secondary to other difficulties rather than being the primary problem. The hypothesis that B experiences a depressed mood largely unrelated to circumstances is not supported by this new information.*

Assessment session 2 (see Figure D2)

> *T resumes the assessment of B's general circumstances and history but first checks how she had felt during her short holiday. He also asks about alcohol consumption and the status of any job applications. T decides not to ask about B's cutting until the therapeutic relationship has consolidated, when B is more likely to be forthcoming.*

B says she was able to stop worrying on holiday. Her friends were supportive. She felt "nothing would really fail." Her mood was better and she experienced only one "panic attack" in anticipation of her return home. She had resumed drinking alcohol but only in a moderate (and normal) quantity.

> *T infers that the beneficial effect on her mood is inconsistent with depression as the primary cause of her problems (Ho6). It seems unlikely that if depressed mood were primary it would be so reactive to circumstances. B feels safer and less worried in the company of friends but experiences a "panic attack" at the thought of coming home. This is evidence to support the hypothesis that acute financial worries and unemployment are playing an important role (Ho4). She seems able to control her drinking, so it is less likely that she has a significant dependency on alcohol. T is confident that B is an honest informant and would not mislead him about these matters.*

B informs T that her boyfriend has ended their relationship because he is not in love with her. In response to being asked how she feels about that, she returns to the theme of "not being in control" (because the man she actually liked didn't take her seriously enough) and not trusting her own judgment.

> *"Being wrong about everything" was one of B's listed problems and so T decides to return to this theme after first asking about attempts to find work. Although T's suggestion to look for work was not, strictly speaking, a homework task, it is important to check whether any suggestions have been acted upon.*

B says she was successful in a first job interview and has been invited for a second round. Several jobs are available. She thinks the jobs are likely to be boring but she will take what's offered. She got excited about a job working in a museum—but doesn't expect to get it. B has also found out about some interesting part-time voluntary work that she could do in addition to a full-time job. A friend has spontaneously offered to help out with her mortgage repayments if necessary.

> *B's resourceful and proactive approach encourages the view that she will need little help from T in this regard. B seems to be doing whatever is possible from a practical point of view. T has not yet explored her complaint that she lacks confidence in her judgments and ends up with the wrong person. To start off this line of inquiry, T asks: "Does she know anyone else who has ended up in this position?"*

B answers: "Yes, my parents are unhappy but they stay together." She considers both of them to be lonely and she sees them every week. B feels close to both of them. B believes that she has made the wrong choice of partners herself and doesn't trust her judgment anymore.

> *T infers that B has the model of an unhappy marriage in her parents but she doesn't seem to take sides. T decides to explore her doubts about her inability to trust herself. As a way into this, he asks about her confidence when she was a child, such as the events that might have triggered her suicide attempt as a teenager, as this is also relevant to a number of hypotheses.*

B says that, "Everything was great until the age of 13 when we moved house." B reports "not being me" after that, and that she was even depressed while in a good relationship with a boyfriend at that time. B had attended a private girls' school and then, for a short time, a high school where she was in the "top echelon." After moving house to a different part of the country, she went back to a junior school then to a mixed-sex high school. B pointed out that this was four schools in 2 years. Her new classmates thought she was "ghastly." This was on account of her refined accent and her respectful attitude towards teachers. B says, "They would never let it go." B also reported being bored because she was a high-achieving pupil in a school that did not seem to reward success.

> *Moving house, and from a private school to several state schools, seems to have been a turning point in B's life. Other children appear to have ridiculed her. The ethos of the state school was, according to her, to show little respect for learning. T suspects that her treatment there amounted to bullying and investigates this hypothesis (Ho7).*

B says "I can't think about it with perspective, or barely think about it at all. I've blanked it out." B confirms that it was bullying that led to a lack of self-worth. She began to cut herself soon after the bullying started. B says that she never regained her former sense of being really alive. The only time she did not feel "heavy and miserable" was in music lessons outside school and when at home.

> *B has confirmed a history of severe bullying, its association with cutting, and a subsequent suppression of memories of what happened. It is of interest that B had not mentioned bullying when seeking help or during the first session, which is surprising given its impact on her. T reasons that several of B's problems could be attributed to post-traumatic stress, Ho8 (e.g. not feeling herself, nightmares, and anxious/depressed mood). T is now interested in how she and her parents coped with this situation, how bad it was, and whether her current nightmares are linked to memories of this period in her life.*

B responds by saying, "I feel I am making up the bullying and feel 'weak' for talking about it. I never tell people about it."

> *B's response explains why she did not mention it earlier. It suggests that she feels responsible for the bullying and blames herself (Ho9). It is consistent with B's way of coping—as indicated before—to be "strong" and deal with any challenge she faces on her own (Ho5). T asks for more details and, in particular, how her parents dealt with the bullying, which might help to explain its influence over her up to the present.*

B described an incident at school in which she "hurt herself badly" and her parents were called. As a result, the school transferred her to a different teaching group where there were fewer bullies. However, the main bully remained in her class. Her mother told her to be nice to him because he was new to the school. When B tried to do this, the bullying increased, on one occasion leading to a fight in the classroom.

> *T infers that the bullying was severe and that the incident of "hurting herself" may have referred to cutting herself at school. The school appears to have been weak in dealing with the situation and her mother's advice was probably counterproductive (Ho10). B may have learned that she had to be "strong," that she was partly responsible for the situation, and that she had to cope on her own. T asks for more details of the bullying.*

B says that the move to the new teaching group did not change the situation and that she had no true friends. Her father never wanted to discuss the situation at school, and her mother therefore felt unsupported. Her mother was aware of her cutting and tried to talk to her about it. She was taken to see a psychologist.

> *The bullying at school appears to have created problems in her parents' relationship. It is possible that B's behavior at the time may have been influenced by relationships at home. T asks how her parents normally deal with stressful events in*

order to find out more about the family. The fact that B was sent to see a psychologist suggests that her parents were at a loss to know what to do.

B says her father is sweet but not a strong person. He never talks about his emotions and when she was a child rarely took it upon himself to organize outings for the family. Her mother sees B's personality as similar to her father's. B says that she also never talks about how she feels. She doesn't like to draw attention to herself and feels she ought to be listening to others. She does not want "to make too much of a fuss" because "things are not usually bad enough to warrant a complaint."

This answer adds to the evidence that B's way of coping is to be strong and stoical, and that she prefers not to share her problems with others (Ho5). T has to bear this in mind in how he manages the therapeutic relationship, given that B is unlikely to want to present herself as vulnerable or to comply with an intervention in which she is placed in a vulnerable position (e.g. a distressing "re-living" technique). T infers that both parents have contributed to how B feels she ought to cope with problems. T asks for more details of her mother's response to the bullying, partly to open up a wider discussion of this clearly important period in B's life.

B says that her mother cannot understand depression or self-harm. She has always conveyed the message that what happened was B's own fault and that she had to change her own behavior. B sounds resentful when recounting that her mother never encouraged her to stand up for herself. The suggestion, rather, was to be passive with the bullies and "ignore them." Her mother simply wanted B "to be liked" and blames herself for not teaching B to achieve this. B says that her parents felt themselves to be a failure, and any request by B for support was interpreted as a further sign that they had failed.

B's way of coping is understandable in light of her upbringing. It would seem that her mother was unable to support B emotionally, gave poor advice, and saw B's problems as a reflection of her own inadequacies (Ho10 supported). T offers this interpretation and asks B to reflect on this in order to help her understand how her present problems might have developed.

B reflects that she was certainly "green" as a child and that if she had children of her own, she would teach them to be "streetwise." However, she also claims that her early childhood had been idyllic. "Not a single bad thing happened." She says that she had always had her mother's attention and that she loved her early school years. For this reason "it was such a shock when we moved."

T infers that B was probably indulged in early childhood and was therefore totally unprepared for the bullying she met in her later schools. T decides to probe still further into her parents' response to the bullying as it seems to have left B to fend for herself almost entirely on her own.

B elaborates that her mother thought that anyone could be convinced to like you, by acting nice, but B now realizes that this is not true. She says her father thought in a similar way. As a child, B thought that if she was liked, she would not be bullied, and that it was therefore safer to be liked.

> *Although B has changed her view that acting nice is the best strategy for being liked, T wonders whether this change of attitude has translated into acting any differently with others. If not, this aspect of her upbringing may still be influencing her current interpersonal relationships and creating difficulties for her. T speculates that a neglect of her own needs (Ho11) in an effort "to be nice" may account for her complaint that she is "not herself" and always feels that "she is wrong" and misjudges people. This avenue of inquiry is reserved for a later occasion. T asks for more details of the nature of the bullying on the assumption that it may have constituted a trauma and that some of B's current complaints are signs of post-traumatic stress (Ho8).*

B goes on to describe how, at the age of 15, she was badly beaten up one night when a girl challenged her to a fight. She was then chased by a large group of schoolchildren. Her own "friends" left her to fend for herself although one girl dragged her away saying that the others would kill her. They took refuge in the police station where she was collected by her parents. The police blamed no one in particular and no charges were laid. B says that her parents didn't know what to do and that she still has dreams of being chased.

> *It seems that this event, and probably others, were traumatic. Her life seemed to have been in danger and she was in a state of extreme fear. Her nightmares appear to be associated with this event and perhaps with other occasions of bullying. T questions her about other examples in order to assess the severity of bullying overall.*

B described holding a party in which a large number of uninvited people gained entry by breaking down the door. Her parents were unable to deal with situation and when one parent later came round to apologize, the event was smoothed over and B felt she couldn't set out her own case.

> *B has now reported other frightening events that support a trauma hypothesis. Her parents seemed to be unable to cope or support her effectively (Ho10) and B was unable to express an assertive point of view despite the intolerable nature of what had happened (Ho11). T comments on the fact that it cannot be easy for B to talk to him about these events because she prefers to be strong and not to reveal personal information. T reminds her of what she had said earlier about not wanting to make a "song and dance" and shows appreciation for the fact that she has spoken about the bullying. T wants B to feel free to open up more about her feelings and way of*

coping with stress. T's comment on her behavior in the session empathizes with the difficulty that B might have in seeing things differently.

B: I felt cold talking about it, like a detached feeling. As if it had happened to someone else.

T infers that B dissociates when recalling memories of the bullying, a phenomenon commonly associated with the recall of traumatic events (Ho8). B has reported that her cutting began at the time the bullying started and T speculates that B may cut herself when in a dissociated state of mind (Ho12). This supplies an opportunity to ask about cutting in the context of its potential meaning. T asks whether she often gets into this detached feeling state and whether it is related to cutting herself.

B: I cut myself when I get angry and frustrated with things that happen. It gives me relief and it doesn't hurt. If I did it just now, it would hurt of course. But these things that frustrate me are not related to the bullying in the past. I feel guilt and embarrassment when I talk about my reaction to the bullying. As if I want to be a weak, victim–type of person.

B denies that cutting is related to bullying. She associates cutting with anger and frustration; these emotional reactions may not be unrelated to her manner of coping with stress or difficult personal interactions. However, she seems to confirm that her state of mind is not a normal one when cutting. B accepts that her original response to the bullying was ineffectual and inappropriate. She appears not to have talked about it, partly to avoid distressing herself (perhaps an avoidance phenomenon, also typically associated with trauma, Ho8) or because, as she says, she doesn't want to present herself as a victim.

As this was the end of the session, T decides to leave B with the opinion that much of her current distress can be interpreted as the effects of post-traumatic stress, a result of bullying at school, as he is now fairly confident of this hypothesis. If B accepts this interpretation, it will prepare the way for introducing her to methods for reducing the effects of traumatic memories. B does not dispute the interpretation. T explains that even though she can reflect rationally on what happened in the past, there is still another part of her mind that is an expression of her original emotional reactions. T explains the need for "emotional processing" of her trauma memories, and proposes that it would be helpful if therapy were to be directed towards helping her to confront and neutralize them.

B then expresses fear at the thought of confronting her memories.

T explains that there are gradual ways of doing this but that they all involve some degree of recall of the memories. T explains that a good way to begin would be to write down the memories she has expressed to him today. T stresses that she should not force herself to do this but just write things down in a notebook, even in a

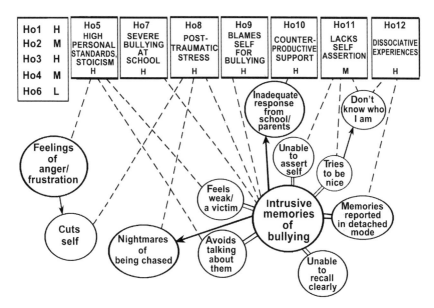

Figure D2 New information and hypotheses from session 2. T is now able to assign levels of confidence to hypotheses. H, M, L = High, Medium, Low.

fragmented form. T reasons that B has avoiding thinking about this period of her life at school and the writing exercise is designed to prompt her recall and bring her more in touch with past experience. Because this is a task that she carries out alone, she does not have to be observed in a distressed and vulnerable state by T, which she might find difficult or lead her to dissociate. There is also evidence that writing about trauma is an effective technique (Pennebaker, 1993). T says that what she has written will be discussed at the next session. B gives the impression that the session has been very helpful and an emotional relief. T is not too concerned that talking about the bullying has left her in a distressed emotional state but he checks what she is doing that evening and at the weekend and is reassured that B is being supported.

Assessment session 3 (see Figure D3)

T first questions B to find out how she felt after the last session in which she talked about the bullying. He wanted to be reassured that B would be able to continue to address this topic.

B: I was just the same—no worse. I was a bit panicky on Sunday but I have been staying at my parents. Talking about the bullying didn't really upset me—I felt detached from it.

T infers that B is still dissociating and perhaps avoiding thinking about the memories. However, she mentions that she has talked to her mother about them, which is a sign that she feels easier about discussing her personal problems.

B: My mother reminded me of the art class incident. She explained it to me. I had completely repressed it. I cut myself all the way up both arms. A girl took to me to the head teacher. My mother was furious. It was the most dramatic and shocking event for her. I suppose she thought the teacher should have been aware of what was happening and stopped it.

T infers that her mother hadn't really done anything that actually helped B, leaving her in the same situation. B's remark that she had no previous recall of this event suggests that there are probably other incidents to be recalled.

B: I did write some things down as you asked me. It was some new events: My first panic attack and the first time I cut myself.

T asks about how she had felt writing it down, both to check that it was not too upsetting and to find out if she had dissociated when writing.

B: It was OK, I wasn't scared to remember. I worked chronologically. It started off quite early—just before my twelfth birthday. I felt sad thinking about myself having to go through this so young.

T reasons that that B is already imposing an adult perspective on her childhood experiences and that this is a sign that she is already beginning to process and restructure her memories.

B (refers to her written notes): Moving house and school. I was sheltered and green. It was shocking for me. Writing things down was revelatory. I could see how schoolwork and events happened in parallel. I was unhappy at school and therefore I didn't learn. And if it was too easy, I was bored. But if I did something well "it was not recognized." People thought I was just good at it anyway. So I just gave up.

B has revealed a different aspect of school life—that she was not learning and not being praised when her work was good.

T: Who was not recognizing you?

B: Not at school nor at home. When I was 12 or 13, I was very good at English. My teacher thought my stories were amazing. She wanted me to take an English examination early, but the school said "no" because it didn't fit in with their timetables. So therefore I got bored.

T infers that B was unable to compensate for the distress caused by bullying through receiving recognition for academic achievements either at school or at home.

B: I did music outside school, and there the people were complimentary and nice. I can see now how it affected me. I wanted to become a musician because I thought I was no good at writing.

T had clearly written quite a lot about events after her move (not all of which was discussed) but the following is worth noting.

B: When I moved house and moved school, it was if everyone knew something I didn't. As if they spoke another language. And I still feel that now. I didn't understand why I was teased. At my first new school, the Primary, it was generally OK. Someone told me that two girls didn't like me. I thought "why"—it surprised me but didn't bother me. Then I went to the mixed-sex school. The first time I cut myself was at home with a penknife by myself. I don't know why I did it. My mother asked me where I had heard about it. When my classmates asked about it at school, I pretended I had been scratched by a rosebush. They teased me because they didn't believe me. I didn't do a lot of cutting at first. My parents didn't really notice. It's all a blank. I don't know if I had heard about cutting from somewhere.

> *T speculates that B may have been bullied because she was perceived as acting oddly. It seems she cannot recall much about it. B had always been liked up to that point and was totally unprepared to be disliked. The feeling of being an outsider has persisted and may explain some of her complaints listed in the first session. The response she received at school has presumably affected her self-image and the doubts she has about her own judgment (Ho13).*

B: My first panic attack was at age 13. With my creative writing, I had lots of stories going around in my head. They were dark stories. When I thought about one in bed, it became real. It was about my bed sheets that gradually became part of my skin. I couldn't pull them off. I couldn't trust my imagination not to hurt me. I had a few more panic attacks later.

> *T is curious about the nature of these attacks. Why does B call them panic attacks? Were they similar to her current panicky feelings? Is this nighttime attack related to her current nightmares and disturbed sleep?*

B: I think my mother called it a panic attack. It lasted about 10–15 minutes. My mother heard me screaming. She was very upset but didn't know what to do with me. I always dreamt a lot and I blurred dreams and stories with reality. My stories became darker and I gave up writing when I was 15. The stories didn't really work and they were misunderstood.

> *T speculates that the dream of the bed sheet becoming part of her body had induced a fear of being confined and unable to escape, similar to a fear of small enclosed places. T asks if this interpretation makes any sense.*

B: My main dream is screaming, with no sound coming out. As if the sheet would muffle it. No one would be aware of my screaming. That dream still comes to me now. When I'm in bed I have a montage of random experiences. The picture flashes and I can't escape the depth of the image.

T wonders whether B was and still is having hypnagogic experiences (hallucina-tions prior to falling asleep, Ho14). Her sensation of being unable to scream out loud (despite attempts to do so) could be an example of sleep paralysis (a con-scious awareness of the flaccid paralysis that occurs normally in a sleeping state, leading to an inability to speak). Another possible hypothesis is that B is expressing in her nightmare her feelings about not being listened to by her schoolteachers or parents (Ho15). T decides to interpret her experiences as hyp-nagogic images or sleep paralysis and encourages B to read up about these phe-nomena on the internet in order to find out if she recognizes them as similar to her own experiences.

B is surprised and intrigued by the interpretation. "There is so much that clutters up my head." B draws the distinction (consistent with the phenom-enon) that her normal dreams are different from the images because the former are story-like, with her as a person in them.

B (returns to her writings): I took some aspirin for a pain at school. Then twice and three times the amount. I thought if I took the lot, my other pains would go away. So I took the whole box and had to go to the Accident and Emergency department of the hospital. I was told off by the nurses at the hospital.

T speculates that B was attempting to get her difficulties acknowledged by acting in this dramatic way (Ho16). The hospital was not sympathetic. T asks how she and others reacted to this event.

B: I reacted with teenage indifference. People were angry with me because I made them cross. I went for some therapy sessions. It was two women at the same time. I think it was a psychologist and a psychiatrist. I don't remember the sessions—I think it was about how to cope.

T infers that B did get noticed and that some people acknowledged that she needed help.

To facilitate recall of the therapy and perhaps other relevant information about events at the time, T asks B to close her eyes and try to recall the physical surround-ings of the therapist's office.

B: The office was opposite my school. It was in an institutional sort of place. They sat opposite me. I don't remember any good feelings. I just felt I was missing out on time I could be at home and away from the school.

T infers that B did not feel listened to, whatever attempts were made. T comments that perhaps people did not explore what was going on below the surface of her difficulties at the time. This was an invitation for B to give an account of her behavior at the time.

B: I was generally hurting myself. I started to cut not just my arms. I made a deeper cut in my wrists and throat—I think to make a bigger effect. I am not sure it was really suicide. I threw myself down the stairs as well, at home. I hit my face on something. I lied about the mark on my cheek and felt smug when others believed my lies. I thought if I broke my arm, that would have been a good one.

It seems that B was escalating her dramatic behavior and T infers that it was designed to draw attention to her problems (Ho16). He attempts to gain evidence for this by asking what she thought she was achieving by these acts.

B: I think it was an instrumental act. People did notice. I had lots of friends even if those friends would still be part of the bully group. I told lies to shock people, like taking heroin.

T reasons that Ho16 is only partially correct. It seems likely that B was also trying to gain popularity by acting outrageously.

T asks B whether she ever discussed her problems with friends in order to find out whether she had any other way of getting noticed or receiving approval.

B: I wouldn't talk to them about that [i.e. cutting]. They wouldn't take sides. It was the bullies versus me.

T infers from her reply that she was socially excluded and that she could not trust even supposed friends. B also reflected on the fact that the bullies, bar one, were girls. B mentioned that she tried to get boys to like her by acting like a boy. She thinks that this explains why she now goes out with men that do not attract her. Her explanation supports the hypothesis that she is still very anxious about being liked and will play a role against her better judgment. B had also written about some other episodes of bullying.

B: I wrote down two other episodes. In the High Street, two girls shouted something at me and I shouted back. They threw me against a shop window and cracked the glass. I also remember carrying a pack of coins to hold in my hand when I made a fist. It was to make your fist more effective.

The process of writing has been successful in prompting B's recall and causing her to reflect with an adult perspective on the past. The level of violence is surprising. The evidence supports the hypothesis that B was blocked from getting any meaningful help or support and had to escalate her dramatic acts in order to be noticed (Ho16). Her father is not mentioned once, emphasizing his psychological absence. B sees historical links with her current behavior without T having to suggest it.

T encourages her to continue to write, utilizing the technique of remembering details of the physical surroundings as a prompt. T remarks that B has not written about the two main traumatic episodes and encourages her to write about these as well. B understands the purpose of what she is doing and believes that it is helping her. She has further job interviews.

T now feels he has sufficient information to be confident that the primary focus of the intervention should be on post-traumatic stress. This does not mean that there is no further need for assessment or no other problems to attend to. Outstanding questions are:

1. Are B's nightmares memories of bullying or are they more closely related to hypnagogic hallucinations or sleep paralysis? If B's nightmares are a component of her post-traumatic response, her nightmares should reduce over time if she is able to process her memories differently.
2. To what extent is B dissociating when she recalls her memories of bullying? Is this likely to be an obstacle to therapy and will it be necessary to focus on this in therapy?
3. To what extent is B suppressing other traumatic memories from her school years and is therefore unable to talk about them?
4. Will B continue to cut herself and will this remain a problem?
5. Does B perceive that she has any problems in her current relationships with friends or boyfriends? Does she try too hard to be liked? Is her tendency to "put on a front" of being capable and invulnerable an aspect of her life that she feels she wants to work on? (She has already started to share her problems with her mother, which indicates a willingness to seek support despite her preferred coping style of not complaining.)

T could have asked B to complete standardized questionnaires to assess, say, depressed mood, signs of post-traumatic stress, and interpersonal problems. These questionnaires could have been administered prior to the first interview and might have been a rapid way of identifying topics for the interview. However, B probably needed time to trust T before revealing much of her history because she hated to appear weak and a victim. Therefore, interviewing probably had distinct advantages in terms of developing B's relationship with T. Questionnaire scores might only have reflected what she was willing to admit at the time.

At this point, there is much about B that T still does not know. T expects to gather further information and modify the formulation as necessary. Jumping forward in time, the following information (listed below) emerged in later sessions. This did in fact change the formulation to some degree.

1. Insomnia. B researched hypnagogic images and sleep paralysis and what she read resonated with her own experiences and helped to normalize them. B began to say that her nightmares and panic attacks "were not so bad." T should really have asked B to keep a diary in order to monitor the

frequency of these problems, after first defining in concrete terms what would count as a "nightmare" or a "panic attack" to be recorded. The fact that he did not do so is an indication of the pressure to work quickly and use the client's time to best advantage to deal with more pressing issues.

2. Dissociation. There was further evidence of B's difficulty getting in touch with her feelings when writing about traumatic events. In one session, and unusual for her, she became very upset when talking about her memories. At the next session, she remembered being upset, and was surprised that she had been upset, but could not recall why. Her tendency to detach herself, and her difficulty in recalling the past, was interpreted for her as a form of avoidance and the possible reasons for it were explored (e.g. a fear of "falling apart," distress in recalling events signifying loss, rejection, and lack of support).

3. Feeling tainted. Perhaps even more significant than physical threat, B reported that she was most lastingly affected by a sense that other schoolchildren regarded her as disgusting. They indicated this by not wanting to be in close physical contact (as if she was "dirty") or by gestures (e.g. "ugh"). She recalled one memory of this type in a "non-static" (i.e. meaning to her non-detached) manner and she said that it still influenced her image of herself. It was presumably an intrusive memory that she re-lived as if presently occurring.

4. Cutting. B later admitted to cutting herself regularly, and also while on her brief holiday. At her first interview, B had not given the impression that this was a frequent behavior (although T had not questioned her in detail about it). B seemed to be reluctant to talk about it and so T dealt with it in a matter-of-fact way and did not show especial concern. As a substitute, B was advised to try to find ways of hurting herself in a milder way. She also attempted to find distracting activities when she had an urge to cut. The problem did not seem to be a major one and gradually became less significant over time.

5. Relationships. Investigation of her memories of bullying highlighted a theme of disloyalty and being "let down," which was still a feature of her relationships with friends. B had earlier stated that she did not know why her mood had changed "for no apparent reason" in the previous year but she later revealed that when rejected by her boyfriend "my confidence fizzled away completely." Therefore, T had underestimated the significance of this break-up of a relationship and the extent to which it was a reason for seeking therapy. Presumably, B had not wanted

to present herself as "weak" or as a "victim" and therefore did not mention the break-up as significant. This illustrates the point that information revealed at interview is heavily filtered by a client and can lead to an inadequate formulation.

6. Responsibility. B felt disloyal to herself after one writing exercise. This exercise had led her to feel sorry for her "teenage self" and she expressed a wish "to want to look after her," whereas formerly this "self" had been "invisible." It was as if she had allowed others to do these things to her teenage self. However, she felt that she "had not looked after her" and subsequently felt guilty and disloyal. B seems to have spontaneously used a technique employed in schema-focused therapy (Young etal., 2003) in which an "adult self" is invited to interact, in a dialog or fantasy, with a "child self." B said: "Everything I did was like carrying a child around with me." T elaborated a lengthy rationale for what B had done on her own initiative, in other words, that she had constructed an image of herself as "another person" because she was now less fused with this earlier image of herself. At the end of this discussion, B felt that she now had "two viewpoints," and felt less responsible and also safer "writing with a bird's-eye view."

7. Managing others' perceptions. B said that one effect of bullying was to be always managing the way other people viewed her. Only recently had she been able to trust her own feelings and act on them but this had led nowhere with the boyfriend who later rejected her. If T had spent more time exploring B's initial complaints of "not trusting her own judgment" and "always getting things wrong" this theme might have emerged earlier. T's failure to do this illustrates that an assessment interview delivers an overload of information. It seemed more important at the time to assess the type and severity of her depressed mood. In the interests of obtaining a comprehensive picture of her problem areas, it might have been better to go through her problem checklist one by one. However, if done mechanically, this strategy might not have fostered a trusting relationship. Moreover, T did not foreclose on a fixed formulation and was able to pick up on significant information as it gradually emerged in assessment and therapy. As already noted, B's preferred coping strategy was to keep problems to herself, to be strong, and not to complain. Under these circumstances, establishing a trusting, safe, and non-judgmental relationship was probably a prerequisite for an adequate formulation to be constructed.

8. Expressing "true" feelings. One aspect of managing others was for B to get them to like her (reminiscent of her mother telling her to be nice to the bullies). B accepted that this might have promoted her image as a victim and exacerbated the bullying. A new therapy focus emerged around expressing her "true feelings" rather than managing others' impressions. However, asserting herself in this way felt very frightening to B, although she was willing to implement some changes in this regard. This intervention necessitated a more detailed assessment of her personal relationships and, in effect, a new formulation of this aspect of her problem.

9. Panic-like feelings. Further light was thrown on B's statement in the first session that a trigger for emotional distress was "not being able to cope," "something I can't do well," and frustration when "not meeting demands." That T did not follow up on this in detail at the time was probably due to information overload (as already noted) and the fact that it was too easy to assimilate this information into a vicious circle model of panic phenomena (representativeness bias, see Chapter 5). In other words, it was assumed that not coping well as a result of her stressed emotional state interfering with what she was doing led her to perceive a greater discrepancy between her performance and the high standards she applied to it, producing even greater distress. In other words, T implicitly adopted this preferred conceptual model of a vicious circle, leading him to attend selectively to the facts. B later revealed that even as a young child, she would lose control if not listened to, and B produced other examples from later in childhood. In other words, this was a feature of her personality that preceded any of the upsetting events of moving house and schools. B reported that she would get extremely frustrated even if one of her parents failed, say, to understand a point in an intellectual argument or the reasons she gave for her aesthetic appreciation of a work of art. Therefore, a characteristic of B's behavior may have predisposed her to react to the change of schools and bullying in the way that she did. B expanded on the meaning of not being understood as "loneliness," at which point she broke into tears. B explained that when not understood she keeps ideas a secret and loses the resolve to communicate. However, without external validation, this leads her to question her own judgment and to lose self-belief. She recalled a number of examples of this phenomenon from her schooldays and the residual anger she still felt about some examples of not having her ideas or contributions acknowledged.

All of the information that emerged after the "assessment phase" illustrates the fact that a richer formulation can always be produced. The new information is not seriously inconsistent with the old formulation, but it points out gaps and weaknesses. New interventions suggest themselves. In B's case, it might have been helpful to work on her ability to express herself without worrying too much about the impression she was creating. If this did not produce any negative consequences, it might have strengthened her confidence in her own judgment. Of course, a client has to see a need for pursuing therapy beyond a certain point. As it happens, B was satisfied when the bulk of her emotional distress was relieved after only five sessions, including the three assessment sessions described above. In T's opinion additional sessions would have been desirable. B may have terminated therapy at this point for financial reasons. B telephoned T five months later to say that she was feeling fine and would get in touch again if she needed further help.

Evaluation of hypotheses in the light of all information

Ho1. A childhood history of abuse/emotional deprivation. [Confirmed in the sense of the trauma of being bullied as a teenager.]

Ho2. B feels uncomfortable with her self-image. [Confirmed, but developed in Hos 5, 11, and 13.]

Ho3. B is at a choice point in her career. [Confirmed.]

Ho4. B is suffering from acute situational stress. [Partially confirmed, but other sources of distress seem to be more important.]

Ho5. Self-critical of her competence, and a need to present herself as able to cope. [Confirmed only in the latter aspect. Does not want to present herself as weak, see also Ho9.]

Ho6. Her complaints are signs of a syndrome of depressed mood as primary cause. [Not supported. Depressed mood appears to be secondary to other difficulties.]

Ho7. Experienced severe bullying as a teenager. [Confirmed.]

Ho8. Some of B's complaints are expressions of post-traumatic stress. [Confirmed.]

Ho9. Blames herself for the bullying. [Confirmed.]

Ho10. Advice from parents on how to cope, and their support, were inadequate. [Strongly supported.]

Ho11. B has difficulty recognizing and expressing her needs in interpersonal situations. [Strongly supported.]

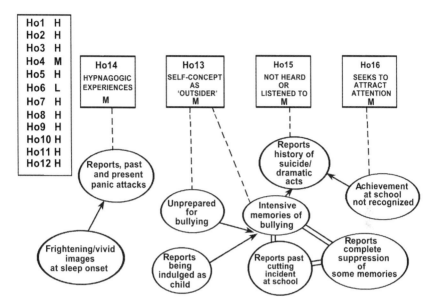

Figure D3 Additions to the ICF diagram after session 3.

Ho12. B experiences dissociative states of mind. [Moderate support.]

Ho13. B has a poorly developed concept of herself as socially successful (i.e. feels an outsider and doubts her own judgment). [Strongly supported.]

Ho14. Nightmares partly related to frightening hypnagogic experiences and sleep paralysis. [Moderately supported.]

Ho15. Nightmares express feelings about not being "heard." [Weakly supported, but not investigated.]

Ho16. Acted as a teenager in a dramatic way to receive attention for problems/distress. [Moderately supported, but possibly sought popularity in this way.]

SECTION E. CHOICE OF INTERVENTION: REVISING THE FORMULATION WHEN AN INTERVENTION FAILS

The aim of formulation is to suggest ways of intervening with a problem and a strategy for helping clients to tackle it. Choice of an intervention is guided by an understanding of the mechanisms that are assumed to be maintaining a problem and sometimes merely by the results of research showing effectiveness of techniques with similar problems. Some points to consider before implementing an intervention are as follows:

1. Does the client understand the rationale of therapy and does he or she want to deal with a problem in the manner suggested? A therapist will have a sense of this from a client's response to any reading material that has been supplied. When an assessment has been conducted collaboratively, the choice of intervention should seem like a natural progression. The formulation will not be perceived as having been imposed but as something that can be used to reach joint decisions about a practical problem at a particular point in time (Harper & Moss, 2003).

2. Are the client's goals for therapy reasonably well defined, even if only specifying a general direction of travel? Client B described in Section D could express no clear idea of what would help. In many cases, the goals of therapy emerge from assessment and discussion.

3. Is there a strategy for working from immediate short-term objectives to longer term goals, that is, towards a satisfactory resolution of the main issues? For instance, client B wished to express her creativity (a long-term goal) but also wanted to earn enough to keep up payments on her home (a short-term objective). Having her own home and finding a partner were also long-term aims. She hinted at a conflict between, on the one hand, achieving this by seeking out a wealthy partner but, on the other hand, not settling for "second best." These were her own pragmatic and existential choices that the therapist simply accepted. Clients can only plan for what they think they want and what compromises they believe they can live with. In the past, B had sought relief from her depressed mood by taking medication. She later realized that this was not the best way to deal with the root causes of her problems and decided not to choose this path again.

4. Is the client motivated to change? It seems to be a general rule that people do not change their behavior unless they have a sufficient incentive to do so. It is therefore essential to explore all sources of motivation, including possible disadvantages of changing as well as the advantages (Miller & Rollnick, 2002). A client may have an unfounded of fear of change and imagine unrealistic obstacles in the way of achieving it. There may be predicted benefits but it is not always possible to foresee all the "follow-on" consequences, some of which may offset any benefit.

5. When deciding what issue to address first (i.e. when selecting the initial "target problem") the following considerations may be helpful:

a. Which problem is the client most motivated to work on?

b. Which problem, if resolved, would bring the client most relief?

c. Which problem would be relatively quick and easy to resolve?

d. What current behavior or environmental stress places a client at risk and demands urgent attention?

e. Which behavior of the client jeopardizes the overall success of therapy and has to be tackled early on? Examples are arriving late (or not at all) for sessions, feelings of hopelessness, lack of commitment to change, inability to pay travel expenses, and use of alcohol or drugs.

f. Which problem interferes most in a client's life?

g. What change, if successfully made, would have the greatest positive impact on other problems?

h. Which problem, if solved, might destabilize a client in other respects, such as relationships with family or partner, or holding on to secure employment?

6. Therapy is easier to conduct when it is directed towards a single objective but it is often necessary to deal with several problems at the same time. Even so, the priority of each one may vary over time. Housing and debt problems may need to be resolved before a client can begin to think about other issues. When working on several fronts, a strategy for doing so has to be decided. For instance, in the course of an ongoing "crisis," a therapist deals with events as they occur but time may be left in the session to switch back to the main problem. From a constructional perspective, working on a problem list one item at a time is not necessarily the best strategy to adopt. It makes theoretical sense to encourage positive strategies for solving a problem while at the same time finding ways to ease distress or diminish self-defeating habits. For instance, a client who tends to criticize a partner may have to learn how to show and receive appreciation while at the same time reducing criticism.

Failed interventions and revisions to a formulation

An intervention can fail for many reasons. It cannot be said to have failed in a technical sense if a client fails to comply with it or subtly undermines it. However, non-compliance might indicate a therapist's failure to prepare a client by fully explaining the rationale of an intervention and dealing sensitively with any reservations a client may have about it. Failure can sometimes be attributed to poor execution of a therapeutic strategy. This need not reflect on the adequacy of the formulation or choice of method.

A failure is of more interest theoretically when a client is well motivated and compliant. In these circumstances, it is more likely that the formulation is at fault. There has to be some means of detecting progress in order for failure to be detected. A therapist should at the very least seek verbal feedback to indicate whether a problem is being resolved or getting worse. Sophisticated and time-intensive measurement is not always necessary. It may simply become obvious within sessions that an intervention is not helpful, or events happening between sessions may indicate this. However, diary ratings or a system of behavioral monitoring makes it easier to detect change.

A formulation is likely to be weak if it is not based on a comprehensive assessment. Even under the best circumstances it may only provide a best guess about which intervention to apply, given that there are always a number of unknowns. In recognition of this uncertainty, an intervention can be introduced in a spirit of experimentation. A client's failure to respond is the usual indication of a need to revise a formulation. Therapy may throw up what could be called "natural experiments" from which lessons can be learned.

An intervention that succeeds does not necessarily validate the formulation on which it is based, but failure, with the exceptions noted above, usually invalidates it. In the case of failure, we know that what was attempted did not work. Through modifying an approach and observing its effect, a therapist sometimes gains a deeper understanding of why the original formulation was inadequate.

An example of a revised formulation following the return of a problem

The following case example illustrates the process of reasoning when choosing an intervention. It shows how the evidence base can be utilized when an intervention fails. Initially, therapy was very effective but the problem returned one year later. The formulation was revised in the light of a reassessment. The second intervention was successful and the client has now largely been free of her problem for several years. The case history illustrates the risks of a narrow conceptualization. The first intervention was chosen on the basis of selecting a procedure known to be generally effective for her problem. This is not an unreasonable basis for decision making but, in retrospect, it was clear that certain relevant factors had not been appreciated at the first assessment.

History
A married woman (M), in her 30s, came for help with intrusive thoughts and associated avoidance of situations that heightened her obsessional fears.

M was the youngest of three sisters born into a working–class family. Her childhood was unhappy. She said she always lived in fear of being scolded by her mother, who was more affectionate towards her older sisters than to her. She described her mother as bullying and never giving praise. She was much closer to her father but he acted in an authoritarian manner, and she described herself as being terrified of him. He had supported her older sisters through university but would not do the same for her. Her older sisters dominated her and regarded her as odd or "a bit mad." This attitude remained into adulthood, with the result that she was often excluded from family affairs or simply expected to fall into requests to help out when needed. As a child, she attempted to assert herself with her mother, and it was partly on this account that she was regarded as "different." However, she always apologized after any act of self-assertion and promised to behave better in future. She also coped by detaching herself emotionally and retreating into literature or the arts. These interests were ridiculed by her family.

Psychological difficulties as an adult

M became severely depressed and anxious at age 20 following the death of her father. She avoided scissors and knives at this time. However, she got married subsequently and has remained happily so. After her marriage, she developed an obsession about contracting HIV, and she also had intrusive thoughts that her marriage would fail. She received 7 years of psychodynamic therapy and also long periods of antidepressant (selective serotonin reuptake inhibitor, SSRI) medication, amounting to 9 years in all. She put off having children for many years and then, when her first daughter was born, suffered a post-natal depression. She was prescribed an SSRI, and again after a second daughter was born. When this daughter was two years old she decided to withdraw from her SSRI and her life "unraveled." When first seen, she was taking a standard dose of a SSRI prescribed by her general physician.

Nevertheless, throughout these early adult years she had put herself through university, had always worked, and had started a business. She decided to seek help privately.

Main presenting problem

M was terrified of harming her children and had intrusive thoughts when left alone with them (e.g. "What if I were to push them off the balcony?" "What if I were to stifle them?"). These thoughts could escalate into an imagined scenario of losing her husband, her children, her business, and a

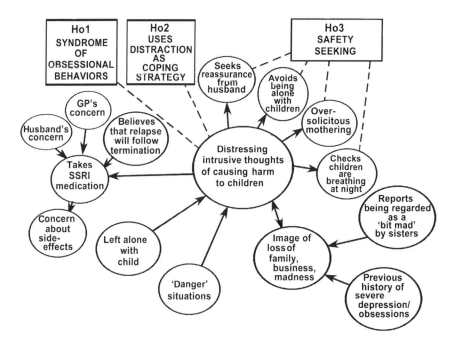

Figure E1 Client M. Formulation diagram after initial assessment.

descent into madness. She avoided ever being left alone with her children, checked whether they were breathing before she went to bed at night, and sought reassurance from her husband that she was a good mother. She tended to keep very busy in order to distract herself and therefore found it very difficult to relax. While on holiday, a realization that she felt "happy" could become a cue for an intrusive thought that her marriage would collapse.

Interventions (see Figure E1)

Therapy adopted techniques that have been found to be successful with obsessions of this nature (Abramowitz, 1998; Foa & Franklin, 2002). These were: (1) Explanation of a cognitive behavioral theoretical rationale with a recommendation to read a self-help book. (2) When experiencing a thought, encouraging acceptance of its presence, without acting upon it, until it had "passed out of her mind." (3) Remaining in situations when her thoughts intruded, rather than escaping to safety. (4) Reducing her avoidance of "dangerous" situations in which the thoughts occurred, and being proactive in seeking them out (e.g. walking across a bridge alone with her daughters). (5) Eliminating the checks that her children were "alive," and avoiding over-solicitous behavior or unnecessary demonstrations of care/affection which seemed to have the function of reassuring herself that she was a good mother. (6) Ending requests for reassurance (mainly from her husband) that she was responsible and caring.

Through a planned series of homework tasks, M was able to reduce her avoidance and increase her exposure to "danger" in the normal activities of caring for her children. In addition, M's beliefs about her qualities as a mother were explored using cognitive therapy techniques, and an attempt was made to restructure her negative view of herself and to replace it with a more realistic appraisal. She allowed herself to be more irritable at times with her own children without feeling that she was failing as a mother. M was also encouraged to be more assertive with her own mother and sisters, and they slowly began to be more accepting of her right to "be herself." The reason for this intervention was to counter their view that she was "unable to cope" or was even "a bit mad," a view that M seemed to have accepted in some measure.

One of M's major fears, reinforced by her husband and general physician, was that she would relapse completely if she were to stop taking her SSRI medication. This medication had helped her in the past. However, she had stopped taking the medication on previous occasions and was willing to tolerate symptoms of withdrawal again. M was aware that the medication had an emotionally deadening effect and led her to put on weight. She was also concerned about cardiac irregularities, for which she was being investigated, and believed that the medication could be a contributing factor.

Given M's belief in the power of medication to suppress her obsessional thoughts, the use of medication could be seen, theoretically, as functioning in the same way as seeking reassurance from her husband or avoiding the "dangerous" situation of being left alone with her children. An interpretation could be made that taking her medication was a form of "safety-seeking behavior," an important component in some cognitive behavioral therapy (CBT) disorder-specific models of obsessive-compulsive disorder (OCD) (Salkovskis, 1999).

Unfortunately, the evidence from outcome studies in which medication is used alone or in combination with CBT does not cast any light on the specific point of whether a client's *belief* in the efficacy of medication could be a significant variable in success. This possibility does not seem to have been investigated in relation to OCD although it is one of the factors taken into consideration in therapy for withdrawal from benzodiazepine drugs (Otto, Pollack, & Barlow, 2000).

Recent evidence suggests that SSRI medication has only a slight effect in reducing obsessional thoughts when used alone, whereas the effect of

CBT by itself or in combination with medication is large (Foa etal., 2005; O'Connor etal., 2006). However, in this latter study, medication had a generally beneficial effect on mood. Therefore, applying these findings to M's case, it was predicted that: (1) If M relapsed following withdrawal of medication, it would be unlikely that this could be explained by the anti-obsessional properties of the medication (which have been shown to be slight). It would be more likely that this would be due to M being deprived of a signal for safety (i.e. an effect mediated psychologically rather than biochemically). (2) If M's mood also became more depressed following withdrawal of medication, one interpretation would be that depression in mood was an effect of the absence of medication (a biochemical effect). (3) If this decline in mood were to be accompanied by an increase in the frequency of her obsessions, a possible interpretation would be that low mood constituted a causal mediator for obsessions in her case.

It seemed plain that medication played a central role in M's beliefs about the obsessions, and M had been taking a SSRI, on and off, for a total of 9 years. As a precondition for learning that she could control her problem using psychological techniques, it was decided to help her to reduce and eventually come off medication despite her physician's belief that "CBT was not powerful enough by itself." In view of her considerable progress after six sessions, and despite the risk that the GP could indeed be right, M decided to reduce her SSRI medication to half the recommended dose. At this point in therapy she was able to dismiss intrusive thoughts fairly easily, did not elaborate on them with further catastrophic ideas, and was regularly doing things in a normal way with her children on her own (i.e. in the absence of another person who made her feel "safe"). After a couple of months on reduced medication, its side-effects were largely eliminated, and she felt revived emotionally (i.e. her mood improved rather than worsened). This suggests that the medication had had no anti-obsessional or mood-enhancing effect.

After 12 sessions, she had been without any medication for three months and her physician stated that he was pleased to have been proved wrong. Given that her obsession was no longer a significant problem, therapy was terminated at this point, with arrangements made for a review several months later.

Subsequent return of obsessions

Given M's long history of episodes of severely disabling obsessions, it may not seem too surprising that she had a recurrence of the problem one year later. In the past, M had received benefit from medication but she has to be regarded as a pharmacological treatment failure in the sense that, when first seen, M suffered a recurrence while being maintained on an adequate dose of an SSRI. According to Cottraux, Martine, Bouvard, and Milliery (2005) "there is no clear consensus on what are, and what to do with, refractory patients." In fact, they cite evidence showing that "as many as 40–60% of OCD patients remain clinically unchanged after an adequate trial of medication." These authors further argue that the customary criteria for benefit from medication are unduly lenient, and that the magnitude of change on the questionnaires employed in evaluation research "will not affect dramatically the life of most of the patients." Therefore, there must remain an element of doubt that medication had ever had any direct effect on M's obsessions, although it may have lifted her mood and increased her ability to cope with them. However, M certainly believed that she would "relapse" without them and the fact that she did so after her first experience of CBT added credence to this belief. Of course, believing that medication is effective could, in itself, bring about a reduction of obsessional behavior through psychological mechanisms (and conversely an increase when medication is withdrawn).

Despite a general recognition that psychological therapy can be effective by itself, the usual recommendation for refractory and severe OCD problems is to increase the level of medication (and to expect a client to take it on a life-long basis), to switch to an alternative medication (e.g. another SSRI, another form of antidepressant, an anti-anxiety agent, or an antipsychotic), or to use several SSRIs in combination. Last-resort options include "intravenous clomipramine or neurosurgery" (Cottraux etal., 2005). However, Sookman and Steketee (2007, 2010) reported good outcomes for clients in whom previous standard CBT methods had not produced benefit. Sookman and colleagues worked on childhood schemas that they believe make a person more vulnerable to develop obsessional behavior. Ten out of their 32 clients overcame their problem completely.

It is certainly not unusual for a client with an obsession to experience its return, and for an obsession to take a completely different form. In the past, M had had obsessional concerns about HIV, sharp objects, and the failure of her marriage. The mere fact that M experienced a return of her fears of harming her daughters does not imply that CBT in her case was "ineffective," any more than one flu remedy would be expected to prevent all future influenza illnesses. If M is prone to develop obsessions, she may have to apply the same techniques repeatedly to deal with them. But rather than interpret recurrences as inevitable for M, it was decided to undertake a new phase of assessment and formulation on the grounds that something had been missed.

Reformulation

M's recurrence of her primary obsession had not taken a new form; as before, it was essentially a fear of being left alone with her children in case she harmed them. However, intrusive thoughts of harming herself or others were now more prominent, leading her to fear the sight of scissors, razors, or other potential implements of attack, or to drive unaccountably into other vehicles on the road. One possible trigger for the return of her obsession was the increased (and realistic) stress of maintaining her business successfully. Another was a serious illness in her mother. She wanted to give up work altogether but decided to continue. Her heavy involvement in work may have explained her feeling that she was living "like an automaton," and also her worry that she was becoming emotionally detached from her husband, family, and friends. She felt "shocked" that CBT had failed and thought that she could not be sure that she would be absolutely safe unless taking medication once again. Her physician did not initially go along with this plan, believing that she could cope. Later he suggested medication but M refused, still aware that it had unwanted side-effects. Of most importance, M also believed that the techniques that had helped her before could help her once again.

Before she could really implement the decision to reapply these CBT techniques, M's obsessional fears and avoidance continued to increase. Consequently, M decided to resume SSRI medication. M was also prescribed a benzodiazepine drug, as needed, to help her cope with occasional "panic attacks." However, M still saw medication as a crutch while continuing to confront her obsessional fears in the same way as before. She challenged herself by spending time alone with her children and accepting her thoughts as a "nuisance," seeing them as part of a OCD condition from which she was suffering, rather than believing in the reality of her imagined disaster scenarios. However, when in the immediate grip of an obsessional thought, she succumbed to all her former fears of potentially causing harm to her children, herself, or others. Her intrusive thoughts also included the following:

- How can I be sure this is OCD?
- I might do something to prove it is not OCD.

The negative implications of her "condition" included the following:

- I am a terrible mother because I can't even be left alone with my children.
- If everyone thinks I'm mad, I might as well give in and be mad.
- I will never work again.
- The children would be better off without me.

The element of the problem that came to the fore in the reassessment was her tendency to throw herself into distracting activity, such as her work, or by inviting a constant stream of visitors to her home. Presumably, these activities deflected attention from intrusive thoughts or an aversive mood state. She came to realize that she was "incredibly driven" and "didn't want to fail," that is, not simply as a mother, but in life in general. This aspect of her attitude to life had not been fully appreciated at first assessment.

It was also apparent that the influence of her family on her view of herself (as ill and incapable) remained strong. The first intervention had focused too narrowly on M's belief that she was a "bad or insufficiently caring mother." Although M had been encouraged to assert her own opinion and stand up for herself with her mother and sisters, and was beginning to do so, it was reasoned that this process had not been taken far enough. M's belief in herself as a good and competent person was still very fragile. Her family was now expressing the opinion that she was "malingering," that she should never have come off medication, and that she was hindering her husband"s advancement at work. Her elder sisters were extremely successful in their own careers, from which the therapist inferred that M felt herself to be under pressure to succeed in order to prove to them that she was equally capable of success. M confirmed this inference by talking about grand plans to grow a large and successful business. This was an idea she was very reluctant to give up.

Viewed systemically and functionally, it was assumed that the views of others, as demonstrated by the opinions they communicated, were internalized by M as her view of herself. While the origins of M's self-concept lay primarily in childhood events, it seemed clear that negative views were still being maintained by current interactions. The concept of herself as an ill person was being communicated by her mother and sisters, and to some extent by her husband and physician, although their opinions were far more pragmatic and based on what they thought she ought to do to cope with her "condition."

The hypothesis was formed that M's intense activity (at work and socially) was highly stressful and producing a raised level central (cortical) arousal in which the frequency of her obsessional thoughts increased. Moreover, her activities served to distract her from intrusive thoughts, and so M was effectively avoiding their complete acceptance. Whether to prove herself as "competent" or "normal" or to distract herself, M's investment in work to the exclusion of other aspects of her life, may have led to a vicious circle of increasing stress, fed by a fear of failure at work, a sense of having to keep her obsessions at bay, and an avoidance of a catastrophic loss of everything she

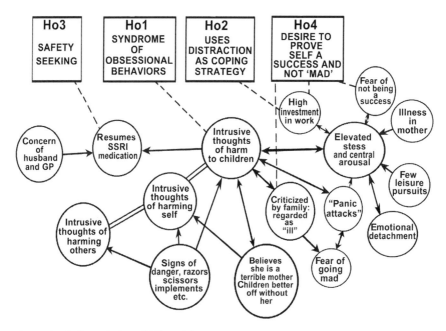

Figure E2 Reformulation of M's problems.

valued. A significant precipitant for the return of her obsession was a business colleague asking her "if she was becoming ill again." M seemed to be focusing more and more of her attention on her obsessional thoughts and their potential consequences, and her intense work and social activity was not being compensated by relaxing leisure pursuits. In fact, M found it a considerable challenge simply to remain alone at home and sit down to read a book.

New interventions

Based on a reformulation (see Figure E2), the following interventions were introduced.

Strengthening a positive self-concept

The aim was to develop an alternative narrative to the one in which she viewed herself as mentally ill, incompetent, and a bad mother. Counterarguments were generated with her and then rehearsed in a reverse roleplay in which the therapist played devil's advocate (Hallam & O'Connor, 2002). It was accepted that M was suffering from an "OCD condition," and that she was more prone to having intrusive thoughts than other people. However, it was argued that the experience of unwanted intrusive thoughts is a common phenomenon and in her case it was one to which she attached exaggerated significance. The aim of rehearsing counter-arguments in a role-play was to strengthen their credibility when she experienced the thoughts at home. The role-play was recorded so that M could listen to herself countering her negative intrusions with positive re-interpretations of their significance. In other words, the therapist, playing devil's advocate, would accuse her of "being a bad mother" of "descending into madness," etc., and M would counter with arguments such as the following:

- My thoughts really are OCD because I have read about OCD.
- The thoughts are frightening and repetitive because of what I believe about what they really mean.
- I am a good mother.
- I only believe I will cause harm because I am afraid of causing harm.
- I fear not being able to cope because as a child I was told I was the unstable one.
- I love my children and they love me.
- People with OCD thoughts do not act on them or cause harm to others.

M was encouraged to continue asserting herself with her mother and sisters, to interact with them on her own terms, and to disengage to some extent from family affairs. M was supported by her husband in this respect. He was encouraged to read a self-help book on obsessions to give him a greater understanding of M's difficulties. He became more proactive in helping M to resist the message of inadequacy she received from her family.

Developing a less "driven" lifestyle

M accepted that she found it very difficult to relax when by herself and that she ought to spend more time in leisure activity. She and her husband planned evenings out together. M decided to downsize her business and work from home, which lessened her financial commitments considerably. M recognized that her business ambitions, however much she still wanted to achieve them, were unrealizable while she was still so vulnerable to her obsessional fears. By working from home, M was forced to confront more "quiet time" and to learn that she could cope without diversionary activity. She began to attend yoga classes.

Subsequent progress

Over a period of nine months, with sessions at approximately monthly intervals, M was able to implement the new therapy plan. Her intrusive thoughts are now either absent or easily dismissed. Her behavior towards her children has normalized completely. In looking back, M stated, "I threw myself manically into something or I collapsed." She feels she now understands better the "dynamics" of the wider family, is able to refuse unreasonable requests, and tends to deal with her sisters in a matter of fact way. She has dissociated herself from her family to some extent, while not blaming them. In her view, M believes that as a child she had to build up a protective wall around herself and therefore became prone to self-doubt with no one to validate her opinions. M is able to take short relaxing breaks when working at home and she enjoys her social activities.

On two points, M has not followed the revised program. With regard to medication, M has continued to take half of her original SSRI daily prescribed dose. This seems to be in deference to her husband's opinion that without it she might "relapse" and he could not bear this to happen. M also found working from home too socially isolating. She took a part-time job and also obtained new business contracts for her self-employment. However, it seems that these extra commitments have not pushed her, as she said, "to over-program myself," and they have not interfered with her home life. M has remained in contact but has not sought any further help in the past 3 years.

Summary

The course of therapy with M illustrates the value of drawing upon evidence-based practice (EBP). The techniques that have been developed for modifying obsessional behavior were effective in her case. However, M's therapy also illustrates that EBP must be applied intelligently, bearing in mind additional problems that prevented its effective implementation. A further examination of the published literature reinforced the view that medication was probably ineffective in her case but this topic had to be approached sensitively given her belief (and that of her husband) that it was safer to continue taking it. Furthermore, there was evidence in the published literature that adverse childhood experiences can create a vulnerability to OCD and that attending to this aspect of a client's problem can be beneficial (as proved to be the case for M). The application of general principles derived from group studies would not have been successful without considerable effort to explore their implications in a collaborative way with

M, who eventually came to accept their relevance. An individual case formulation (ICF) was drawn up and presented to her in diagrammatic form. The formulation process was drawn out over 20 months. In total M received 26 sessions of therapy, a relatively modest investment considering the impact of the problem over the course of her own life, on that of her family, and on her ability to maintain her business. It is also modest in terms of the length of previous psychodynamic and drug therapies. In this light, any proposal to reduce the cost of therapy by introducing briefer and cheaper forms of manualized EBP (MEBP) must be carefully weighed up against their actual effectiveness.

A successful case example can always be dismissed as "anecdotal evidence." However, when the reasoning that goes into making decisions is exposed for public examination, and a better explanation cannot be produced to account for the facts as presented, the desire for "proof" becomes dogmatic. The actions taken in many areas of public life are contested—such as the introduction of new social policies, investments in new ventures, and the investigation of the causes of accidents. The solutions to problems that beset individual human beings are of a similarly contestable nature. Once it is accepted that personal problems are not caused by eradicable "disorders," any proposed solution will have its advantages and disadvantages.

Abramowitz, J. S. (1998). Does cognitive-behavioral therapy cure obsessive-compulsive disorder? A meta-analytic evaluation of clinical significance. *Behavior Therapy, 29*, 339–355.

Addis, M. E., Wade, W. A., & Hatgis, C. (1999). Barriers to dissemination of evidence based practices: Addressing practitioners' concerns about manual-based psychotherapies. *Clinical Psychology: Science and Practice, 6*, 430–441.

Ahearn, W. H., MacDonald, R. P. F., Graff, R. B., & Dube, W. V. (2007). Behavior analytic teaching procedures: Basic principles, empirically derived practices. In P. Sturmey, & A. Fitzer (Eds.). *Autism spectrum disorders: Applied behavior analysis, evidence, and practice* (pp. 31–83). Austin, TX: Pro-Ed Inc.

American Psychiatric Association. (1980). *Diagnostic and statistical manual of mental disorders* (3rd ed.). Washington, DC: APA.

American Psychiatric Association. (2002). *Diagnostic and statistical manual of mental disorders* (4th ed.). Washington, DC: APA.

Anderson, H., & Goolishian, H. (1992). The client is the expert: A not-knowing approach to therapy. In S. McNamee, & K. J. Gergen (Eds.). *Therapy as social construction* (pp. 25–39). London: Sage.

Anderson, T., Ogles, B. M., Patterson, C., Lambert, M. J., & Vermeersch, D. A. (2009). Therapist effects: Facilitative interpersonal skills as a predictor of therapist success. *Journal of Clinical Psychology, 65*, 755–768.

Andersson, G. (2009). Using the Internet to provide cognitive behavior therapy. *Behaviour Research and Therapy, 47*, 175–180.

Andrews, G., & Titov, N. (2009). Hit and miss: Innovations and the dissemination of evidence based psychological treatments. *Behaviour Research and Therapy, 47*, 974–979.

Angus, L., & Kagan, F. (2007). Empathic relational bonds and personal agency in psychotherapy: Implications for psychotherapy supervision, practice and research. *Psychotherapy: Theory, Research, Practice, Training, 44*, 371–377.

APA Presidential Task Force on Evidence-Based Practice. (2006). Evidence-based practice in psychology. *American Psychologist, 61*, 271–285.

Avdi, E., & Georgaca, E. (2007). Narrative research in psychotherapy: A critical review. *Psychology and Psychotherapy, 80*, 407–419.

Bakhtin, M. M. (1981). Discourse in the novel. In M. M. Bakhtin (Ed.). *The dialogic imagination. Four essays by M. M. Bakhtin* (pp. 259–422). Austin: University of Texas Press.

Baldwin, S. A., Wampold, B. E., & Imel, Z. E. (2007). Untangling the alliance-outcome correlation: Exploring the relative importance of therapist and patient variability in the alliance. *Journal of Consulting and Clinical Psychology, 75*, 842–852.

Bandura, A. (1969). *Principles of behavior modification*. New York: Holt, Rinehart and Winston.

Barber, J. P., & Crits-Christoph, P. (1993). Advances in measures of psychodynamic formulations. *Journal of Consulting and Clinical Psychology, 61*, 574–585.

Barlow, D. H. (2010). Negative effects from psychological treatments. *American Psychologist, 65*, 13–19.

Barlow, D. H., & Carl, J. R. (2011). The future of clinical psychology: Promises, perspectives, and predictions. In D. H. Barlow, & P. E. Nathan (Eds.). *The Oxford handbook of clinical psychology* (pp. 891–911). New York: Oxford University Press.

Barlow, D. H., Allen, L. B., & Choate, M. L. (2004). Toward a unified treatment for emotional disorders. *Behavior Therapy, 35*, 205–230.

Barlow, D. H., Craske, M. G., Cerny, J. A., & Klosko, J. S. (1989). Behavioral treatment of panic disorder. *Behavior Therapy, 20*, 261–282.

Barlow, D. H., Nock, M. K., & Hersen, M. (2008). *Single case experimental designs: Strategies for studying behavior change* (3rd ed.). Boston: Allyn and Bacon.

Barlow, D. H., & Nock, M. K. (2009). Why can't we be more idiographic in our research? *Perspectives on Psychological Science, 4*, 19–21.

Baron, R. M., & Kenny, D. A. (1986). The moderator-mediator variable distinction in social psychological research: Conceptual, strategic, and statistical considerations. *Journal of Personality and Social Psychology, 51*, 1173–1182.

Beck, A. T. (1970). *Depression: Causes and treatment*. Philadelphia: University of Pennsylvania Press.

Beck, A. T. (1976). *Cognitive therapy and the emotional disorders*. New York: International Universities Press.

Beck, A. T., & Steer, R. A. (1993). *The Beck Anxiety Inventory Manual*. San Antonio, TX: The Psychological Corporation.

Becker, C., Zayfert, C., & Anderson, E. (2004). A survey of psychologists' attitudes towards utilization of exposure therapy for PTSD. *Behaviour Research and Therapy, 45*, 819–828.

Bennett-Levy, J. (2006). Therapist skills: Their acquisition and refinement. *Behavioural and Cognitive Psychotherapy, 34*, 57–78.

Bernard, C. (1957). *An introduction to the study of experimental medicine [1865]*. New York: Dover Publications. [Translated by H. C. Greene, introduced by L. J. Henderson, with a foreword by I. B. Cohen.]

Beutler, L. E. (2000). David and Goliath: When empirical and clinical standards of practice meet. *American Psychologist, 55*, 997–1007.

Beutler, L. E., Moleiro, C., & Talebi, H. (2002). How practitioners can systematically use empirical evidence in treatment selection. *Journal of Clinical Psychology, 58*, 1199–1212.

Beutler, L. E., Blatt, S. J., Alimohamed, S., Levy, K. N., & Angtuaco, L. (2006). Participant factors in treating dysphoric disorders. In L. G. Castonguay, & L. E. Beutler (Eds.). *Principles of therapeutic change that work* (pp. 13–63). New York: Oxford University Press.

Bhaskar, R. (1979). *The possibility of naturalism: A philosophical critique of the contemporary human sciences*. Brighton, UK: Harvester Press.

Bickman, L. (1999). Practice makes perfect and other myths about mental health services. *American Psychologist, 54*, 965–978.

Blackburn, I. M., James, D. L., & Reichelt, F. K. (2000). *The revised cognitive therapy scale*. www.ebbp.org/resources/CTS-R.pdf. Accessed 26 February 2012.

Blackledge, J. T. (2003). An introduction to relational frame theory: Basics and applications. *The Behavior Analyst Today, 3*, 421–433.

Bohart, A. C., & House, R. (2008). Empirically supported/validated treatments, a modernist ideology. I. Dodo, manualization, and the paradigm question. In R. House, & D. Loewenthal (Eds.). *Against and for CBT: Towards a constructive dialogue*. Ross-on-Wye, UK: PCCS Books.

Bower, P., & Gilbody, S. (2005). Stepped care in psychological therapies: Access, effectiveness and efficiency. *British Journal of Psychiatry, 186*, 11–18.

British Psychological Society. (2011). *Good practice guidelines for the use of psychological formulation*. Leicester, UK: BPS.

Bromley, D. B. (1986). *The case-study method in psychology and related disciplines*. Chichester, UK: John Wiley & Sons Ltd.

Brown, T. A. (2007). Temporal course and structural relationships among dimensions of temperament and DSM-IV anxiety and mood disorder constructs. *Journal of Abnormal Psychology, 116*, 313–328.

Brown, T. A., & Barlow, D. H. (2009). A proposal for a dimensional classification system based on the shared features of the DSM-IV anxiety and mood disorders: Implications for assessment and treatment. *Psychological Assessment, 21*, 256–271.

Bruch, M., & Bond, F. W. (Eds.). (1998). *Beyond diagnosis: Case formulation approaches in CBT*. Chichester, UK: John Wiley & Sons Ltd.

Cannon, B. (2003). Sartre's contribution to psychoanalysis. In R. Frie (Ed.). *Understanding experience: Psychotherapy and post-modernism* (pp. 27–51). London: Routledge.

Carlbring, P., Ekselius, L., & Anderson, G. (2003). Treatment of panic disorder via the internet: A randomized trial of CBT vs applied relaxation. *Journal of Behavior Therapy and Experimental Psychiatry, 34*, 129–140.

Carlbring, P., Maurin, L., Törngren, C., Linna, E., Eriksson, T., Sparthan, E., Strååt, M., Marquez von Hage, C., Bergman-Nordgren, L., & Andersson, G. (2011). Individually-tailored, Internet-based treatment for anxiety disorders: A randomized controlled trial. *Behaviour Research and Therapy, 49*, 18–24.

Carr, D. (1997). Narrative and the real world: An argument for continuity. In L. P. Hinchman, & S. K. Hinchman (Eds.). *Memory, identity, community: The idea of narrative in the human sciences* (pp. 7–25). Albany, NY: SUNY Press.

Carr, D. (1986). *Time, narrative and history*. Bloomington, IA: Indiana University Press.

Caspar, F., Berger, T., & Hautle, I. (2004). The right view of your patient: A computer-assisted, individualized module for psychotherapy training. *Psychotherapy: Theory, Research, Practice, Training, 41*, 125–135.

Castonguay, L. G., & Beutler, L. E. (2006). *Principles of therapeutic change that work* (pp. 13–63). New York: Oxford University Press.

Chorpita, B. F., & Regan, J. (2009). Dissemination of effective mental health procedures: Maximizing return on a significant improvement. *Behaviour Research and Therapy, 47*, 990–993.

Clark, D. M. (1986). A cognitive approach to panic. *Behaviour Research and Therapy, 24*, 461–470.

Clark, D. M. (2011). Implementing NICE guidelines for the psychological treatment of depression and anxiety disorders: The IAPT experience. *International Review of Psychiatry, 23*, 375–384.

Clark, D. M., Salkovskis, P. M., Hackman, A., Middleton, H., Anastasiades, P., & Gelder, M. G. (1994). A comparison of cognitive therapy, applied relaxation and imipramine in the treatment of panic disorder. *British Journal of Psychiatry, 164*, 759–769.

Clark, D. M., Layard, R., & Smithies, R. (2008). Improving access to psychological therapy: Initial evaluation of the two UK demonstration sites. *London School of Economics Centre for Economic Performance*. Available at www.iapt.nhs.uk. Paper no. 1648.

Clark, D. M., Layard, R., Smithies, R., Richards, D. A., Suckling, R., & Wright, B. (2009). Improving access to psychological therapy: Initial evaluation of two UK demonstration sites. *Behaviour Research and Therapy, 47*, 910–920.

Corey, G. (2009). *Theory and practice of counseling and psychotherapy*. Belmont, CA: Brooks/Cole.

Corrie, S., & Lane, D. A. (2010). *Constructing stories, telling tales*. London: Karnac.

Cottraux, J., Martine, A., Bouvard, M. A., & Milliery, M. (2005). Combining pharmacotherapy with cognitive-behavioral interventions for obsessive-compulsive disorder. *Cognitive Behaviour Therapy, 34*, 185–192.

Craske, M. G., Kircanski, K., Zelikowsky, M., Mystkowski, J., Chowdhury, N., & Baker, A. (2008). Optimizing inhibitory learning during exposure therapy. *Behaviour Research and Therapy, 46*, 5–27.

Craske, M. G., Roy-Byrne, P. P., Stein, M. B., Sullivan, S., Sherbourne, C., & Bystritsky, A. (2009). Treatment for anxiety disorders: Efficacy to effectiveness to implementation. *Behaviour Research and Therapy, 47*, 931–937.

Crits-Christoff, P., Wilson, G. T., & Hollon, S. D. (2005). Empirically supported psychotherapies: Comment on Westen, Novotny and Thompson-Brenner (2004). *Psychological Bulletin, 131*, 412–417.

Cukrowicz, K. C., Timmons, K. A., Sawyer, K., Caron, K. M., Gummelt, H. D., & Joiner, T. E. (2011). Improved treatment outcome associated with a shift to empirically supported treatments in an outpatient clinic is maintained over a ten-year period. *Professional Psychology: Research and Practice, 42*, 145–152.

Curtis, J. T., & Silberschatz, G. (2007). The plan formulation method. In T. D. Eells (Ed.). *Handbook of psychotherapy case formulation* (2nd ed., pp. 198–220). New York: Guilford Press.

Cushman, P., & Gilford, P. (2000). Will managed care change our way of being? *American Psychologist, 55*, 985–996.

Dannahy, L., Hayward, M., Strauss, C., Turton, W., Harding, E., & Chadwick, P. (2011). *Journal of Behavior Therapy and Experimental Psychiatry, 42*, 111–116.

Davies, P., Thomas, P., & Leudar, I. (1999). Dialogical engagement with voices: A single case study. *British Journal of Medical Psychology, 72*, 179–187.

Davison, G. C. (2000). Stepped care: Doing more with less? *Journal of Consulting and Clinical Psychology, 68*, 580–585.

DeGrandpre, R. J. (2000). A science of meaning: Can behaviorism bring meaning to psychological science? *American Psychologist, 55*, 721–739.

Department of Health. (2010a). Attitudes to mental illness. *London: Department of Health research report No. JN207028.*

Department of Health, & Realising the benefits, The IAPT programme at full roll out. (2010b). Reference 13495 http://www.dh.gov.uk/publications. Accessed 10 2012.

Dobson, K. S., & Khatri, N. (2000). Cognitive therapy: Looking backward, looking forward. *Journal of Clinical Psychology, 56*, 907–923.

Donley, J. E. (1911). Freud's anxiety neurosis. *Journal of Abnormal Psychology, 6*, 126–134.

Doss, B. D. (2004). Changing the way we study change in psychotherapy. *Clinical Psychology: Science and Practice, 11*, 368–386.

Dougher, M. J. (1998). Stimulus equivalence and the untrained acquisition of stimulus functions. *Behavior Therapy, 29*, 577–591.

Dozois, D. J. A., Seeds, P. M., & Collins, K. A. (2009). Transdiagnostic approaches to the prevention of depression and anxiety. *Journal of Cognitive Psychotherapy: An International Quarterly, 23*, 44–59.

Dryden, W. (2007). *Dryden's handbook of individual therapy* (5th ed.). London: Sage.

Dudley, R., Kuyken, W., & Padesky, C. A. (2011). Disorder specific and trans-diagnostic case conceptualization. *Clinical Psychology Review, 31*, 213–244.

Duncan, B. L. (2002). The legacy of Saul Rosenzweig: The profundity of the dodo bird. *Journal of Psychotherapy Integration, 12*, 32–57.

EBPP. (2006). Evidence-based practice. Presidential task force. *American Psychologist, 61*, 271–285.

Eells, T. D. (2010). The unfolding case formulation: The interplay of description and inference. *Pragmatic Case Studies in Psychotherapy, 6*, 225–254.

Eells, T. D., Lombart, K. G., Kendjelic, E. M., Turner, L. C., & Lucas, C. P. (2005). The quality of psychotherapy case formulations: A comparison of expert, experienced, and novice cognitive-behavioral and psychodynamic therapists. *Journal of Consulting and Clinical Psychology, 73*, 579–589.

Eells, T. D., Lombart, K. G., Salsman, N., Kendjelic, E. M., Schneiderman, C. T., & Lucas, C. P. (2011). Expert reasoning on psychotherapy case formulation. *Psychotherapy Research, 21*, 385–399.

Elkin, I., Falconnier, L., Martinovitch, Z., & Mahoney, C. (2006). Therapist effects in the National Institute of Mental Health treatment of depression collaborative research program. *Psychotherapy Research, 16*, 144–160.

Elkin, I., Shea, M. T., Watkins, J. T., Imber, S. D., Sotsky, S. M., Collins, J. F., Glass, D. R., Pilkonis, P. A., Leber, W. R., Docherty, J. P., Fiester, S. J., & Parloff, M. B. (1989). National Institute of Mental Health treatment of depression collaborative research program: General effectiveness of treatments. *Archives of General Psychiatry, 46*, 971–982.

Ellard, K. K., Fairholme, C. P., Boisseau, C. L., Farchione, T. J., & Barlow, D. H. (2010). Unified protocol for the transdiagnostic treatment of emotional disorders: Protocol development and initial outcome data. *Cognitive and Behavioral Practice, 17*, 88–101.

Ellis, A. (1962). *Reason and emotion in psychotherapy*. Oxford: Lyle Stuart.

Emmelkamp, P. M.G., Bouman, T. K., & Blaaw, E. (1994). Individualized versus standardized therapy: A comparative evaluation with obsessive-compulsive patients. *Clinical Psychology and Psychotherapy, 1*, 95–100.

Emmelkamp, P., Ehring, T., & Powers, M. B. (2010). Philosophy, psychology, causes and treatments of mental disorders. In N. Kazantzis, M. A. Reinecke, & A. Freeman (Eds.). *Cognitive and behavioral theories in clinical practice* (pp. 1–27). New York: Guilford Press.

Epling, W. F., & Cheney, C. D. (2008). *Behavior analysis and learning* (4th ed.). New York: Psychology Press.

Erickson, D. H., Janeck, A. S., & Tallman, K. (2009). Transdiagnostic group CBT for anxiety: Clinical experience and practical advice. *Journal of Cognitive Psychotherapy: An International Quarterly, 23*, 34–43.

Evans, I. M. (1972). A conditioning model of a common neurotic pattern: Fear-of-fear. *Psychotherapy: Theory Research and Practice, 9*, 238–241.

Evans, I. M. (1986). Response structure and the triple-response-mode concept. In R. O. Nelson, & S. C. Hayes (Eds.). *Conceptual foundations of behavioral assessment*. New York: Guilford Press.

Evans, I. M. (1993). Constructional perspectives in clinical assessment. *Psychological Assessment, 5*, 264–272.

Evers, C. W., & Wu, E. H. (2006). On generalising from single case studies: Epistemological reflections. *Journal of Philosophy of Education, 40*, 511–526.

Eysenck, H. J. (1952). The effects of psychotherapy: An evaluation. *Journal of Consulting Psychology, 16*, 319–324.

Eysenck, H. J. (Ed.). (1964). *Experiments in behaviour therapy*. Oxford: Pergamon Press.

Eysenck, H. J. (1981). *A model for personality*. New York: Springer.

Fairburn, C. G., & Cooper, Z. (2011). Therapist competence, therapy quality, and therapist training. *Behaviour Research and Therapy, 49*, 373–378.

Faust, D. (1991). What if we had really listened? Present reflections on altered pasts. In D. Cicchetti, & W. M. Grove (Eds.). *Thinking clearly about psychology* (pp. 185–215). Minneapolis: University of Minnesota Press.

Fauth, J., Gates, S., Vinca, M. A., Boles, S., & Hayes, J. A. (2007). Big ideas for psychotherapy training. *Psychotherapy: Theory, Research, Practice, Training, 44*, 384–391.

Fishman, D. (1999). *The case for pragmatic psychology*. New York: New York University Press.

Foa, E. B., & Franklin, M. E. (2002). Psychotherapies for obsessive-compulsive disorder: A review. In M. Maj, N. Sartorius, A. Okasha, & J. Zohar (Eds.). *Obsessive-compulsive disorder*. Chichester, UK: John Wiley & Sons Ltd.

Foa, E. B., Liebowitz, M. R., Kozak, M. J., Davies, S., Campeas, R., Franklin, M. E., Huppert, J. D., Kjernisted, K., Rowan, V., Schmidt, A. B., Simpson, H. B., & Tu, X. (2005). Randomized, placebo-controlled trial of exposure and ritual prevention, clomipramine, and their combination in the treatment of obsessive-compulsive disorder. *American Journal of Psychiatry, 162*, 151–161.

Follette, V., Palm, K. M., & Rasmussen Hall, M. L. (2004). Acceptance, mindfulness and trauma. In S. C. Hayes, V. M. Follette, & M. M. Linehan (Eds.). *Mindfulness and acceptance: Expanding the cognitive-behavioral tradition*. New York: Guilford Press.

Follette, W. C., Naugle, A. E., & Linnerooth, P. J. (1999). A functional alternative to traditional assessment. In M. J. Dougher (Ed.). *Clinical behavior analysis* (pp. 99–125). Reno, NV: Context Press.

Fowers, B. J. (2005). Psychotherapy, character, and the good life. In B. Slife, J. Reber, & F. C. Richardson (Eds.). *Critical thinking about psychology: Hidden assumptions and plausible alternatives* (pp. 39–59). Washington, DC: APA Press.

Frank, G. (1984). The Boulder model: History, rationale, and critique. *Professional Psychology: Research and Practice*, *15*, 417–435.

Frank, J. D., & Frank, J. B. (1991). *Persuasion and healing: A comparative study of psychotherapy* (3rd ed.). Baltimore: Johns Hopkins University Press.

Freedman, J., & Combs, G. (1996). *Narrative therapy: The social construction of preferred realities*. New York: W. W. Norton.

Gambrill, E. D. (2005). *Critical thinking in clinical practice: Improving the quality of judgments and decisions* (2nd ed.). Hoboken, NJ: John Wiley & Sons Inc.

Gambrill, E., & Littell, J. H. (2010). Do haphazard reviews provide sound directions for dissemination efforts? *American Psychologist*, *65*, 927–935.

Garb, H. N., & Boyle, P. A. (2003). Understanding why some clinicians use pseudoscientific methods. In S. O. Lilienfeld, S. J. Lynn, & J. M. Lohr (Eds.). *Science and pseudoscience in clinical psychology* (pp. 17–38). New York: Guilford Press.

Garfield, S. L. (1997). Brief psychotherapy: The role of common and specific factors. *Clinical Psychology and Psychotherapy*, *4*, 217–225.

Garske, J. P., & Anderson, T. (2003). Toward a science of psychotherapy research: Present status and evaluation. In S. O. Lilienfeld, S. J. Lynn, & J. M. Lohr (Eds.). *Science and pseudoscience in clinical psychology* (pp. 145–175). New York: Guilford Press.

Gellatley, J., Bower, P., Hennessy, S., Richards, D., Gilbody, S., & Lovell, K. (2007). What makes self-help interventions effective in the management of depressive symptoms? Meta-analysis and meta-regression. *Psychological Medicine*, *37*, 1217–1228.

Geller, J. D. (2005). Style and its contribution to a patient-specific model of therapeutic technique. *Psychotherapy: Theory, Research, Practice, Training*, *42*, 469–482.

Gelso, C. J., & Carter, J. A. (1994). Components of the psychotherapy relationship: Their interaction and unfolding during treatment. *Journal of Counseling Psychology*, *41*, 296–306.

Ghaderi, A. (2006). Does individualization matter? A randomized trial of standardized (focused) versus individualized (broad) cognitive behavior therapy for bulimia nervosa. *Behavior, Research and Therapy*, *44*, 273–288.

Gifford, E. V., Tavakoli, S., Weingardt, K. R., Finney, J. W., Pierson, H. M., Rosen, C. S., Hagedorn, H. J., Cook, J. M., & Curran, G. M. (2012). How do components of evidence-based psychological treatments cluster in practice? A survey and cluster analysis. *Journal of Substance Abuse Treatment*, *42*, 45–55.

Gilbert, P. (2010). *The compassionate mind*: London: Constable.

Glover, G., Webb, M., & Evison, F. (2010). Improving access to psychological therapies: A review of the progress made by sites in the first rollout year. *North East Public Health Observatory* www.iapt.nhs.uk. Accessed 12.06.12.

Godoy, A., & Gavino, A. (2003). Information-gathering strategies in behavioral assessment. *European Journal of Psychological Assessment*, *19*, 204–209.

Goldiamond, I. (1974). Toward a constructional approach to social problems. *Behaviourism*, *1*, 1–84.

Goldfried, M. R. (1980). Toward the delineation of therapeutic change principles. *American Psychologist*, *35*, 991–999.

Goldfried, M. R. (2009). Searching for therapy change principles: Are we there yet? *Applied and Preventive Psychology*, *13*, 32–34.

Goldfried, M. R., & Davila, J. (2005). The role of relationship and technique in therapeutic change. *Psychotherapy: Theory, Research, Practice, Training*, *42*, 421–430.

Gordon, P. K. (2007). A comparison of two versions of the Cognitive Therapy Scale. *Behavioural and Cognitive Psychotherapy*, *35*, 1–11.

Greist, J. H., Marks, I. M., Baer, L., Kobak, K. A., Wenzel, K. W., Hirsch, M. J., Mantle, J. M., & Clary, C. M. (2002). Behavior therapy for obsessive compulsive disorder guided by a computer or by a clinician compared with relaxation as a control treatment. *Journal of Clinical Psychiatry*, *63*, 138–145.

Gwynne Jones, H. (1961). Specific conditioning treatment of enuresis nocturna. *Developmental Medicine and Child Neurology*, *3*, 227–236.

Hallam, R. S. (1974). Extinction of ruminations: A case study. *Behavior Therapy*, *5*, 565–568.

Hallam, R. S. (1976a). The Eysenck Personality Scales: Stability and change after therapy. *Behaviour Research and Therapy*, *14*, 369–372.

Hallam, R. S. (1976b). A complex view of simple phobias. In H. J. Eysenck (Ed.). *Case histories in behaviour therapy*. London: Routledge, Kegan and Paul.

Hallam, R. S. (1985). *Anxiety: Psychological perspectives on panic and agoraphobia*. London: Academic Press.

Hallam, R. S. (1992). *Counselling for anxiety problems*. London: Sage Publications.

Hallam, R. S. (2009). *Virtual selves, real persons: A dialogue across disciplines*. Cambridge: Cambridge University Press.

Hallam, R. S. (2011). IAPT causes split between Frankie and Johnny. *Clinical Psychology Forum*, *220*. April.

Hallam, R. S. (2012). Disordered selves. *Contemporary Social Science*, *7*, 1–17.

Hallam, R. S., & O'Connor, K. (2002). A dialogical approach obsessions. *Psychology and Psychotherapy*, *75*, 333–348.

Hardy, G. E., Cahill, J., Stiles, W. B., Ispan, C., Macaskill, N., & Barkham, M. (2005). Sudden gains in cognitive therapy for depression: A replication and extension. *Journal of Consulting and Clinical Psychology*, *73*, 59–67.

Harper, D., & Moss, D. (2003). A different kind of chemistry? Reformulating "formulation." *Clinical Psychology Forum*, *25*, 6–10.

Harré, R., & Van Langenhove, L. (1999). *Positioning theory: Moral contexts of intentional action*. Oxford: Blackwell.

Hayes, S. C. (2011). Future of cognitive behavioural therapies: A debate between Stephen Pilling. Steve Hayes & David Veale. *CBT Today*, *39(1)*. March.

Hayes, S. C., & Brownstein, A. J. (1986). Mentalism, behavior-behavior relations, and a behavior-analytic view of the purposes of science. *The Behavior Analyst*, *9*, 175–190.

Hayes, S. C., & Strosahl, K. D. (Eds.) (2004). *A practical guide to acceptance and commitment therapy*. New York: Springer.

Hayes, S. C., Barnes-Holmes, D., & Roche, B. (Eds.) (2001). *Relational frame theory: A post-Skinnerian account of human language and cognition*. New York: Kluwer Academic/Plenum Publishers.

Hayes, S. C., Luoma, J. B., Bond, F. W., Masuda, A., & Lillis, J. (2006). Acceptance and commitment therapy: Model, processes and outcomes. *Behaviour Research and Therapy*, *44*, 1–25.

Haynes, S. N., & O'Brien, W. H. (2000). *Principles and practice of behavioral assessment*. New York: Kluwer Academic.

Haynes, S. N., Leisen, M. B., & Blaine, D. D. (1997). Design of individualized behavioral treatment programs using functional analytic clinical case models. *Psychological Assessment*, *9*, 334–348.

Held, B. S. (1995). *Back to reality: A critique of postmodern theory in therapy*. New York: W. W. Norton.

Hersen, M. (Ed.). (2004). *Psychological assessment in clinical practice: A pragmatic guide*. New York: Brunner-Routledge.

Hill, C. E. (2005). Therapist techniques, client involvement, and the therapeutic relationship: Inextricably intertwined in the therapy process. *Psychotherapy: Theory, Research, Practice, Training*, *42*, 431–442.

Hill, C. E., Stahl, J., & Roffman, M. (2007). Training novice therapists: Helping skills and beyond. *Psychotherapy: Theory, Research, Practice, Training*, *44*, 364–370.

Hollon, S. D., & DeRubeis, R. J. (2009). Mediating the effects of cognitive therapy for depression. *Cognitive Behaviour Therapy*, *38*, 43–47.

Horowitz, M. (2005). *Understanding psychotherapy change: A practical guide to configurational analysis*. Washington, DC: American Psychological Association.

Hubble, M. A., Miller, S. D., Duncan, B. L., & Wampold, B. E. (Eds.) (2007). *The heart and soul of change: Delivering what works in therapy* (2nd ed.). Washington, DC: American Psychological Association.

Hunsley, J. (2007). Addressing key challenges in evidence-based practice in psychology. *Professional Psychology: Research and Practice, 38*, 113–121.

Jacobson, N. S., Schmaling, K. B., Holtzworth-Monroe, A., Katt, J. L., Wood, L. F., & Follette, V. M. (1989). Research-structured vs clinically flexible versions of social learning-based, marital therapy. *Behaviour, Research and Therapy, 27*, 173–180.

Jacobson, N. S., Dobson, K. S., Truax, P. A., Koerner, K., Gollan, J. K., Gortner, E., & Prince, S. E. (1996). A component analysis of cognitive-behavioral treatment for depression. *Journal of Consulting and Clinical Psychology, 64*, 295–304.

James, G. W. B. (1940). Anxiety neurosis. *Lancet, 239*, 561–564.

Jennings, L., & Skovholt, T. M. (1999). The cognitive, emotional, and relational characteristics of master therapists. *Journal of Counseling Psychology, 46*, 3–11.

Jose, A., & Goldfried, M. R. (2008). A transtheoretical approach to case formulation. *Cognitive and Behavioral Practice, 15*, 212–222.

Kahneman, D., & Tversky, A. (1973). On the psychology of prediction. *Psychological Review, 80*, 237–251.

Kanfer, F. H., & Saslow, G. (1965). Behavioral analysis: An alternative to diagnostic classification. *Archives of General Psychiatry, 12*, 529–538.

Kaslow, N. J., Rubin, N. J., Bebeau, M. J., Leigh, I. W., Lichtenberg, J. W., Nelson, P. D., Portnoy, S. M., & Smith, I. L. (2007). Guiding principles and recommendations for the assessment of competence. *Professional Psychology: Research and Practice, 38*, 441–451.

Kazdin, A. E. (2008). Evidence-based treatment and practice. *American Psychologist, 63*, 146–159.

Kazdin, A. E. (2011). Evidence-based treatment research: Advances, limitations, and next steps. *American Psychologist, 66*, 685–698.

Kendjelic, E. M., & Eells, T. D. (2007). Generic psychotherapy case formulation training improves formulation quality. *Psychotherapy: Theory, Research, Practice, Training, 44*, 66–77.

Keyes, C. L. M., & Lopez, S. J. (2005). Positive directions in diagnosis and interventions. In C. R. Snyder, & S. J. Lopez (Eds.). *Toward a science of mental health: Handbook of positive psychology* (2nd ed., pp. 45–59). New York: Oxford University Press.

Kiropoulos, L. A., Klein, B., Austin, D. W., Gilson, K., Pier, C., Mitchell, J., & Ciechomski, L. (2008). Is internet based CBT for panic disorder and agoraphobia as effective as face-to-face CBT? *Journal of Anxiety Disorders, 22*, 1273–1284.

Kirsch, I. (2009). *The emperor's new drugs: Exploding the antidepressant myth*. London: The Bodley Head.

Knapp, S., & Vandecreek, L. (2007). Balancing respect for autonomy with competing values with the use of principle-based ethics. *Psychotherapy: Theory, Research, Practice, Training, 44*, 397–404.

Koerner, K. (2007). Case formulation in dialectical behavior therapy for borderline personality disorder. In T. D. Eells (Ed.). *Handbook of psychotherapy case formulation* (2nd ed., pp. 317–348). New York: Guilford Press.

Kraus, D. R., Castonguay, L., Boswell, J. F., Nordberg, S. S., & Hayes, J. A. (2011). Therapist effectiveness: Implications for accountability in patient care. *Psychotherapy Research, 21*, 267–276.

Kuyken, W. (2006). Evidence-based case formulation, is the emperor clothed? In N. Tarrier (Ed.). *Case formulation in cognitive behaviour therapy: The treatment of challenging and complex cases*. Hove: Routledge.

Kuyken, W., Padesky, C. A., & Dudley, R. (2009). *Collaborative case conceptualization: Working effectively with clients in cognitive-behavioral therapy*. New York: Guilford Press.

Kuyken, W., Fothergill, C. D., Musa, M., & Chadwick, P. (2004). The reliability and quality of cognitive case formulation. *Behaviour Research and Therapy, 43,* 1187–1201.

Lambert, M. (2007). Presidential address: What we have learned from a decade of research aimed at improving psychotherapy outcome in routine care. *Psychotherapy Research, 17,* 1–14.

Lang, P. J. (1968). Fear reduction and fear behavior: Problems in treating a construct. In J. M. Schlien (Ed.). *Research in Psychotherapy* (Vol. 3, pp. 90–102). Washington, DC: American Psychological Association.

Leavitt, H. M., & Williams, D. C. (2010). Facilitating client change: Principles based upon the experience of eminent psychotherapists. *Psychotherapy Research, 20,* 337–352.

Leeming, D., Boyle, M., & Macdonald, J. (2009). Accounting for psychological problems: How user-friendly are psychosocial formulations? *Clinical Psychology Forum, 200,* 12–17.

Lindsley, O. R. (1959). Reduction in rate of vocal psychotic symptoms by differential positive reinforcement. *Journal of the Experimental Analysis of Behavior, 2,* 269.

Linehan, M. M. (1993). *Skills training manual for treating borderline personality disorder: Diagnosis and treatment of mental disorders.* New York: Guilford Press.

Littell, J. H. (2010). Evidence-based practice: evidence or orthodoxy? chapter 6, In B. L. Duncan, S. D. Miller, B. E. Wampold, & M. A. Hubble (Eds.). *The heart and soul of change: Delivering what works in therapy* (2nd ed, Chapter 6). Washington, DC: American Psychological Association.

Longmore, R. J., & Worrall, M. (2007). Do we need to challenge thoughts in cognitive behavior therapy? *Clinical Psychology Review, 27,* 173–187.

MacIntyre, A. (1981). *After virtue.* Notre Dame, IA: University of Notre Dame Press.

Maddux, J. E. (2005). Stopping the "Madness"; Positive psychology and deconstructing the illness ideology and the DSM. In C. R. Snyder & S. J. Lopez (Eds.). *Handbook of positive psychology* (pp. 13–25). New York: Oxford University Press.

Magyar-Moe, J. L. (2009). *Therapist's guide to positive psychological interventions.* San Diego: Academic Press.

Mair, M. (2000). Psychology as a discipline of discourse. *European Journal of Psychotherapy, Counselling, and Health, 3,* 335–347.

Mansell, W., Harvey, A., Watkins, E., & Shafran, R. (2009). Conceptual foundations of the transdiagnostic approach to CBT. *Journal of Cognitive Psychotherapy, 23,* 6–19.

Marchand, E., Stice, E., Rohde, P., & Becker, C. B. (2011). Moving from efficacy to effectiveness trials in prevention research. *Behaviour Research and Therapy, 49,* 32–41.

Marks, I. M., Hallam, R. S., Philpott, R., & Connolly, J. (1976). *Behavioural psychotherapy: An advanced clinical role for nurses.* London: RCN Research Series.

Martell, C. R., Dimidjian, S., & Hepman-Dunn, R. (2010). *Behavioral activation for depression: A clinicians' guide.* New York: Guilford Press.

Martin, D. J., Garske, J. P., & Davis, M. K. (2000). Relation of the therapeutic alliance with outcome and other variables: A meta-analytic review. *Journal of Consulting and Clinical Psychology, 68,* 438–450.

Marzillier, J., & Hall, J. (2009). The challenge of the Layard initiative. *The Psychologist, 22*(5), 396–399.

McFall, R. (2007). On psychological clinical science. In T. A. Treat, R. R. Bootzin, & T. B. Baker (Eds.). *Psychological clinical science: Papers in honor of Richard McFall* (pp. 363–396). New York: Psychology Press.

McHugh, R. K., & Barlow, D. H. (2010). The dissemination and implementation of evidence-based psychological treatments. *American Psychologist, 65,* 73–84.

McHugh, R. K., Murray, H. W., & Barlow, D. H. (2009). Balancing fidelity and adaptation in the dissemination of empirically-supported treatments: The promise of trans-diagnostic investigations. *Behaviour Research and Therapy, 47,* 946–953.

McKay, K. M., Zac, E. I., & Wampold, B. E. (2006). Psychiatrist effects in the psychopharmacological treatment of depression. *Journal of Affective Disorders, 92,* 287–290.

McLeod, J. (2010). *Case study research in counselling and psychotherapy.* London: Sage.

McLeod, J., & Lynch, G. (2000). "This is our life": Strong evaluation in psychotherapy narrative. *European Journal of Psychotherapy, Counselling, and Health, 3,* 389–406.

McNulty, J. K., & Fincham, F. (2012). Beyond positive psychology? Toward a contextual view of psychological processes and well being. *American Psychologist, 67,* 101–110.

Meehl, P. E. (1954). *Clinical vs statistical prediction.* Minneapolis: University of Minnesota Press.

Meyer, V. (1966). Modification of expectations in cases with obsessional rituals. *Behaviour Research and Therapy, 4,* 273–280.

Miller, R. B. (2005). Suffering in psychology: The demoralization of psychotherapeutic practice. *Journal of Psychotherapy Integration, 15,* 299–336.

Miller, R. B. (2009). The logic of theory and the logic of practice. *Pragmatic Case Studies in Psychotherapy, 5,* 101–107.

Miller, R. B. (2011). Real clinical trials (RCT)—Panels of psychological inquiry for transforming anecdotal data into clinical facts and validated judgments: Introduction to a pilot test with the case of "Anna." *Pragmatic Case Studies in Psychotherapy, 7,* 6–36.

Miller, W. R., & Rollnick, S. (2002). *Motivational interviewing: Preparing people for change* (2nd ed.). New York: Guilford Press.

Miller, S. D., Hubble, M. A., & Duncan, B. L. (2007). Delivering what works. In M. A. Hubble, S. D. Miller, B. L. Duncan, & B. E. Wampold (Eds.). *The heart and soul of change: Delivering what works in therapy* (2nd ed., pp. 421–429). Washington, DC: American Psychological Association.

Mohr, D. C. (2009). Telemental health: Reflections on how to move the field forward. *Clinical Psychology: Science and Practice, 16,* 343–347.

Moore, P. (2007). Formulation diagrams: Is there more than meets the eye? *Clinical Psychology Forum, 174,* 9–12.

Morgan, A. (2000). *What is narrative therapy? An easy to read introduction.* Adelaide: Dulwich Centre Publications.

Morgan, D. L., & Morgan, R. K. (2001). Single-participant research design. *American Psychologist, 56,* 119–127.

Muller, J. M. (2011). Evaluation of a therapeutic concept diagram. *European Journal of Psychological Assessment, 27,* 17–28.

Mumma, G. H. (1998). Improving cognitive case formulations and treatment planning in clinical practice and research. *Journal of Cognitive Psychotherapy: An International Quarterly, 12,* 251–274.

Mumma, G. H., & Mooney, S. R. (2007). Comparing the validity of alternative cognitive case formulations: A latent variable, multivariate time series approach. *Cognitive Therapy and Research, 31,* 451–481.

Nezu, A. M., Nezu, C. M., & Cos, T. A. (2007). Case formulation for the behavioral and cognitive therapies. In T. D. Eells (Ed.). *Handbook of psychotherapy case formulation* (2nd ed., pp. 349–378). New York: Guilford Press.

Nezu, A. M., Nezu, C. M., & Lombardo, E. (2004). *Cognitive-behavioral case formulation: A problem-solving approach.* New York: Springer.

Nezu, A. M., Nezu, C. M., Peacock, M. A., & Girdwood, C. P. (2004). Case formulation in cognitive-behavior therapy. In M. Hersen, S. N. Haynes, & E. M. Herby (Eds.). *The comprehensive handbook of psychological assessment, Behavioral assessment* (Vol. 3, pp. 402–426). New York: John Wiley.

Norcross, J. C. (Ed.). (2011). *Psychotherapeutic relationships that work.* New York: Oxford University Press.

Norcross, J. C., & Goldfried, M. R. (2005). *Handbook of psychotherapy integration* (2nd ed.). Oxford: Oxford University Press.

Norcross, J. C., & Lambert, M. J. (2011). Evidence-based therapy relationships. In J. C. Norcross (Ed.). *Psychotherapeutic relationships that work* (pp. 3–21). New York: Oxford University Press.

Norcross, J. C., Vandenbos, G. R., & Freedheim, D. K. (2011). *History of psychotherapy* (2nd ed.). Washington, DC: American Psychological Association.

O'Brien, W. H. (2010). Evaluating case formulation decision-making and therapist responsiveness: A perspective from the area of behavioral assessment and case formulation. *Pragmatic Case Studies in Psychotherapy, 6*, 293–306.

O'Brien, W. H., & Carhart, V. (2011). Functional analysis in behavioral medicine. *European Journal of Psychological Assessment, 27*, 4–16.

O'Connor, K., Aardema, F., & Pélissier, M.-C. (2005). *Beyond reasonable doubt: Reasoning processes in obsessive-compulsive disorder and related disorders*. Chichester, UK: John Wiley & Sons Ltd.

O'Connor, K., Aardema, F., Robillard, S., Guay, S., Pélissier, M.-C., Todorov, C., Borgeat, F., Leblanc, V., Grenier, S., & Doucet, P. (2006). Cognitive behaviour therapy and medication in the treatment of obsessive-compulsive disorder. *Acta Psychiatrica Scandinavica, 113*, 408–419.

Okiishi, J., Lambert, M. J., Nielson, S. L., & Ogles, B. M. (2003). Waiting for supershrink: An empirical analysis of therapist effects. *Clinical Psychology and Psychotherapy, 10*, 361–373.

Orlinsky, D. (2006). Comments on the state of psychotherapy research (as I see it). *North American SPR Newsletter*. June 2006.

Ormel, J., Riese, H., & Rosmalen, J. G. M. (2012). Interpreting neuroticism scores across the adult life course: Immutable or experience-dependent set points of negative affect? *Clinical Psychology Review, 32*, 71–79.

Orwin, A. (1973). "The running treatment": A preliminary communication on a new use for an old therapy (physical activity) in the agoraphobic syndrome. *British Journal of Psychiatry, 122*, 175–179.

Otto, M. W., Pollack, M. H., & Barlow, D. H. (2000). *Stopping anxiety medication: Panic control therapy for benzodiazepine discontinuation, patient workbook*. San Diego, CA: Academic Press.

Padesky, C. A. (1997). *Collaborative case conceptualization (DVD)*: www.padesky.com. Accessed 15.06.2012.

Paivio, S. C., Holowaty, K. A.M., & Hall, I. E. (2004). The influence of therapist adherence and competence on client reprocessing of child abuse memories. *Psychotherapy: Theory, Research, Practice, Training, 41*, 56–58.

Paul, G. (1966). *Insight vs. desensitization in psychotherapy*. Stanford, CA: Stanford University Press.

Paul, G. (1967). Strategy of outcome research in psychotherapy. *Journal of Consulting Psychology, 31*, 109–118.

Payne, M. (2007). Narrative therapy. In W. Dryden (Eds.). *Dryden's handbook of individual therapy* (5th ed., pp. 410–423). London: Sage.

Peck, D. F. (2010). The therapist-client relationship, computerized self-help and active therapy ingredients. *Clinical Psychology and Psychotherapy, 17*, 147–153.

Pennebaker, J. W. (1993). Putting stress into words: Health, linguistic, and therapeutic implications. *Behaviour Research and Therapy, 31*, 535–548.

Persons, J. B. (1989). *Cognitive therapy in practice: A case formulation approach*. New York: Norton.

Persons, J. B. (2005). Empiricism, mechanism, and the practice of cognitive-behavior therapy. *Behavior Therapy, 36*, 107–118.

Persons, J. B. (2008). *The case formulation approach to cognitive-behavior therapy*. New York: Guilford Press.

Peterson, R. L., & Trieweiler, S. J. (1999). Scholarship in psychology; The advantage of an expanded vision. *American Psychologist, 54*, 350–355.

Prochaska, J. O. (1979). *Systems of psychotherapy: A transtheoretical analysis*. Homewood, IL: Dorsey.

Proudfoot, J., Shapiro, D. A., Ryden, C., Everitt, B., Goldberg, D., Mann, A., Tylee, A., Marks, I., & Gray, J. A. (2004). Clinical efficacy of computerised cognitive–behavioural therapy for anxiety and depression in primary care: Randomised controlled trial. *British Journal of Psychiatry, 185*, 46–54.

Raimy, V. (Ed.). (1950). *Training in clinical psychology*. New York: Prentice Hall.

Reed, G. M. (2006). What qualifies as evidence of effective practice? Clinical expertise. In J. C. Norcross, L. E. Beutler, & R. F. Levant (Eds.). *Evidence-based practices in mental health: Debate and dialogue on the fundamental questions* (pp. 13–23). Washington, DC: American Psychological Association.

Richards, D. A., & Suckling, R. (2008). Improving access to psychological therapy: The Doncaster demonstration site organisational model. *Clinical Psychology Forum, 181,* 9–16.

Rose, N. (1998). *Inventing our selves: Psychology, power, and personhood*. Cambridge: Cambridge University Press.

Rosen, G. M., & Davison, G. C. (2003). Psychology should list empirically supported principles of change (ESPs) and not credential trademarked therapies or other treatment packages. *Behavior Modification, 27,* 300–312.

Rosen, G. M., Glasgow, R. E., & Moore, T. E. (2003). Self-help therapy. In S. O. Lilienfeld, S. J. Lynn, & J. M. Lohr (Eds.). *Science and pseudoscience in clinical psychology* (pp. 399–424). New York: Guilford Press.

Rosenwald, G. C. (1988). A theory of multiple case research. *Journal of Personality, 56,* 239–264.

Ross, L. (1977). The intuitive psychologist and his shortcomings: Distortions in the attribution process. In L. Berkowitz (Ed.). *Advances in experimental social psychology* (Vol. 10, pp. 173–240). Orlando, FL: Academic Press.

Roth, A., & Pilling, S. (2007). *The competencies required to deliver effective cognitive and behavioural therapy for people with depression and anxiety disorders*: www.ucl.ac.uk/CORE.

Rubin, A., & Parrish, D. (2007). Challenges to the future of evidence-based practice in social work education. *Journal of Social Work Education, 43,* 405–428.

Ruscio, A. M., & Holohan, D. R. (2006). Applying empirically supported treatments to complex cases: Ethical, empirical, and practical considerations. *Clinical Psychology: Science and Practice, 13,* 146–162.

Salkovskis, P. M. (1999). Understanding and treating obsessive-compulsive disorder. *Behaviour Research and Therapy, 37,* 29–52.

Salkovskis, P. M. (2002). Empirically grounded interventions: Cognitive-behavioural therapy progresses through a multi-dimensional approach to clinical science. *Behavioural and Cognitive Psychotherapy, 30,* 3–9.

Salter, A. (1949). *Conditioned reflex therapy: The direct approach to the reconstruction of personality*. New York: Creative Age Press.

Sarbin, T. R. (1998). Believed in imaginings: A narrative approach. In J. de Rivera & T. R. Sarbin (Eds.). *Believed-in imaginings: The narrative construction of reality* (pp. 15–30). Washington, DC: APA Publications.

Sarbin, T. R., Taft, R., & Bailey, D. E. (1960). *Clinical inference and cognitive theory*. Oxford: Holt, Rinehart, and Winston.

Sawyer, R. K. (2003). Non-reductive individualism. Part II: Social causation. *Philosophy of the Social Sciences, 33,* 202–224.

Schiepek, G. (2003). A dynamic systems approach to clinical case formulation. *European Journal of Psychological Assessment, 19,* 175–184.

Schneider, B. H., & Byrne, B. M. (1987). Individualizing social skills training for behavior-disordered children. *Journal of Consulting and Clinical Psychology, 55,* 444–445.

Schulte, D., & Eifert, G. H. (2002). What to do when manuals fail? The dual model of psychotherapy. *Clinical Psychology: Science and Practice, 9,* 312–328.

Schulte, D., Kunzel, R., Pepping, G., & Schulte-Bahrenberg, T. (1992). Tailor-made versus standardized therapy of phobic patients. *Advances in Behaviour Research and Therapy, 14,* 67–92.

Seale, C. (1999). *The quality of qualitative research*. London: Sage.

Segal, Z. V., Williams, J. M. G., & Teasdale, J. D. (2002). *Mindfulness-based cognitive therapy for depression: A new approach to preventing relapse*. New York: Guilford Press.

Seligman, M. E. P. (2002). Positive psychology, positive prevention, and positive therapy. In C. R. Snyder & S. J. Lopez (Eds.). *Handbook of positive psychology* (pp. 3–9). New York: Oxford University Press.

Shafran, R., Clark, D. M., Fairburn, C. G., Arntz, A., Barlow, D. H., Ehlers, A., Freeston, M., Garety, P. A., Hollon, S. D., Ost, L. G., Salkovskis, P. M., Williams, J. M. G., & Wilson, G. T. (2009). Mind the gap: Improving the dissemination of CBT. *Behaviour Research and Therapy, 47*, 902–909.

Shakow, D. (1976). What is clinical psychology? *American Psychologist, 31*, 553–560.

Shapiro, D. A., Barkham, M., Rees, A., Hardy, G. E., Reynolds, S., & Startup, M. (1994). Effects of treatment duration and severity of depression on the effectiveness of cognitive-behavioral and psychodynamic-interpersonal psychotherapy. *Journal of Consulting and Clinical Psychology, 62*, 522–534.

Shapiro, J. P. (2009). Integrating outcome research and clinical reasoning in psychotherapy planning. *Professional Psychology: Research and Practice, 40*, 46–53.

Shapiro, M. B. (1961). The single case in fundamental clinical psychological research. *British Journal of Medical Psychology, 34*, 255–262.

Sharpless, B. A., & Barber, J. P. (2009). A conceptual and empirical review of the meaning, measurement, development, and teaching of intervention competence in clinical psychology. *Clinical Psychology Review, 29*, 47–56.

Sholomskas, D. E., Syracuse-Siewert, G., Rounsaville, B. J., Ball, S. A., Nuro, K. F., & Carroll, K. M. (2005). We don't train in vain: A dissemination trial of three strategies of training clinicians in cognitive–behavioral therapy. *Journal of Consulting and Clinical Psychology, 73*, 106–115.

Singer, J. A., & Bonalume, L. (2010). Toward the scientific study of autobiographical memory narratives in psychotherapy. *Pragmatic Case Studies in Psychotherapy, 6*, 215–222.

Skinner, B. F. (1953). *Science and human behavior.* New York: Macmillan.

Sluckin, W. (1954). *Minds and machines.* Harmondsworth: Penguin.

Smits, J. A., Powers, M. B., Berry, A. C., & Otto, M. W. (2007). Translating empirically supported strategies into accessible interventions: The potential utility of exercise for the treatment of panic disorder. *Cognitive and Behavioral Practice, 14*, 364–374.

Sookman, D., & Steketee, G. (2007). Directions in specialized cognitive behavior therapy for resistant obsessive compulsive disorder: Theory and practice of two approaches. *Cognitive and Behavioral Practice, 14*, 1–17.

Sookman, D., & Steketee, G. (2010). Specialized cognitive behavior therapy for treatment resistant obsessional compulsive disorder. In D. Sookman & R. L. Leahy (Eds.). *Resolving impasses to symptom remission* (pp. 31–74). New York: Routledge.

Spek, V., Cuijpers, P., Nyklíček, I., Riper, H., Keyzer, J., & Pop, V. (2007). Internet-based cognitive behaviour therapy for symptoms of depression and anxiety: A meta-analysis. *Psychological Medicine, 37*, 319–328.

Spring, B., & Neville, K. (2011). Evidence-based practice in clinical psychology. In D. H. Barlow & P. E. Nathan (Eds.). *The Oxford handbook of clinical psychology* (pp. 128–149). New York: Oxford University Press.

Stiles, W. B. (2002). Assimilation of problematic experiences. In J. C. Norcross (Ed.). *Psychotherapy relationships that work: Therapist contributions and responsiveness to patients* (pp. 357–365). New York: Oxford University Press.

Stiles, W. B. (2005). Case studies. In J. C. Norcross, L. E. Beutler, & R. F. Levant (Eds.). *Evidence-based practices in mental health: Debate and dialog on the fundamental questions* (pp. 57–64). Washington, DC: American Psychological Association.

Stiles, W. B., Leiman, M., Shapiro, D. A., Hardy, G. E., Barkham, M., Detert, N. B., & Llewelyn, S. (2006). What does the first exchange tell? Dialogical sequence analysis and assimilation in very brief therapy. *Psychotherapy Research, 16*, 408–421.

Stip, E., & Letourneau, G. (2009). Psychotic symptoms as a continuum between normality and pathology. *Canadian Journal of Psychiatry, 54*, 140–151.

Stricker, G., & Trierweiler, S. J. (1995). The local clinical scientist: A bridge between science and practice. *American Psychologist, 50*, 995–1002.

Stuart, S., & Robinson, M. (2003). *Interpersonal therapy: A clinician's guide*. London: Arnold.

Sturmey, P. (2007). *Functional analysis in clinical treatment*. San Diego, CA: Academic Press.

Sturmey, P. (2008). *Behavioral case formulation and intervention: A functional analytic approach*. Chichester, UK: Wiley-Blackwell.

Summers, R. F. (2003). The psychodynamic formulation updated. *American Journal of Psychotherapy, 57*, 39–51.

Tang, T. Z., DeRubeis, R. J., Hollon, S. D., & Amsterdam, J. (2007). Sudden gains in cognitive therapy of depression and depression relapse/recurrence. *Journal of Consulting and Clinical Psychology, 75*, 404–408.

Tarrier, N., & Calam, R. (2002). New developments in cognitive-behavioural case formulation. Epidemiological, systemic and social context: An integrative approach. *Cognitive and Behavioural Psychotherapy, 30*, 311–328.

Teachman, B. A., & Clerkin, E. M. (2010). A case formulation approach to resolve treatment complications. In M. W. Otto & S. G. Hofmann (Eds.). *Avoiding treatment failures in the anxiety disorders* (pp. 7–30). New York: Springer Publications.

Trepka, C., Rees, A., Shapiro, D. A., Hardy, G. E., & Barkham, M. (2004). Therapist competence and outcome of cognitive therapy for depression. *Cognitive Therapy and Research, 28*, 143–157.

Tsai, M., Kohlenberg, R. J., Kanter, J. W., Kohlenberg, B., Follette, W. C., & Callaghan, G. M. (2009). *A guide to functional analytic psychotherapy; Awareness, courage, love and behaviorism*. New York: Springer.

Turk, D. C., & Salovey, P. (Eds.). (1988). *Reasoning, inference, and judgments in clinical psychology*. New York: Free Press.

Twohig, M. P. (2009). Acceptance and Commitment Therapy for treatment-resistant post-traumatic stress disorder: A case study. *Cognitive and Behavioral Practice, 16*, 243–252.

Twohig, M. P., Hayes, S. C., Plumb, J. C., Collins, A. B., Hazlett-Stevens, H., & Woidneck, M. R. (2010). A randomized clinical trial of acceptance and commitment therapy vs progressive relaxation training in the treatment of obsessive compulsive disorder. *Journal of Consulting and Clinical Psychology, 78*, 705–716.

Vallis, M. T., Shaw, B. F., & Dobson, K. S. (1986). The Cognitive Therapy Scale: Psychometric properties. *Journal of Consulting and Clinical Psychology, 54*, 381–385.

Vertue, F. M., & Haig, B. D. (2008). An abductive perspective on clinical reasoning and case formulation. *Journal of Clinical Psychology, 64*, 1046–1068.

Vitaliano, P. P., Russo, J., Carr, J. E., Maiuro, R. D., & Becker, J. (1985). The Ways of Coping Checklist: Revision and psychometric properties. *Multivariate Behavioral Research, 20*, 3–26.

Wampold, B. E. (2007). Psychotherapy; The humanistic (and effective) treatment. *American Psychologist, 62*, 857–873.

Wampold, B. E. (2010). *The basics of psychotherapy: An introduction to theory*. Washington DC: American Psychological Association.

Wampold, B. E., & Bhati, K. S. (2004). Attending to the omissions: A historical examination of evidence-based practice movements. *Professional Psychology: Research and Practice, 35*, 563–570.

Wampold, B. E., Hollon, S. D., & Hill, C. E. (2011). Unresolved questions and future directions. In J. C. Norcross, G. R. Vandenbos, & D. K. Freedheim (Eds.). *History of psychotherapy* (2nd ed., pp. 333–356). Washington, DC: American Psychological Association.

Watkins, E. R. (2009). Depressive rumination: Investigating mechanisms to improve cognitive behavioural treatments. *Cognitive Behaviour Therapy, 38*, 8–14.

Watson, D. L., & Tharp, R. G. (1989). *Self-directed behavior: Self-modification for personal adjustment*. Pacific Grove, CA: Brooks/Cole.

Webb, C. A., DeRubeis, R. J., & Barber, J. P. (2010). Therapists' adherence/competence and treatment outcome: A meta-analysis. *Journal of Consulting and Clinical Psychology*, *78*, 200–211.

Weisz, J. R., Weersing, V. R., & Henggeler, S. W. (2005). Jousting with straw men: Comment on Westen, Novotny and Thompson-Brenner (2004). *Psychological Bulletin*, *131*, 418–426.

Wells, A. (2008). *Metacognitive therapy for anxiety and depression*. New York: Guilford Press.

Westbury, C. F. (2010). Bayes' rule for clinicians: An introduction. *Frontiers in Psychology*, *1*, 1–7.

Westen, D., Novotny, C. M., & Thompson-Brenner, H. (2004). The empirical status of empirically supported psychotherapies: Assumptions, findings, and reporting in controlled clinical trials. *Psychological Bulletin*, *130*, 631–663.

Westen, D., & Weinberger, J. (2004). When clinical description becomes statistical prediction. *American Psychologist*, *59*, 595–613.

Westen, D., & Weinberger, J. (2005). In praise of clinical judgment: Meehl's forgotten legacy. *Journal of Clinical Psychology*, *61*, 1257–1276.

Westra, H. A., Constantino, M. J., Arkowitz, H., & Dozois, D. J.A. (2011). Therapist differences in cognitive-behavioral psychotherapy for generalized anxiety disorder: A pilot study. *Psychotherapy*, *48*, 283–292.

Whisman, M. A. (1993). Mediators and moderators of change in cognitive therapy of depression. *Psychological Bulletin*, *114*, 248–265.

Whitaker, R. (2010). *Anatomy of an epidemic: Magic bullets, psychiatric drugs, and the astonishing rise of mental illness in America*. New York: Crown Publishers.

Williams, S. L., & Falbo, J. (1996). Cognitive versus performance-based treatments of panic and agoraphobia. *Behaviour Research and Therapy*, *34*, 253–263.

Wilson, G. T. (1998). Manual based treatment and clinical practice. *Clinical Psychology: Science and Practice*, *5*, 363–375.

Wilson, G. T. (2007). Manual-based treatment: Evolution and evaluation. In T. A. Treat, R. R. Bootzin, & T. B. Baker (Eds.). *Psychological clinical science: Papers in honor of Richard McFall* (pp. 105–132). New York: Psychology Press.

Wilson, N. (2003). Commercializing mental health issues: Entertainment, advertising, and psychological advice. In S. O. Lilienfeld, S. J. Lynn, & J. M. Lohr (Eds.). *Science and pseudoscience in clinical psychology* pp. 425–560). New York: Guilford Press.

Wolitzky, D. L. (2007). The role of clinical inference in psychoanalytic case formulation. *American Journal of Psychotherapy*, *61*, 17–36.

Wolpe, J., & Turkat, I. D. (1985). Behavioral formulation of clinical cases. In I. D. Turkat (Ed.). *Behavioral case formulation* (pp. 5–36). New York: Plenum Press.

Wong, Y. J. (2006). Strength-centered therapy: A social constructionist, virtues-based psychotherapy. *Psychotherapy: Theory Research, Practice, Training*, *43*, 133–146.

Wright, S., & Truax, P. (2008). Behavioral conceptualization. Adults, In M. Hersen & J. Rosqvist (Eds.). *Handbook of psychological assessment, case conceptualization, and treatment* (Vol. 1, pp. 48–75). New York: John Wiley & Sons Inc. Chapter 3.

Yanchar, S. L. (2009). Case studies and non-abstractionist theorizing. *Pragmatic Case Studies in Psychotherapy*, *5*, 71–79.

Yates, A. J. (1958). The application of learning theory to the treatment of tics. *Journal of Abnormal and Social Psychology*, *56*, 175–182.

Young, J. E., Klosko, J. S., & Weishaar, M. (2003). *Schema therapy: A practitioner's guide*. New York: Guilford Publications.